# *RISE UP!*

# WHEN LIFE GETS YOU DOWN,

# RISE UP!

# KACEY McCALLISTER

Covenant Communications, Inc.

*To all those who have struggled on this adventure called life.*
*There have been some crazy turns, huh?*

Front cover image © Ted Warren
Back cover Spartan race image © Aaron Tharp

Cover design copyright © 2019 by Covenant Communications, Inc.
Design and formatting by Hannah Bischoff

Published by Covenant Communications, Inc.
American Fork, Utah

Printed in the United States of America
First Printing: April 2019

25 24 23 22 21 20 19    10 9 8 7 6 5 4 3 2 1

ISBN:978-1-52440-927-2

# TABLE OF CONTENTS

# AUTHOR'S NOTE

THIS BOOK IS MANY THINGS. It's an autobiography, a bit of comic relief, and hopefully a source of inspiration and encouragement. More than any of those things, though, it's a testament to the message to rise up. When I started my business, I called it Rise Up, but it is more than just a way to provide for my family. It is a movement that aims to challenge the way we see our challenges. It is a way of life that takes these challenges we face day after day and encourages us to not only get through them but to use them to help ourselves become better than we were before. Our challenges can lift us up rather than be allowed to beat us down.

In school I was an awful writer. My English teachers would have laughed at the thought of me writing a book. Even though I usually got *A*s in English class, it took a huge amount of effort to get even a *B-* on a writing assignment. Every time I would sit down to write, my brain would go into a mad scramble like a rat in a cage trying to find a way out. While in college I would sit down for hours trying to write a simple one-page paper, only to come out of it with a few sentences that didn't even make sense. I dreaded English more than any other subject. But when it came time to share my story, I knew I had to be the one to write it. I could have hired someone else to write the story of my life, but for me that would have been giving up on myself.

Writing this book has been one of the hardest things I've ever done. It was super stressful and required a mountain of time and effort. But everything that is worthwhile in life is the same way. If it is hard, then there is a pretty good chance it will be worth the effort in the end. I have been amazed at the growth, both in my personal and professional life, that has occurred from the simple act of hitting some keys. When I began this process I was only able to type using one finger at a time to carefully tap out words. Time and patience were required to improve my typing speed. It took even longer for those words to make coherent sentences. I am constantly amazed to look back and see just how far I have come and to realize that the striving and the pain was worth it.

If you've glanced at the cover of this book, you know I don't have legs. I am a double amputee. But that is not who I *am*. I am an accomplished athlete, a husband, a father, a builder, a writer, and a motivational speaker. I was not born naturally talented at anything (except being a redhead). If anything, I was born to work, and work hard. I know nothing is impossible when you put your mind to it. Many times throughout my life I was met with disbelief and even scorn when I set out to do something a kid without legs shouldn't be able to do. But in the wise words of my dad, "*Can't* never did anything; *won't* never will."

So as I show in this book how I have overcome the most difficult things in my life, the whole point I hope to make is that *you* can. So get out there, and Rise Up!

# FOREWORD

As FOUNDER AND CEO OF the world's largest and greatest obstacle-course racing company, Spartan Race, I have had the distinct honor of observing humans from across the world challenge themselves to face their fears and then crush them. When Kacey asked me to author the foreword to his book, it was an easy yes! Kacey is a double amputee who participates in Spartan races all over the country—but you don't notice he's missing anything, because he doesn't let you. His abilities are all you see.

Kacey is not only a humble spirit but an absolute contender in life on this planet. His perspective, grit, determination, and simple kindness are exactly what the world needs more of. As a fellow author, I have learned that having the right perspective on your passion and life's work is critical. Sharing one's story with millions of people is an important and coveted responsibility, and I can think of no better teacher than Kacey to share his message of rising up!

It is only our minds that prevent us from overcoming our fears. Through his strength and persistence, Kacey shows the world that anything is possible. Rising to the occasion is not a matter of lip service—it's a way of life. As he crossed the finish line of the 2018 Spartan Race World Championship Beast in Tahoe, California, Kacey jokingly commented, "Joe, you need to find something that can break me—this didn't."

He shows up, and he gets it done. From the mountains of Seattle, Washington, to Olympic Valley in Tahoe, California, there is great reverence in the capability and spirit of determination. I believe in Kacey's spirit and wisdom, and I am proud to be a part of this inspiring work. It's now my personal mission to seek the event that will have Kacey talking about the challenge for a lifetime. Maybe a twenty-four-hour ULTRA event in Iceland? Hard to tell.

—Joe De Sena

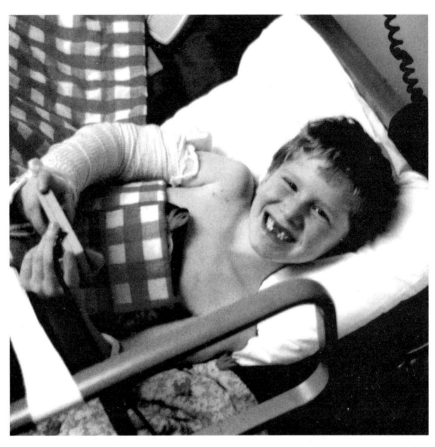

# CHAPTER 1
## THE ACCIDENT

*"Strength does not come from physical capacity. It comes from an indomitable will. Strength does not come from winning. Your struggles develop your strengths. When you go through hardships, and decide not to surrender, that is strength."*
—*Mahatma Gandhi*[1]

In life, there is often a defining moment we credit for determining the course of our fate. That kind of puts the pressure on that one moment, doesn't it? The truth is there is not just one moment. In fact, there are many times in our lives when situations, naysayers, or bad luck threaten to keep us from living up to our potential. When we decide to rise up, we decide to define our own lives. As we face each of these moments in life, we find ways to overcome them and grow stronger because of them.

I WAS BORN ON SEPTEMBER 11, 1986, in Kemmerer, Wyoming, a town in the middle of nowhere where the closest shopping was an hour away at the Walmart in Evanston. For the first few years of my life, I had only one older brother, Keith, and we were about as close as two brothers could be. We didn't grow up inside; we grew up outside, finding never-ending ways to entertain ourselves. We filled our days playing hide-and-seek, kick the can, ghost tag, capture the flag, and just living the life of kids before electronics ruled our lives. We would play outside for hours until our mom called us in for dinner. Even when the snow blanketed the ground, we were never short on activities, whether we went sledding on a nearby hill, went ice skating, built forts and igloos, or had snowball fights.

---

1 "The Doctrine of the Sword," *Young India,* 11 Aug 1920.

We went everywhere and got into everything together, including, oftentimes, getting into trouble. Because of the size of the town, there wasn't much we could get into without someone telling our parents what we were up to. Once, while still in diapers, Keith ended up downtown about a mile away on his Big Wheel. Thankfully, someone recognized him and called my mom. She, of course, had just let him go out to play in the backyard while she did some dishes and laundry, never realizing he'd taken himself on a field trip.

For three years it was just Keith and me, and then our sister, Whitney, was born. Once she was old enough, she was a welcome addition to our adventures. Whitney was dragged into wrestling matches, mud fights, sledding, and plenty of backyard sports. We in turn entertained her by playing dolls with her.

Then, in another couple of years, our younger brother, Kirt, came along. He was a blond little ball of joy. He would join me and Keith in any way he could, which at the time meant sitting on the floor holding a basketball while his older brothers ran around pretending to be Michael Jordan. I enjoyed taking care of him as Mom's big helper, whether that meant grabbing the diaper and wipes or bringing in the groceries. It was fun to find ways to make him laugh. I was not the only one who enjoyed having a new brother. He was soon designated as Whitney's new playmate, even playing dress-up with her (and when I say dress-up, I do mean she made him wear dresses). He was our little brother. We all called him Shorty. He was the tagalong to his big brothers and sister.

Growing up, the four of us were taught through word and action that family was more important than anything else. We always ate dinner together, and not in front of the TV but sitting at the dinner table or counter as a family and sharing stories about our days. Come Sunday we'd head off to church as a family.

Church has always been a big part of my life. My mom comes from a long line of members of The Church of Jesus Christ of Latter-day Saints, dating back to the early days of the Church, even before the pioneers made their way to Utah. My dad's family joined the Church when he was thirteen, and it wasn't long before he fell in love with the gospel and the joy it brought him. I also took to church with the unadulterated joy of a child. I loved to read and hear the stories from the scriptures, imagining myself as Daniel in the den of lions in the Old Testament, Nephi building a boat in the Book of Mormon, or Paul preaching before the kings of the world in the New Testament. In Sunday School I was the energetic child singing each song as loudly as possible and shooting my hand into the air at every opportunity because I knew the answers and could relate to every story.

One of the biggest tenets of our religion is the importance of sharing the gospel with others through missionary work. The day we were traveling to see my uncle off on his mission just five days before Christmas was the Sunday that changed my life forever.

The day before my uncle's farewell talk in church, we loaded up the car and drove three hours to my grandma's house, which was a short walk from the church building.

The next morning we hustled to get ready for church. Only when we were ready to go were we allowed to have breakfast. We sat down at my grandma's old wooden table to have pancakes. The best part about them was her homemade syrup; I don't know what made it taste so good, but I like to think it was made with that little bit of love grandmas mix in.

After breakfast we walked across the street to the church building. It was a crisp Utah winter day, and the chill nipped at my cheeks as I shoved my hands into my coat pockets and stomped my red cowboy boots. (In Wyoming every self-respecting boy had a nice pair of cowboy boots specifically for church. I had received this particular pair of spiffy boots on my birthday just a few months prior, and I wore them with great pride.) My boots crunched over the snow and asphalt as my family and I crossed the twenty-four feet of road to the red-brick building.

I really don't remember what my uncle spoke about that day, but what I do remember is knowing that I too wanted to serve a mission when I grew up. After he finished his farewell talk, my uncle walked up to me and stuck out his hand for a firm handshake.

"Kacey, do you want to be a missionary?" he said.

Now, you have to understand that I was, am, and forever will be a goofy, stubborn redhead.

Putting my hands on my hips, I said, "No, I'm a missionary now!" referring to the lyrics of my favorite Sunday School song, "I Want to Be a Missionary Now." Little did I know a more appropriate song would soon be, "I hope they call me on a mission when I have grown a foot or two."[2]

After church was over our family gathered outside to begin the walk back to Grandma's house. By the time I made it to the sidewalk with Mom and Dad, the rest of my siblings were already across the road. I was stuck on the same side of the street as my parents, and man, did they like to talk. In an effort to get them moving, I hopped into my mom's arms. It didn't take long before she was tired of holding a wiggly six-year-old and put me down to stand next to her.

"Okay, Kacey," she said. "There are two cars coming and a truck."

Sure enough the two cars rushed by, but before the truck passed safely, the unthinkable happened: I sprinted across the road with no warning.

I sped across the small divided highway, and within a few steps I was in the middle of the road, where I paused for just an instant before attempting to sprint the rest of the way across the road, stepping directly in front of the oncoming truck. Unfortunately this was not a small pickup truck or even a fully loaded work truck. It was an eighteen-wheeler that was bearing down on my little six-year-old body. Before my mom and dad could react, I was gone from sight. The crowd around my mom pulled her away from the scene to shield her from the sight of my body going through the wheels of the semi. As they pulled her away, she informed them very calmly that she knew I was dead.

This is one of the great times in life when God's power is clear to see. For months before this moment, my mother had an unsettling feeling that something tragic was going to happen to someone she loved. At first she

---

2 "I Hope They Call Me on a Mission" by Newel Kay Brown © by Intellectual Reserve, Inc., *Children's Songbook*, 169.

thought it would be my dad who would die, but after a while she had the sickening premonition that it would actually be one of her children. When I took off across the road, she knew the moment had come.

I had no such foreknowledge. In fact, I don't remember running across the road at all. I only remember a flash of light. People who've lived through near-death experiences often talk about seeing a light at the end of a tunnel. There was no tunnel for me, but there definitely was a white flash. Now, that may have been a side effect of my head hitting the pavement or the snow as it flew by, but I like to think it was God speaking to me and that the conversation went a little something like this:

*God:*
    *"Hey, Kacey."*
*Me:*
    *"Hi, Heavenly Father. Am I dead?"*
*God:*
    *"No, but I wanted to let you know you are going to lose your legs."*
*Me:*
    *"Will I find them?"*
*God:*
    *"No, Kacey, it doesn't work that way. You won't get them back—not for a while. This is so you can do great things and be an inspiration to others."*
*Me:*
    *"Really? That's awesome! I won't have to buy shoes!"*
*God:*
    *"Kacey, you will show people that anything is possible."*
*Me:*
    *"Like fitting into small places?"*
*God:*
    Sigh. *"Sure, Kacey. Like that."*

Okay, maybe it didn't go like that, but hey, it could have happened.

I have no recollection of the pain of the accident or of any part of it. All the details were told to me later.

My dad, who had chased after the slowing truck, rushed over to my broken body, picked me up in his arms, and started talking to me about Christmas and all the things I wanted to get—anything he could say to distract me. Soon I was surrounded by friends and neighbors offering helping hands and warm hearts. Someone nearby called for an ambulance. My dad put his hands on my head and gave me a priesthood blessing that I would live. The ambulance soon arrived and rushed me away with Dad by my side. My mother had to first see that the rest of her children were in good hands before following us to the hospital.

The local hospital served a town of only about four thousand people, so it wasn't equipped to handle a small child who had just gone through a veritable meat grinder. The next closest hospital was Primary Children's Hospital in Salt Lake City, a three-hour drive through a twisting, windy canyon. We didn't have that kind of time, so the paramedics took Mom and me to the local airport, where I was loaded onto a small Life Flight plane and flown out.

With the temperature dropping every minute, moving me to the plane was an exercise in caution. Due to the trauma and blood loss, my blood pressure kept dropping to zero, so the EMTs had to monitor me every step of the way. Meanwhile, I was refusing to stay still. The medications they had pumped through my veins were not strong enough to knock me out, and I kept trying to sit up. It was only then that my mom finally allowed herself to believe I would actually live. She saw her stubborn-as-nails redheaded son fighting to live and started to hope I would defy the odds and win the battle of semi versus six-year-old.

We got to Salt Lake in under an hour, and I was quickly transferred to a waiting helicopter. The helicopter took off from the airport directly toward Primary Children's Hospital. Even with the wind and snow coming from all sides, the pilot set the aircraft down safely on top of the building. Up to that point, I still had no memory of the events. Later my parents told me everything they could remember about that day.

My first memory of the accident was when they pulled me from the helicopter. I could feel the beat of the rotor blades as the wind swept over my skin. The bitter cold sliced through the blankets that enveloped me, and muffled voices floated down to me through a haze. I couldn't focus on any one voice, and there was only one thought that could get through: *It's cold*, not, *I wonder why I am coming out of a helicopter.* Nope. My first post-traumatic thought was, *It's cold.*

Outside the helicopter in the freezing weather, they quickly hooked me up to oxygen only to find that the tank was empty. They placed me back into the helicopter to wait for a new one. When the new one was brought out, I was once again pulled from the helicopter and reattached to the oxygen. This time the tank was full, but the connector was wrong, and once again they had to return me to the helicopter. My mom, standing next to me, still in her dress and heels, prayed as her little boy was placed into the freezing wind time and time again. She held her frustration inside, knowing she needed to be strong and stay by my side. Finally the third set of oxygen worked, and I was rushed into the hospital. The warmth of the building surrounded me as the medical staff rushed me down the halls to the waiting operating room to continue the fight to save my life.

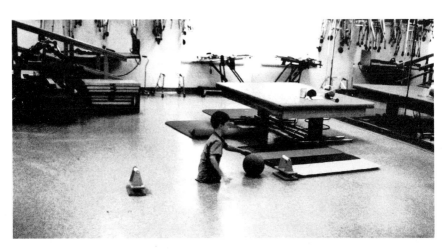

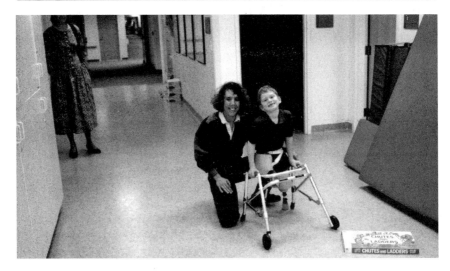

# CHAPTER 2
## A WILL TO LIVE

*"And once the storm is over, you won't remember how you made it through,*
*how you managed to survive. You won't even be sure whether the storm is really over.*
*But one thing is certain. When you come out of the storm,*
*you won't be the same person who walked in. That's what this storm's all about."*
—*Haruki Murakami*[3]

Some say I've coped so well because I was a young child when I lost my legs and was able to quickly adjust, but I believe it was something much more than that. I believe it was my Heavenly Father watching out for me and guiding me to where I should be.

Do I know His entire plan for me? No. But I do know He has led me and guided me through the tough times in my life so I could fulfill my purpose here on Earth.

One of those purposes is to inspire others to find joy in life regardless of the situation they may find themselves in. Life is meant to be full of joy. Yeah, there are hard times that happen to everybody, but that's just part of life. God doesn't want us to come home to Him the same way we left; He wants us to learn and grow.

THE FIGHT TO SAVE MY life was not an easy one. The doctors and nurses had a very unusual situation on their hands. After all, they were faced with treating a little boy who, by all intents and purposes, should not have survived being struck by a vehicle weighing nearly eighty thousand pounds.

---

3 *Kafka on the Shore*, New York: Knopf, 2005.

The shock from the impact alone should have been more than enough to take me out, but my little body would not give in to a silly thing like logic.

While I was in surgery, my parents paced the floor, waiting for any news on my condition. During a break in surgery a nurse came to talk to my parents. She told them I had woken up during surgery and she was the one who had sat with me and held my hand. Her heart was touched as I visited and talked with her for a while until I once again fell back under the influences of the drugs. She was crying as she told my parents that if there was any issue at home and they were unable to care for me, she would gladly take care of me as long as they needed her to. With a quiet word of gratitude from my mom, the nurse returned to the doctors who persisted in repairing my damaged body.

Against all odds the doctors were able to stabilize me enough to assess and control the damage. My right arm was shattered, there was road rash on the back of my head about the size of a quarter, and my left leg had been severed six inches below the hip. Then there was my right leg, which was broken in seven places and dangled from my body, attached only by a small strip of flesh no thicker than a couple of decks of playing cards. The surgeons had two options: remove the right leg altogether; or attempt to reattach the leg and risk tissue rejection, which could result in major complications at best and, at worst, death. Ultimately it was decided that amputation was the better option.

When they removed my leg, there were some major issues that needed to be addressed. The largest one was how to cover the stub. In most instances doctors are able to cut a little higher than needed and use the extra skin and muscle to wrap under so the stub has plenty of protection. My right side was so severely damaged, however, that there was no skin left for them to use. The only course was to perform a skin graft. Fortunately, the highway patrol officers had returned to the scene of the accident and found the rest of my leg wedged in between two of the semi's wheels. The doctors needed every last bit of my skin for the graft.

Usually when a skin graft is applied, skin is taken from a person's stomach, back, or butt. Luckily there was enough skin from my amputated legs to cover the graft. My mom sat down next to my bed, looking at her little boy. My face was bruised and scratched up. There were scabs dotting my head, and my arm was in a cast. She held my hand as Dr. O'Neil came in to tell her about the issues dealing with the graft of my right stub.

"Mrs. McCallister, we hope the skin we recovered from his right leg will attach to the stump of the left leg; the next two weeks are going to be the most telling for the graft," Dr. O'Neil told my mom.

"What if it doesn't take?" she asked, fully aware that if the skin did not take, my recovery would be longer and harder.

Dr. O'Neil let out a slow sigh and sat down opposite her. "If the skin doesn't take, we will have to use skin from his stomach," he said. "But let's hope it doesn't come to that. Using skin from the stomach would be very painful for him, as well as increase the risk of infection." He stood and walked toward the door. "Mrs. McCallister, we are doing everything we can to give your boy a full and happy life."

---

I WAS NEVER MEANT TO HAVE LEGS,
BUT THAT DIDN'T MEAN I COULDN'T BE HAPPY.

---

So she prayed, and others prayed right along with her. When the time came to look at the wound's progress, Mom stared on in silent horror. The entire right stub was a mottled black-and-red mass that looked like something out of a war film. To her surprise, however, the doctor was quite pleased with what he saw.

"This looks really good, Mrs. McCallister," Dr. O'Neil said as he peeled back the layers of my bandages.

"Really?" my mom said with more than just a little suspicion tinting her voice.

"This is exactly what we want to see at this point," he replied. "In fact, this is much better than we could have hoped for."

Relief flooded over Mom's entire being, visibly washing away the stress, her shoulders relaxing and the color returning to her face. Her prayers had been answered.

The medical team tried to keep me sedated as much as possible, but after a couple of days it was time to reduce the medication and allow me to fully wake up. My mom sat by my side as much as possible. There were times when I would wake up for a few minutes and look up at my mom. Seeing the concern on her face, I would rub her hand and tell her it would be all right. I would continue this until once again falling back asleep.

This part of the event was very hazy for me. All I remember is waking up in a dreamlike state and feeling the call of nature. I sat up in bed, grabbed my blanket around me, and tried to make the trip to the bathroom. It was only then that I realized I could not stand up. At about that time, a nurse walked into my room.

"Kacey," she said. "You don't have legs anymore."

*That explains why I can't stand up,* I thought. *Wait a sec. How am I going to get to the bathroom?*

Then, like a puff of smoke, the dream vanished. When I woke up again, I lay in bed for a minute staring up at the ceiling, unable to sit up or make any attempt to leave my bed. Remembering my "dream," I reached down to feel where my legs should have been. At first all I felt were the bandages that encased my lower body. As my hand traveled lower I felt it—or *didn't* feel it. There were no legs for me to feel.

The next thing I heard was my mom's voice, repeating what the nurse had said. "Kacey," she said with a nervous tremor in her voice. "You don't have legs anymore."

I simply nodded my head and fell back asleep.

A lot of people go through a period when they mourn the loss of limbs and their former lifestyle, but I never felt this way. I was ready to start this new adventure. The only real moment of pause I had was when I took a moment to reassess my dream of growing up to be a bronc rider. In Wyoming almost every little boy grew up with the dream of becoming a cowboy or a rodeo star or both. After losing my legs I thought long and hard about it and decided to give that dream up because they would have to tie me onto the saddle. I would just have to find other dreams that would be just as awesome.

I would soon find out I had cut my tongue into a few different pieces. My four front teeth had also been knocked out. Pair that with the multitude of scrapes, bruises, and dents on my face, and I had quite the set of mementos from my game of chicken with the semi. With only five days until Christmas, I could one-up the popular Christmas song and say, "All I want for Christmas is my four front teeth."

One thing that helped keep the joy of Christmas present were the gifts that kept showing up in my room. If anyone is considering experiencing a life-altering accident, I highly recommend doing so right before Christmas because boy, did my hospital room fill up. Stuffed animals filled every square inch of space. One of my favorites was a big white bear dressed like a police officer that was sent by the highway patrolmen who were at the scene of my accident. Another favorite was a Nintendo Gameboy. At home we didn't have a video game system because my mom thought they were time-wasters and made you brain-dead, but in the hospital I got to play video games as much as I wanted (well, except when my mom was there).

I also developed a love of music books—not books with notes and lines, but singalong books given to me by the many visitors who came to my room. I would listen to them for hours on end. This helped me pass the time when I was separated from my family. My mom and dad had been by my side for most of time I was in the hospital, but it took a while before I saw my best friend, my oldest brother, Keith. The loss of my brother's companionship hit me the hardest. Everybody else had been to visit and offer words of encouragement, but it had been two weeks, and Keith still had not made it into my hospital room. I was heartbroken. Keith and I had spent almost every second together outside of school prior to my accident. We had run all over the neighborhood all summer long. And now he was too scared to see me. My other siblings had come into the room without a shred of worry. Given that Kirt was one and Whitney was three, I am not sure they even realized what was going on. But Keith, eight years old at the time, had been standing out in the hall for days, refusing to come in. He was worried. What had happened to his little brother? He knew something horrible had happened. Was his best friend going to be the same, or would he be a completely different person? If I didn't have my legs anymore, would that mean I couldn't play anymore?

It wasn't until my mom knelt down and looked him straight in the eye and said, "Keith, your brother needs you" that he finally decided to give it a shot. When they entered the room, Keith stood behind Mom, peeking his head out to see what had become of his brother.

I saw him, and my heart leaped with joy. It was my best friend! He had finally come! I couldn't wait to show him all the cool stuff I'd gotten for Christmas.

"Hey, Keith, is that you?" I said.

"Yeah," he said tentatively.

"Get on over here!" I yelled.

Keith ran over to the bed to see if I was okay. Looking me over, he examined the empty area where my legs should have been.

"So you don't have your legs anymore?" Keith asked with more wonder than fear in his voice.

"Nope. But I'm still me—just shorter," I responded. And just like that it was as if we had never been separated. He spent every second he could glued to my side. It probably helped that I had a new Gameboy. What better way for brothers to spend time together than bonding over video games? We also spent time playing board games, telling jokes, and watching movies. Then, way sooner than either of us wanted, the reunion was over. My mom told Keith it was time to go home.

"No, Mom! Please, let me stay," he begged, not knowing what would happen if he left his brother again.

"It's okay, Keith; he will be okay, but there is no place here for you to stay," Mom said, trying to get him off the bed.

"I can stay with Kacey," he reasoned, pleading.

"Keith, I know you want to be next to your brother, but we have to go. I swear we'll be back as soon as we can," she promised, pulling him off the bed. Mom leaned down and gave me a kiss on the head before turning to leave. She practically had to drag Keith out of the room. I was glad to have my brother back and disappointed he had to leave.

The room seemed extra silent after his departure. Once again I was alone. I was alone for most of my hospitalization, not because my parents did not want to be there, but because they couldn't be there constantly. It was a two-hour drive from Kemmerer, Wyoming, to Salt Lake City. Dad had to work, and Mom had three other kids she needed to take care of. But whenever she could find neighbors or relatives to watch my siblings, she was right there by my side.

Besides feeling lonely, I really hated the nurses sticking me with a pushpin and squeezing my fingers to get enough drops of blood to fill their little slides. Even worse, I hated being stuck in bed. All I could do was lay there. It might sound like a blast to sit around watching TV and playing games, but I felt like a prisoner stuck behind the bars of a cell.

Nobody likes a hospital stay, and I was no different. I was stuck there while being poked and prodded all day long. It seemed like the medical staff were always finding new ways to try and torture me. My stubs were initially left open so gravel and dirt could drain from the wounds. This had to be done before the doctors could close them up. To keep them clean, I had to have a catheter and a colostomy. The catheter was uncomfortable, but the colostomy was worse. It was awkward, it smelled bad, and it had to be cleaned multiple times a day. I didn't like it at all. My personality, though, would not let me dwell on what was bad about the situation. It didn't take long for me to find the jokes in having such a thing on my stomach. Using humor was how I coped with dealing with the colostomy. I tried to stay positive through the hardest times, and laughing and joking was my way of doing it.

To break up the monotony, one day shortly after Christmas, a nurse wheeled my bed to a row of windows that overlooked the Salt Lake Valley. This was a fairly major undertaking considering I was still hooked up to about a dozen different cords, all of which had to come along for the ride. But she rolled me right up to the glass, locked the wheels in place, and propped me up from my usual horizontal position so I could look out over the city. I had not been able to do more than lift my head off my pillow for days, so when I saw the sight from that overlook, it stuck with me. It was as if a million stars had fallen out of the sky, rolled down the mountains, and settled into a magical valley. I no longer felt like I was stuck in a cold, boring hospital. It now felt like it could be part of a magical kingdom on a hill. What a great thing to see at Christmastime, when my entire world had just been turned onto its head.

In late January I was finally released so I could continue healing in the comfort of my own home for a couple of months. It had been nearly thirty days since my accident, and I was more than ready to see the outside world again. Since I still couldn't sit up in bed, my parents set my bed up in the living room so I could be around everybody. This was a monumental change from being sequestered away at the hospital, plus I was no longer being poked and prodded by medical staff—double bonus! I couldn't wear shorts while my stubs healed and was basically hanging out in the living room in my underwear, so Keith even made a little tent over my stubs to give me some privacy.

Keith stayed by my side for as long as he could, but he couldn't stay home with me all day. School was in full swing. So during the daytime I didn't have much to do except lie in bed and read books and play video games (since I was limited to lying around all day, Mom let up on the video game ban). Between the unlimited access to video games and a constant supply of books, I don't know which took up more of my time. As much as I enjoyed playing Nintendo, I was also a fanatic about reading. In the evening time my first-grade teacher, Mrs. Dikeman, stopped by the house to give me the schoolwork I had missed that day and teach me the lessons I had missed. I enjoyed seeing my teacher, and it was nice to feel included in class, even if I couldn't be there in person.

After a month at home and hundreds of books later, I returned to the hospital for another stay to experience the joys of therapy. Staying in the hospital full-time was not very fun. There were tons of tests, medications, and every now and again another surgery. It was not all bad though; I loved therapy and hanging out with other kids. In between our therapy sessions, we would gather in the breakroom and play video games, watch movies, mess around, and tell jokes. I loved telling jokes and making people laugh. I started collecting jokes, especially any that had to do with missing limbs. I thought they were so funny. I would get my jokes from books, from other people, and even from Laffy Taffy. I loved helping doctors, nurses, and especially patients leave with a smile on their face.

During this time period there were a few people who left me with a smile on my face. One of the biggest activities in the McCallister home was watching sports, and that meant basketball, football, and every four years, the Olympics. As a little kid I dreamed of meeting the greatest athletes and of course being one myself one day. As I was in the hospital I got to meet some of them. First was Olympic gold medalist Mary Lou Retton. She came into my room and talked with me. She told me there wasn't anything I couldn't do. Several days later I got to meet one of the best basketball players of all time. It was Michael Jordan's right-hand man and longtime teammate, Scottie Pippen. As I basked in the coolness of the moment, I wondered what it would take for me to be a great athlete. Never did it cross my mind that I couldn't do sports now that I was in a chair. I was a kid who believed anything was possible, and I was stubborn enough to pull it off. After these visits I went back to my therapy knowing that someday I would get out of that hospital and become a great athlete.

It was frustrating to be back in the hospital without my family, and I looked for any activity that would relieve the boredom. I actually came to enjoy rehab because it meant I got to get out of my bed and start doing things other kids were doing: playing with balls, running obstacle courses, and learning to play games like baseball and basketball without legs became the best part of my days and made the hospital feel less like a prison.

Hands down the best day in rehab was the day I arrived to find, sitting in the middle of the room, sparkling like a gem, my new wheelchair. It wasn't really new—it had been used by many before me—but for the time being it was all mine. For me a wheelchair was not just a mode of transportation; it was freedom. Up to that point I had been in a very clunky hospital wheelchair that required someone else to push me around. I didn't like other people having to push me. I tried to get the older wheelchair down the hall by myself, but I think it was made by a caveman because it felt like it weighed a thousand pounds. It took a ton of energy to even make it down the hall. This new chair would be like driving a sports car versus a tricycle. I was ready to jump in and peel out. But I had to wait for the instructions.

"To go forward, you push the wheels forward," the therapist instructed. "To go backward, you push the wheels backward."

A nod and an impatient grunt were the only responses she received from me.

"To turn, hold one wheel and push the other wheel," she continued patiently.

"Okay, okay," I said. I was barely listening to her way-too-long and boring explanation. "Can I go now?"

"To turn quickly, you can push one wheel forward while pulling the other one back," the therapist carried on, despite my obvious impatience.

When I let out a sarcastic gasp of amazement, she finally realized she'd better let me go.

Zoom!

I flew all around the hospital that day. Up and down ramps, across a huge sky bridge, up and down the halls, and in and out of rooms. I didn't stop until the nurses pried my hands off the wheels to make me eat dinner and go to bed.

I should have been really excited to do it all again the next day; however, there was a big problem: I could not move. I was so sore my entire body felt like it had gotten hit by a semi again. My dad came into the room and asked me how I was doing.

"I can't move, Dad," I said.

"Why can't you move?" he said.

"I'm sore," I said, trying to stretch my aching muscles. I tried to sit up, thought better of it, and lay back down.

"You're not *that* sore," he replied.

"The only things that don't hurt are my eyelids," I said, adding a moan and closing my eyes for maximum effect.

"It won't last forever," he said with a laugh as he slapped my shoulder. "Nothing can hold you back for long."

He was right. The next day I was back in my chair, and even though I was wincing in pain, I was terrorizing hospital staff and patients alike, blasting up and down the hallways. My desire to cruise around under my own power far outweighed my aches and pains. Not only did I quickly become a pro at using the wheelchair, but I was just as quick to master the exercises that allowed me to get out of my chair and run around using just my arms. The wheelchair was absolute freedom for me. I was no longer dependent on where other people wanted me to go; if I wanted to roll down to the game room, I could. If I wanted to go look at the amazing fountain in the front entrance, I could do that too. Anywhere I wanted to go, anything I wanted to do, I could. That is what having a chair felt like.

Not every part of therapy was my cup of tea though. I hated working with my prosthetic legs. Prosthetic legs (or, as I called them, fake legs) are different for every person. Many people find freedom in their new legs, but that was not how it felt for me.

When it comes to fitting fake legs, the more real leg you have to attach the piece to, the better off you are, particularly when it comes to getting the joints right. For instance, if you still have your knee, there is a lot that can be done to make sure your fake leg functions almost the same as the real thing. As you go farther up the leg, you lose more and more functionality. On the left side, I had a little piece of a stub they were able to put a standard prosthetic on, but my right leg was amputated all the way up to the hip, so there was no socket to attach to, which made the prosthetic seem more like a torture device than a useful limb.

The prosthetic consisted of a bucket, open on two sides, that I would sit in. At the top of the bucket was a hard strap that went around my back before being cinched down to itself in the front. The whole thing was made out of hard plastic and made me hot, sweaty, and altogether uncomfortable. The left side was almost as bad. It was a typical tube-style leg that required me to lube up with lotion or talcum powder so I could slide my stub in at the precise angle to attach to the locking mechanism at the bottom. Once all the pieces were together, it was like learning to drive a backhoe. Every movement of my stubs caused the fake legs to spasm through the air. The only things that kept me upright were the two crutches I clung to for dear life. I hated my fake legs.

Despite the fact that I was so obviously opposed to using my new legs, my mom had her mind set on the fact that I would be walking through life, not rolling around in a wheelchair. More than that, she saw me going off to serve a two-year mission wearing fake legs. So, oh yes, she made me wear them. Even when she saw me crying and couldn't bear the sight of my tears, she knew in her mind I needed to keep practicing with those legs. I had a different plan in mind—that being not wearing my legs—and I tried to get out of them at every available opportunity.

One day, while I wheeled around the hospital looking for something to do, I came across a new patient I hadn't met yet. Since I was a long-time resident of the hospital and was always looking for new playmates, I curiously peeked into the hospital room to see if the new patient wanted to play with me. This new patient was a little girl, about my age, named Cambria. Cambria had undergone surgery to relieve swelling on her brain after she'd run into a parked car with her bike while racing with some boys in her neighborhood (she won the race, of course). After her surgery she couldn't bring herself to look at the scar that ran along her hairline across the front of her head. She called it her bloody braid. The scar disturbed her so greatly that anything that reflected her image—mirrors, shiny balloons, TV monitors—had to be removed from her sight. She became so depressed and despondent about her appearance that she stopped eating and her mother and doctors became seriously concerned about her mental health.

As I rolled past Cambria's room, I saw the little girl lying in her bed. I made a sharp turn and wheeled up to her bed, ready to introduce myself.

"Hey, I'm Kacey. Do you want to play?" I said with all of my redheaded charm.

Cambria turned her face away and shook her head.

"Are you all right?" I said. "What's wrong with you?"

Cambria reached over to grab a piece of paper and handed it to me without letting me see her face. It was a crayon drawing of her with the bloody braid in plain view.

"Is that what you look like?" I asked.

Cambria nodded.

"Well, I don't care," I said. "Let's go play."

Cambria lifted her head, with a surprised look on her face.

"Okay," she said.

And that was all it took—we were off and playing. It wasn't long before her condition improved dramatically. She started eating and responding to people and treatments, and after a few days she was allowed to go home. I missed her. Another friend had come and gone. It was just part of life while living in the hospital. Every day I got stronger and more hopeful that I would be the one who was sent home next. Sometimes it seemed like I would never leave the hospital. It kind of became a second home. The only break I got was when I was allowed to leave the premises for the day. This didn't happen very often, especially since it wasn't until rehab was almost over that I was allowed to leave at all.

My first outing was epic in its simplicity. My dad and Keith picked me up, and we loaded into the cab of Dad's gray 1986 Ford pickup. When my dad asked me where I wanted to go, I immediately thought of food. Living in Kemmerer, we didn't go out to eat very much, but anytime we traveled, we would always stop at the same fast-food restaurant. They had everything a kid could want: chicken nuggets, little plastic toys, and a giant play place.

"McDonald's!" I shouted. With an echoing cheer from my brother, we pulled out of the hospital parking lot. Driving through Salt Lake City in the daytime is so much better than looking at it through the big glass windows of the hospital. We put on some tunes and cruised our way down to the closest Mickey *D*'s. As we were pulling into the parking lot, I had a revelation.

"Dad!" I yelled. "I can park in the handicap spots now!"

"No, you can't!" Keith responded immediately.

"Yes, I can," I retorted.

"No, you can't," he said again, sticking to his guns.

"Yes, I can," I said. "I have a wheelchair!"

"No, you can't," he insisted. There was no doubt in my brother's mind that I would not be a disabled kid in a wheelchair. I would be just as able as anybody else to do anything I wanted.

At McDonald's we ordered our food and played on the play structure, which included me getting out of my wheelchair, climbing the stairs, jumping into the ball pit, and going down the slide. I played with my brother like I had before my accident—just without my legs. We then drove back to the hospital, my home away from home, where I once again said goodbye to my father and brother.

As far as my siblings were concerned, there wasn't anything I couldn't do, despite my physical condition. In fact, they were always the first to tell me to do it myself. Well, okay, Keith kept telling me to do it myself. Whitney was really nice—maybe even too nice. Whenever I asked her to help me with something, she would, whether it was bringing me a snack, doing my chores, or generally doing just about anything else I asked her to do. Was I taking advantage of my sister? Yes, yes I was.

One time, while taking a break from my hospital therapies, I went to see disabled athletes play tennis. It was really cool to see them whipping around the tennis court in fancy wheelchairs, playing just as fast as or faster than people who had absolutely nothing wrong with them. As they whipped around the court, I knew I wanted to be just like them one day—maybe not as a tennis player but definitely as an athlete. I knew at that point there was no sport I wouldn't be able to conquer. I might succeed in a different way than I'd imagined, but nothing was going to stop me. I knew as soon as I was out of the hospital I was going to start playing sports.

The same day I finished therapy and left the hospital for good, my dad and I entered a race. We raced in the Governor's Cup, a half-mile loop around the capitol building in Salt Lake City. I did it in my wheelchair with my dad running beside me. I was the slowest one there, but I finished by myself. My dad was there to help if needed, but I did the whole thing on my own only a few months after losing my legs. I felt triumphant. I knew I had found my passion in life. I loved to be active. There was no time to sit around and feel sorry for myself. No wheelchair would be able to limit who I could become. I was mobile, and nothing was going to stop me.

Running in that race was the best thing I could have done upon coming out of the hospital. I was no longer worried about what the future would hold because I knew I had the ability to compete. I found out, though, that life is not just about getting stronger; it is also about finding ways to do things others would consider impossible. Coming home from the hospital had many challenges beyond the basics of healing.

Now I had to figure out how to be a regular kid again.

# CHAPTER 3
## LEARNING HOW TO LIVE AGAIN

*"Can't never did anything; won't never will."*
—*Bernie McCallister, my father*[4]

Before I was officially released from the hospital, my doctors told my parents something that would change my life. They told my parents not to do things for me. On the surface this seems kind of cruel. A young boy has just lost his legs, and the medical professionals are telling the people who love him most that they should refrain from helping him. In reality this was one of the greatest gifts my parents could ever share—they forced me to learn how to do things for myself.

When you rely on others to do things for you, you limit what you're able to do. Developing a strong work ethic, dealing with failure, overcoming disappointment and frustration—all these lessons learned are blessings throughout your life. My parents wanted me to be able to accomplish anything I set my mind to.

When I returned home from the hospital, I was expected to participate in household chores just like everybody else. While mom was busy teaching us the importance of sharpening our domestic skills, Dad made sure we understood what hard work looked like outside of the home. Around our house you didn't say *can't*, not even to chores. *Can't* was considered a bad word. My dad would always say, "*Can't* never did anything; *won't* never

4 Personal notes in possession of author.

will." I thought it was just a stupid saying dads are always spewing out, but over the years I have come to realize the wisdom in that statement. He meant if you are telling yourself you can't, you will never be able to do anything because you are too afraid to try. Won't is an even worse form of can't. It is the refusal to even make an attempt.

Cleaning my room, doing laundry, and washing dishes were only the beginning of our list of chores. We were expected to do whatever we were asked to do, whether it was mowing the lawn, walking the dog, shoveling dirt and bark dust, helping collect rocks for a retaining wall, planting, weeding, watering, or participating in service for other people. Work was never a choice; it was an expectation.

One of the most challenging items on my list of chores was making my bed, especially considering I had to sit on the bed while making it. Adding to this complexity was the fact that we had a bunk bed. Putting on the fitted sheet was the hardest part of all (not that it isn't a pain for most people). Figuring out how to accomplish this task with my new body taught me how to think through a problem. I couldn't just throw the sheet on and hope it worked. I had to put one corner on and then pull the sheet to the next corner. And I couldn't simply jump off the bed to finish. Instead I had to jump on the already-made side to pull the fitted sheet the rest of the way over. In the end, it wasn't the tidiest bed ever made, but my mom didn't get picky about the wrinkles.

Another seemingly minor task that required creative problem-solving was how to reach light switches. One day my uncle Kirt came over to visit, and I wanted to show him my room, but the lights were off. I started scooting along the floor, making my way to the light switch but was clearly too short to reach it in the usual way. Observing my movements, my uncle offered to turn the lights on for me.

"No, no. Let him do it," my dad said, intervening.

"But he can't reach the light switch from the ground," my uncle said, reaching for the switch.

"Just watch," my dad told him, holding up a hand as I scooted into the room to retrieve a baseball bat.

With the baseball bat firmly in hand, I scooted over to the switch, and with the extended reach afforded by the bat, I turned on the lights.

My dad turned to my uncle with a grin on his face. "See? I told you he could do it," he said.

To my uncle's credit, he never again doubted I could accomplish a difficult task.

This wasn't the only time I had to rely on ingenuity to successfully complete daily tasks. To make a sandwich or wash the dishes, I had to get up on the counter. To do this I would stretch my arms up to the top of the counter and pull myself up. Getting down from the counter was the fun part. Instead of lowering myself onto a chair or bracing my body with my arms, I would fling myself off the counter and land on my hands while swinging my body under me. This worried my parents greatly, not so much for *my* safety (I also did this off the top of my bunk bed) but for my little brother's safety. At the time he wasn't even two years old, but since we were about the same height (since I had no legs), he figured he could do it too. He would leap off the counter from a full standing position. He survived, but it certainly scared the pants off my parents. I got a stern talking to about being careful in front of my impressionable little brother.

After a while chores became so commonplace they barely registered on the scale of things I worried about; I was much more excited to return to school. Because the accident happened over Christmas break, I already knew my first-grade classmates and couldn't wait to see them again. Thanks to the home visits from my teacher, Mrs. Dikeman, I wasn't behind on my schoolwork. I also wasn't worried about how the other kids would see me. Either they would accept me, or they wouldn't; I was ready to be back in school.

When my first day back to school arrived, I was excited. I was going to see all the friends I hadn't seen for months. Plus I was going to be back in a place that made sense rather than sitting in a hospital playing games by myself and being poked and prodded by doctors and nurses. I was able to push my own wheelchair, and now I finally got to head back for all of my favorite things: books, P. E., recess, and especially school lunch. I was ready to be back.

There was one part of school I was *not* ready for: getting on the short bus. Before my accident all I had to do was walk onto the bus and pick a seat, and off we went. On my first day back to school, it felt like just getting on the bus took longer than my first surgery. First the bus came to a stop and the driver got out to open the door using the biggest remote control I had ever seen to lower a motorized ramp. The ramp took forever to peel itself out of the door and unfold onto the ground. After rolling onto this torturously slow platform, the mechanism creeped its way back up by closing a mini gate and rising upward until it was level with the bus door. Then, and only then, could I roll onto the bus. Once on the bus I was subjected to the joys of waiting for the bus driver to place straps and restraints on my chair so I wouldn't go flying around the bus. All in all, the boarding process probably took about ten minutes—a lifetime for an impatient six-year-old.

Imagine someone needing a ride, but before they can get in the car, they have to wait for their ninety-five-year-old grandmother to open the door even though they are capable of doing it themselves. It takes a minute for her to pull the door open, and they have to wait until the opening is wide enough for them to get in. Once they are inside the car, they have to allow her to buckle them up, which means she's not only getting in their personal space but taking forever to do it.

Even though boarding that bus was more painful than watching face paint dry on a mime, I was excited when we finally reached our destination. The bus driver barely had a chance to unbuckle me before I flew off the ramp and pushed myself into school for the first time in months.

Because we lived in such a small town, all of my classmates knew who I was and what had happened, and they were ready to make me feel right at home. My desk was ready and waiting for me to fill it with my school supplies. There was a big *hello* at the start of class, and then our school day continued, as it always had, with reading time, music class, recess, and lunch.

I also discovered new ways to play out on the playground with my friends. I was never in my chair for very long. In fact, I became a favorite at the end of the school day because everybody wanted to volunteer to help me out to the bus.

Even though everybody made me feel like I was once again part of the school, I still felt left out when it came to things I couldn't do because of my physical limitations, like learning how to swim. I had never really learned how to swim before the accident, and now, without legs, I felt awkward. While I was up for joining my classmates for almost any other activity, I was not quite ready to take on the challenge of swimming lessons. My hesitations stemmed not just from my accident but also from some severe inner-ear trauma. I had lost almost all my hearing in my right ear as a baby because of frequent ear infections, so I avoided getting water in my ears. So when all the other elementary students were walked down to the pool, I rode the bus home.

Faced with putting up with the same degrading boarding process day in and day out while my classmates splashed around in a pool, I decided it was time for me to have a little fun of my own. I decided to play a little game with my captor (aka the bus driver). I became boneless. If you don't know the boneless game, it goes like this: You pretend you don't have any bones and allow your body to go completely limp. If someone tries to pick you up, you gather mass from the universe to make yourself heavier and that much harder to lift. What makes it even more interesting is there is only so much bonelessness you can achieve while strapped into a wheelchair. Being a redhead, I was extra stubborn, which was like a power-up for my boneless skills.

Apparently the bus driver did not know this game and became extremely concerned that something was truly wrong with me. As any professional boneless player knows, this makes the game that much more exciting.

"Kacey," the bus driver said with legitimate concern in her eyes. "Are you okay?"

*Flop!*

She sat me back up.

"Can you sit up?" she said looking me over for injury.

*Flop!*

She propped my body back into a sitting position.

"Kacey, I need you to sit up for me," she said, her voice sounding less concerned and more impatient.

Again I responded by drooping my body over the seat belt, adding some drool for good measure. You can never go too far with this game.

Eventually I arrived home in one piece. What my six-year-old self didn't realize was by playing the boneless game, I had set a chain of events in motion. The bus attendant, physical therapist, and counselor got together and decided I needed a chest restraint. The chest strap was a piece of foam covered in plastic that spanned the height and width of my chest. At each corner it had a strap and buckle so it could anchor to corresponding buckles on my wheelchair. This new form of torture was implemented on the way to school the next day.

I was not dumb. I knew this piece of medical equipment was meant for children who are unable to hold themselves upright on their own. I was humiliated, embarrassed, and frankly, quite mad.

"Mom!" I yelled as I came through the front door the next day.

"What? And don't yell in the house," she said, as she came out of the kitchen brushing flour off her hands. Cooking for friends and family was not just something my mom saved for special occasions but something that happened daily. When she wasn't cooking for us, she was preparing treats and meals for sick Church members, relatives, neighbors, parents of newborns, or people who just needed a happy thought sent their way. But at my dramatic entrance, all thoughts of cooking were temporarily set aside.

"I am never taking the bus again!" I informed her, banging my hand on the arm of my wheelchair for emphasis.

"Why? What happened?" she asked, her brow furrowing in concern.

"They treated me like a cripple," I said.

"What do you mean they treated you like a cripple?" she asked. "What did they say?"

I relayed the whole embarrassing ordeal to her.

"Kacey, I am so busy. I can't take you to school every day," she said. "I have other kids at home who need to be taken care of. I am not going to be your taxi service. If you are not going to take the bus to school, you will have to find some other way to get there."

"Fine. Then, I'll wheel to school," I said, raising my voice to prove my determination.

"Kacey, there is snow and ice outside," Mom replied calmly.

"I don't care," I said. "I'll get there anyway."

"Okay, as long as I don't have to take you," she said.

She called the bus service and told them I would be pushing my wheelchair to school. She knew full well this might end badly. The possibility I would end up stranded in a snowdrift was highly likely. But she also knew I would need to figure out how to do things on my own and discover by trial and error if I could do something. She also understood how stubborn I could be and opted to give me the benefit of the doubt.

The next morning I got up, packed my lunch, layered on my winter clothes, and headed out the door. The bus was sitting there, as it always was, waiting for me. Apparently the school district was under the impression I might have second thoughts and decide to board the torment train at the last minute. Oh, I wish I could have seen the look on the bus driver's face as I wheeled right on by.

I was excited to push my way to school. For the first hundred feet of sidewalk, it was easy going, but then I ran into some things that made me have to dig deep for that stubborn streak and continue on. Some of the curbs did not have a ramp for me to roll up, so I had to find a driveway or another way to get onto the sidewalk. While most homeowners had cleared the snow away from the sidewalks in front of their houses, there were still slick ice patches to maneuver over, and I had to approach them very slowly to avoid spinning out in my wheelchair. Piles and drifts of snow could mostly be avoided, but in some cases I had to push through them. When the snow came up to my push rims, it made my hands freeze, but I continued on. Nothing was going to stop me. By the time I got to school, I was cold, tired, and more than a little bit sore. It had taken me nearly twenty minutes, which if you count the time it took to load and unload me from the bus was probably about the same amount of time as an average bus ride. But I never rode the bus again. From then on I wheeled myself to school regardless of the weather—rain, sun, snow, or wind. Nothing could stop me from showing the school I could do it on my own.

Although I didn't realize it at the time, I was preparing for life as a motivational speaker from the moment I got out of the hospital, proving I could do things others would think impossible day after day. Many people around me saw that I had not only survived what should have killed me but had moved forward and begun to thrive. After the accident I was asked to speak in front of groups with my mom at events, sometimes in front of as many as several hundred people. One such event, when I was seven years old, was the Festival of Trees in Salt Lake City, an annual fundraiser hosted by the hospital where I'd recovered. The hall was filled with what seemed like hundreds of trees, each decorated to outshine the next, and everyone was dressed in their finest holiday attire. After we strolled through the display, my parents and I were ushered up to the stand so I could give my speech.

The director of the festival said a few words, and then he turned to me. I had memorized what I was going to say and had practiced it a few times already, so, using my fake legs, I walked up to the lectern like a pro to share the story of my accident and recovery. I was a natural performer. It seemed like I spoke for an hour, but after about three minutes I was done. There was a roar of applause as I walked back to sit with my parents. I was shaking with adrenaline. I had just spoken to a giant room packed with people in fancy clothes. What a thrill to have people hanging on my every word. I had been nervous when I started, but by the end I had gained confidence in myself.

After a few more words from other people, the director brought me forward again. This was the part I had been waiting for. The lights for all the sparkling trees turned off. The only lights that could be seen were dim ones on the walls of the hall. In front of me sat a huge metal switch. I reached out and wrapped my little hand around the great-big wooden handle. With a tug, I pulled the switch over. Immediately the Christmas trees turned on in a wave of light, and the crowd cheered. It was like Christmas morning, except instead of one tree, there were hundreds.

After the event was over and we were driving home, my parents told me how well I had done. "Kacey, you are going to get a lot more opportunities to speak," Dad said. He could already see what was in store for me.

"Really, Dad?" I said with more than a hint of skepticism. "It was fun, but why would I be asked to speak more?"

"People will want to hear your story. And you are really good at telling it," he said. I wasn't sure what he meant. I filed the conversation away. As a little boy I didn't care about motivating others with my story; I was interested in having fun, which of course meant video games and sports. In the hospital I'd had all the video games I could want, but now I was ready to get back into sports.

The accident had left me weak and small, but within months of being out of the hospital, I started playing baseball. It was great to start doing a sport with my classmates. I played T-ball from my wheelchair, with my dad tagging along to help me when I needed it. It made me feel like I was alive instead of a cripple wasting away in a chair.

My dad grew up in a houseful of boys. He was always trying to one-up his brothers, especially in sports. In high school he was a super all-around athlete excelling at any sport he tried. As a dad he still played in the local softball leagues and was excited to get his boys playing baseball as well. Usually he would be on the side, yelling as loudly as anybody else. But this time he was not on the sideline; he was on the field, pushing me around the bases. I would swing the bat—*Ping!*—and then, like a race car speeding off the start line, my dad would propel my chair into motion, causing me to fling my bat aside so I could grip the handrests as he barreled down the baseline.

"Dad! Slow down! Slow down!" I yelled the first time this happened. I couldn't help it; I was terrified.

"No! We're gonna win!" he yelled back, turning on the jets.

I latched on to the armrests as if my life depended on it. As we sped by, kids on the other team jumped out of the way to escape the madman charging down the baseline.

"Tag him out!" the coach from the other team yelled.

"I don't want to tag him out!" said one of the kids, as tears ran down his face. He wanted no part of getting run down by my father.

I was thrilled to be back playing sports. I knew I would not spend my life in a wheelchair. I would not be limited in what I could do because of a little thing like losing my legs. I was going to be just like everybody else. If everybody else was playing baseball, well then, sign me up.

---

NOTHING COULD STOP ME.
EACH NEW SUCCESS GAVE ME MORE CONFIDENCE.

---

I was also not willing to rely on my dad for locomotion for the rest of my life. By the following season, I was out of my wheelchair and playing baseball from the ground. My biggest problem was making it to first base. I could hit the ball as well as, if not better than, most, but I was slow getting to the bases. After putting some thought into it, I discovered that if I hit left-handed, I was on the other side of the plate and, hence, two feet closer to first base.

I also had an interesting running style. My usual way of walking when out of my chair could be called a scoot. I put both my arms forward and then swung my body through my arms. When I ran, it became much more of a gallop. I turned my body sideways and flung my body forward before planting my butt and bringing my hands forward. This became a basic skill for many of the sports I participated in throughout my life.

I was figuring out how to live without legs. Nothing could stop me. Each new success gave me more confidence. Household chores? Check.

Going to school on my own? Check. Wearing fake legs? (Grumble.) Check. Flying leaps off the counter? Check. Playing baseball? Double check.

Then, without warning, my world was flipped upside down. My dad got an offer to be a partial owner in a tire store. This in itself wasn't the bad news. The part that stunk was that the tire store was located in Oregon. At eight years old, I was going to have to adjust to a whole new life. Again.

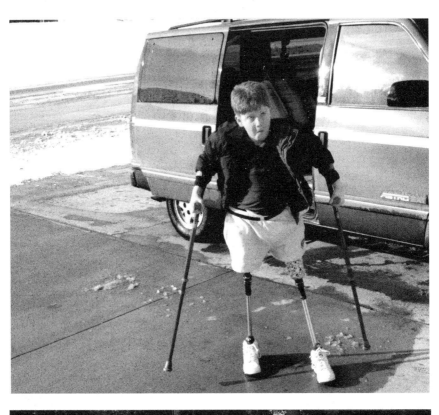

# CHAPTER 4
## MOVING TO OREGON

*"It is the same with people as it is with riding a bike. Only when moving can one comfortably maintain one's balance."*
—*Albert Einstein*[5]

Change happens. We are not supposed to live the same way we did a year, a month, or even a day ago. As we live, we learn. New opportunities come all the time, and we have just a couple of options when they do: we can ignore them and hope we aren't changed too much, or we can take those life lessons and learn from them to become better. To progress, we have to take the turns in the road of life and keep moving forward.

MY MOM GREW UP IN a military family, so she knew plenty about moving from place to place. She had us packed up and ready to go in no time. As we headed out, Dad drove the U-Haul while Mom followed in our Astro van, and I gazed out the window at the changing landscape.

"Mom," I said as Kemmerer's hills faded into the background. "I am going to move back here when I grow up."

As we made our way through Wyoming, Utah, Idaho, and eastern Oregon, I saw the same view I had seen my entire life: brown grass swaying in the breeze, cows on the open range swishing their tails back and forth, and rolling hills that would soon be covered in snow. I just knew I was going to miss it. But as we crossed the mountains and came into the Columbia Gorge, I started to see something different. There were trees. Not one or

---

5 Walter Isaacson, *Einstein: His Life and Universe*, New York: Simon & Schuster, 2007, 565.

two, but lots of them. I began to realize there was something different about Oregon. I just didn't know yet if it was going to be a good different.

When we first arrived we stayed in an old house owned by some family friends in Dallas, Oregon, while my parents were finding a house closer to my dad's store. The friends who owned it did not live in it, so it was not exactly move-in ready when we got there. The entire property was surrounded by grass so tall you could get lost in it, the paint was peeling, and a tire swing drifted in the breeze as if waiting to be used by a child who no longer existed. Inside, the kitchen floor had a tilt so pronounced that when we ate pancakes the syrup slid over to the edge of the plate. The creepiest part, though, was the spiders. I am not talking about the kind of thing where you come across a spider every once in a while. This was an honest-to-goodness infestation that was so bad my sister would wake up with dozens of spider bites. Most of our stuff was in storage, so we were sleeping on air mattresses and in sleeping bags, which made us easy targets. My parents had to bug-bomb the place a few times before we were able to go to bed without the fear of being gobbled up by the creepy crawlies.

Even though it was like a scene from shows I was never allowed to watch, my mom handed us brooms and rags, and in no time we turned it into a cozy little house where we found plenty of ways to keep ourselves busy. We didn't have any friends yet and our toys were packed away, so we relied on each other for entertainment. We did have a TV, but it only got one channel. Mom made sure to keep us away from the tube as much as she could, but I figured out a way around this. Since I was always the first to get up, I could watch TV until Mom woke up. I also discovered that the earlier I woke up, the more TV I got to watch. This only worked to a point. If I got up *too* early, the only thing playing was some workout show. I hated having to watch people stretch their legs before I could watch cartoons.

It didn't take long for us to figure out it was more fun to be outside than to sit around watching one channel on TV. At first we just played in the tall grass and pushed each other in the tire swing, both of which turned out to be not nearly as creepy as I'd first imagined. Then, when we finally pulled our bikes (I rode a handcycle) out of storage, we started exploring.

Dallas is in the middle of the Oregon hills, and you could be out in the countryside in no time, biking through landscapes that made postcards pale in comparison. We had moved from the dull and dusty wasteland of Wyoming to a lush and fertile enchanted forest. It was green, like, everywhere. There were streams and grass and flowers, and fruits and berries grew as far as the eye could see—blueberries, blackberries, strawberries, marionberries, apples, plums, cherries, apricots, and on and on and on. I also remember finding the coolest seed known to man. It was called the helicopter seed, and we would collect them in mass and fling them in the air to watch them twirl down to the ground.

Even more breathtaking than all of Oregon's greenery was my first trip to the beach. To get there, we drove up and over the Cascade Mountains, which were so densely packed with trees it seemed as though we were driving through a green, leafy tunnel. As soon as we exited the tunnel, the ocean was laid out before us. At first we didn't even see the sand. All we could see was the horizon, where the ocean met the sky. This was the first time in my life when I truly began to comprehend the curvature of the earth. As we got closer, we rolled down the window to let in the salty smell of the sea air and the sound of the crashing waves. We stopped and piled out of the car, and I looked around in amazement, taking in the scene around me: the coastal trees, gnarled and misshapen by the wind; the sand in every crevice of the sidewalk; and, of course, the ocean itself. It was pure magic.

Using a wheelchair in the sand is a tough workout, so I'd brought along my skateboard instead. I jumped out of the van and cruised down the paved path to the beach. When it got too tough to roll the skateboard in the sand, I would simply hop off my board and scoot on the ground while pulling the skateboard along behind me. Depositing my board near the rest of our stuff, I took off across the sand on my hands, feeling its dry warmth turn hard and wet as I closed in on the water's edge. My mom made sure we knew to be careful in the water, arming us with admonitions like "Never turn your back on it," "Watch out for the riptide," and "The water is stronger than you think."

We took these lessons to heart and barely even touched the water on that first trip. The minute any wave more than an inch or two high came our way, we yelled and ran away.

I loved to dig holes in the sand. What was even better than digging holes was burying each other in those holes. What was even better than *that* was using the holes to play pranks. I'd jump down into a hole so only the top half of my body showed and waited for a random person to walk past. Right as they'd look down to laugh at how deep I was buried, I'd leap out of the sand and run across the beach. Shouts of surprise and sometimes startled screams would follow me as I continued down the beach. Every once in a while, instead of running off I'd turn around and frantically start digging in the hole, yelling in a fake panic, "Where are my legs?"

As the sun started to set that day, we gathered our belongings and made our way up to the car. Rolling my skateboard up from the beach was a lot harder than going down, but I didn't care. I had just spent my first day on an Oregon beach with my family.

The summer before my fourth-grade year was rapidly coming to a close, and it was once again time for me to make my appearance at school as the kid in a wheelchair. I was worried, but my fears were soon banished. I made new friends and had caring teachers who made me feel right at home. Before we had made it to Halloween, my parents found a permanent home, and we moved again.

Moving the second time wasn't as bad. We all knew it was coming and were ready to be settled. Pulling up to the new house in Keizer was nothing like pulling up in front of the Spider House. This time around, when we pulled up in our van, I was pleasantly surprised to find a cream-colored house with a small lawn in front and an even bigger lawn in the back. As we entered the house, my siblings and I fanned out to lay claim on our bedrooms. The modest three-bedroom house left no chance for having our own rooms, so Keith and I claimed the bigger of the kids' bedrooms and started planning whose stuff would go where. As excited as we were about the house, we were even more excited to see what our new school was going to be like.

This time going to a new school was not nearly as intimidating as it had been before. We'd already started a new school once since moving to Oregon, and this time we knew we wouldn't be changing schools again for a while. The elementary school was less than a half mile from our house, and we got to walk there every morning. My fourth-grade teacher's name was Mrs. O'Neil. I was super excited by this due to the fact that the really cool reporter friend from *Teenage Mutant Ninja Turtles* was named April O'Neil.

I really enjoyed the schoolwork for the most part, but because my mom made me wear my fake legs every day, it was hard for me to enjoy recess (and there's very little you look forward to more than playground time when you're in fourth grade, except maybe pizza Friday). My mom, of course, thought recess was the perfect opportunity for me to practice using my legs. I disagreed wholeheartedly. I could play tetherball and more tetherball. I couldn't climb on the playground equipment. I couldn't keep up with the kids playing soccer. Wall ball and foursquare get really tough when you are rooted to one spot and your arms are attached to thin metal poles.

Eventually I figured if I had to wear my legs on the playground, I'd do something I wanted to do instead of watching everybody else play games I couldn't participate in. So I became that kid in the corner who reads books while everybody else runs around playing games of freeze tag and red rover. Eventually even this got old. I wanted to play like everybody else.

My self-esteem was falling to an all-time low. Being in a wheelchair was more than enough reason for me to be singled out, but the issue wasn't my wheelchair. When I was in the chair, I had choices. I could choose to get out of my chair. I could choose to zoom around in my chair. I could choose to do handstands. Because of that freedom, I knew who I was. I didn't know who I was when I was wearing my legs. When I was wearing my legs, my choices were limited. When I wore my legs, I saw myself as a slow-moving cripple, and that changed how I viewed the world. I felt left out and picked on. When I wore my legs, I couldn't play any of the games the other kids were playing. I couldn't run around in P. E. if we ever went outside. I would be placed on the sideline to watch, or one of the students would be assigned to play a game with me. I was the kid who needed "special attention." I was also gaining weight. I had always liked to eat, and now, with the limited movement, I was putting on the pounds.

After a couple of months, I finally broke down and decided to let my mom know how miserable it was for me to feel so isolated from my peers.

"Mom, I am sick of wearing my legs," I complained after school one day. "I can't do very much with them on."

"Kacey, you are going to be able to walk anywhere one day! You just need to practice walking with them," Mom replied, exasperation creeping into her voice.

"I really want to be able to play at recess," I said in the most pathetic way possible. "Can I at least take my legs off to play with the other kids?"

"What do you do now?" Mom said.

"Sit and read books under the covered area," I said.

"Okay, we will talk to your teacher about letting you take off your legs for recess," Mom said. "But only during recess, Kacey. You need to make sure you put them right back on when you're back in class."

If my legs snapped on and off like the legs of my sister's dolls, it would have made things a whole lot easier, but technology in the mid-'90s wasn't quite there yet. My right leg had to be strapped into place with plenty of underwear coverage to prevent a plastic-to-skin interaction. After that, the other leg had to be put on using lotion to create a seal as well as to make it slippery enough for the stub to slide down into the socket. Needless to say, it was a challenge to find lotion at school.

The first few times I took my legs off for recess, I was more than happy to put them back on because I had won the battle—I was free to be a regular kid on the playground. But soon I discovered the longer I waited to put them back on, the longer I didn't have to wear them. It got to the point where I was testing how far I could push my teachers before they forced me to put them back on. Sometimes I would push the issue so much it would pretty much be time for the next recess and, before you knew it, the day was over and I still hadn't put my legs back on. This was fine by me. Then I made a grave error. I returned home without my legs on.

"Why don't you have your legs on?" Mom said, folding her arms across her chest and taking a firm stance in front of me when I came through the front door.

"I don't know," I said. "I never got around to putting them back on."

"What do you mean you didn't get around to putting them back on?" Mom said, clearly not satisfied with my lame explanation. "You are supposed to put them on right after recess!"

"I know, Mom. I'll do better," I said. After that I made sure to have my legs on by the time I got home.

She knew me well enough to know I had purposely avoided putting them back on. That was not the last time either. Despite the best efforts of the adults in my life, I found as many reasons as I could to get out of

---

THERE WAS SOMETHING INTRINSICALLY SATISFYING ABOUT THE THRILL OF A JOB WELL DONE.

---

wearing my legs. In my legs I felt limited and crippled. When I was out of my legs, though, I was able to do so much more.

Once I was out of my legs, the world opened up to me; I was finally free. It felt like the first time I got to ride in a wheelchair; I had a mobility I didn't have when my legs were on. I could swing across monkey bars or play four square, wall ball, soccer, basketball, jump rope, hopscotch, kickball, or dodge ball, or I could pretend to be a Power Ranger on the top of the play structure. I chose who and what I wanted to be.

I hated wearing my legs, but it was teaching me that even if you hate something, there is a strength that comes from working at it. My legs required me to work at standing. They required me to work really hard to figure out how to walk. They even required me to figure out how to sit down. Everything with the legs was hard. Yet there is a saying: "I can do hard things." My mom understood this. She didn't know if I would use my legs in the future, but she did know I needed the opportunity to. And to have that chance, I needed to wear them all the time, so I was forced to wear them every day to school (I took them off the second I got home) and four hours every day during the summertime to practice.

So I learned to work at a very young age, and I loved it. There was something intrinsically satisfying about the thrill of a job well done.

# CHAPTER 5
# HARD WORK IS MY SUPERPOWER

*"Opportunity is missed by most people
because it is dressed in overalls and looks like work."*
—*Author Unknown*[6]

Nowadays people are convinced that to be successful you need to become a viral sensation on the Internet. In reality, it is the small victories that nobody hears about that translate into lifelong success. At this time in my life I did things that I considered were normal and humdrum. But they weren't. How many kids wake up early and go out in the bitterly cold rain or snow to deliver papers? Well, I was one of those kids. My parents instilled a strong work ethic in me, and I gladly volunteered for any job I came across, and it wasn't because I needed the money. Even as a young boy, I understood that true happiness and success comes not from the green in your pocket but from the sense of accomplishment of a job well done.

SOON AFTER WE MOVED TO Keizer, I started looking for ways to make money. I was nine years old, and I had been preparing to be a missionary; I'd need enough to pay my own way. I also knew I wanted to go to college one day, and even as an elementary student, I understood college didn't come cheap. There aren't many jobs on the market for a kid in elementary school, but a friend let Keith and me help on his paper route. After a few weeks he ended up giving us his morning paper route.

---

6 "Opportunity Is Missed Because It Is Dressed in Overalls and Looks Like Work," Quote Investigator, posted August 13, 2012, https://quoteinvestigator.com/2012/08/13/overalls-work/.

I put my early-riser skills to good use and got to work. I proceeded to deliver my fifty newspapers around the neighborhood. It was no easy task to start. I was up every morning at five to wrap and stuff the papers into waterproof bags (it was Oregon, after all), and then they were crammed into a special bag my mom had sewn for me that fit on the front of my chair. One newspaper is pretty light, but with my bag full it felt like I had an entire library of textbooks sitting on my lap.

One of the biggest challenges was getting up a giant hill by our house. Without papers on my lap, I could get up the hill just fine, but with them it was tough going. I put on my thinking cap to figure out how to solve this latest obstacle. I couldn't have my parents push me up the hill every morning.

I tried zigzagging up the hill. That worked, but it took way too long. I tried putting the papers on the back of my chair. That just made me tip over. Finally I tried going up backward. Yep, that did it. I was able to get up the hill by myself. It was slow going, but at least I could make it up on my own. Going up and down that hill gave me more muscles. I was getting strong. This paper route that had not one, but two hills on its path forced me to train my muscles to work. I got better and stronger every day. After a month of going backward, I was able to tackle the hill going forward.

This marked one of the first times in my post-accident life that I'd come across something that had temporarily stumped me. The paper route taught me I could hold down a taxing job when I got older because I had successfully figured out how to navigate and push through the challenges this job had presented without help or guidance. Even when I had to sit on my hands between houses to get them warm enough to get to the next house, I kept on delivering those papers. Handing off the route to a "more abled" person never crossed my mind.

One day while I was flinging papers, I saw an ad for a dachshund I thought would be a perfect addition to my life. I have always loved dogs, but the dogs we had were always my dad's dogs and mostly Labrador retrievers. Walking them was like getting pulled around by a four-wheeler. I kind of had to hold on and make sure I didn't die. A dachshund seemed like a better match for me. After I'd finished that morning's route, I approached my mom to test the waters while she was making breakfast.

"Mom, can I have a dog?" I said.

She gave me a mom look I knew meant absolutely not.

"No, I am not getting you a dog," she replied.

My parents were never the kinds to buy us things just because. We had to work for it.

"No, Mom," I said. "I am going to buy her with my first paper-route check."

"Kacey, you're going to have to feed her," she said.

"I know, Mom," I replied calmly. I knew all of the things that were coming in this conversation, and I had my responses ready.

"And walk her," she continued.

"Yep, got it," I said.

"And she will be an outside dog," Mom said, drawing her final line in the sand. Mom hated having dogs inside the house.

"I agree to all the terms and conditions, Mom," I said, mentally ticking off potential names for my new pet.

"Okay, you can get the dog," Mom said.

The dachshund, which probably weighed no more than seven pounds, came with a spiked collar and a name to match. I decided her name would no longer be Spike but Suzie Q, after the snack cakes. Getting her with my first paper-route check was very gratifying for me. I had done all the hard work to get the money, and now I was able to get my own dog. I learned a lesson that day: hard work pays off. Even if sometimes the reward isn't easily visible. Getting up before everyone else every morning was hard. But I have never been afraid of hard things.

As soon as I got done with my route, I hurried to get to school an hour early. Why an hour early? I had joined the choir. I was not a gifted singer by any stretch of the imagination. I loved it though. I was that kid in music class and Sunday School singing at the top of my lungs to every song. I mentioned that when I was in the hospital people had brought me singalong books on tape. I would memorize every song and sing it over and over and over again.

We sang a compilation of Broadway show tunes, many of which I knew already because we grew up watching musicals like *The Sound of Music*, *Oklahoma*, *West Side Story*, *Grease*, and *Newsies*. Everyone in my house loved to sing. I never realized I sang too loudly or was not hitting the right notes. I really didn't know until I was an adult that I probably shouldn't be singing a solo. But over the years I did get better and learned quite a bit about music.

I loved singing, but how I had always identified myself was by my ability to be active. My mom and dad had instilled in us kids the love of being active and playing sports. At nearly six feet tall, our mom was always taller than those around her, and she used her height to her advantage, mastering volleyball, softball, and dance. Dad was slightly shorter but equally athletic and competed in baseball, basketball, football, wrestling, hunting, and any other sport he could get involved in.

For me it was baseball for a few years, but as elementary came to a close, I started looking at other sports options. Before I knew it I was trying out for the local youth basketball league. Keith was trying out, so I decided I wanted to as well. I knew I was not the best player out there, but there was no way I was the worst either. I was able to get out of my wheelchair and chase the other players up and down the floor. Passing the ball was a cinch. I could dribble the ball as well as anybody else and loved guarding my opponents. When it came to shooting, however, I could not sink a shot to save my life. That was not surprising, considering I sat less than three feet off the ground. I worked hard in tryouts to show I could accomplish anything.

After tryouts were over, the director invited my parents to his home to talk. When they got there, they found out just how hard it would be for me to get to play basketball.

"Mr. and Mrs. McCallister, we recommend Kacey not play basketball," said the director.

"He wants to play," Mom said. "Let him play."

"I don't know if it would be the best situation for him," he said, trying his best to be tactful.

"He wants to play. Let him play," Mom repeated, refusing to go along with the idea that I should be asked to stop doing something I enjoyed.

"We don't want him to get hurt," the director said.

"He will be all right," Mom insisted. "One, he is a tough kid. Two, he doesn't care if he gets hurt; he just wants to play. Three, let him play."

"We are worried about the legal ramifications if he gets injured," he said, finally getting to the real issue at hand.

"That's why there are waivers," Mom replied, losing her patience. "*Let him play.*"

"Once again, we recommend he doesn't play," the man repeated. My parents battled with him for another thirty minutes, trying to get him to let me play, but he never changed his mind.

Well, I didn't get to play that year, but I was never one to sit around and feel sorry for myself. All I could do was buck up and show people what I was capable of. I wasn't ready to throw in the towel on my burgeoning basketball career just yet.

The following year there were new directors, so we figured maybe they would see that I would be a great addition to their program. I pushed myself even harder than the year before, and with the extra strength from pushing my wheelchair up and down the hill for my morning paper route, I was that much stronger.

Despite my solid performance, the new directors stood firm, basically saying, "We don't want to get sued because your crippled son wants to do something everybody else gets to do."

When this happened the first time, we were merely disappointed. This time we were mad. As we exited the building, I had a thought.

"Mom," I said. "Do you think the paper would like to write a story about a kid playing basketball without legs?"

I was always reading headlines in the papers I delivered about people accomplishing "the impossible." I was okay with attempting the impossible, and I knew I could inspire others.

"Yes, Kacey, I think they would," she said with fire and determination in her voice that foreshadowed the battle brewing in her head.

"Well, these guys will feel pretty silly when I make the papers playing for somebody else," I said as we got into the car.

Mom hunted down a recreational league for boys my age. It didn't take her long to find one at the local Boys and Girls Club.

"How can I help you?" said the guy at the front desk.

"I want to play basketball," I said, looking him right in the eyes.

"Okay, here is the form," he said, barely looking up from his computer screen.

"You mean I can play?" I said.

"I can check with my boss, but there shouldn't be a problem," he replied, stepping away from the desk to go find his boss.

We waited on pins and needles; my hands were sweaty with anticipation. I kept glancing at the door. It seemed like it was taking forever. Finally he returned with a determined look on his face. I knew what was coming. Another disappointment.

"Yes, you can play," he said, smiling at me. "We don't stop anyone from playing."

I was so excited. The battle was over, and we'd won. I was going to play basketball like everybody else. I don't think I stopped smiling for a week.

The season turned out to be everything I wanted and more. What made it especially good was our coach, Coach Cheeseburger. His real name was not actually Cheeseburger, but that's what we called him. He earned this nickname after eating a ton of cheeseburgers. It wasn't until his name was called on picture day that we learned his name was actually John Witherspoon. Cheeseburger, or Cheese for short, was a big guy. He stood at six feet tall and had a nice big belly that entered the room before he did.

Cheese was not the most polished coach out there. He worked as a mechanic and always came to practice with grease embedded in the grooves of his hands. His battered plaid jacket always had a hole or two in it, and his dirty hair curled out of the bottom of an equally dirty ball cap. But he gave me an outlet to express my love of sports. I found out years later that Cheeseburger was the second coach they called to take me on their team. The first coach didn't want to have me on his team because he figured winning was just too important, so Cheese got the second call. He had a way of making every one of us feel loved and cared-for with his good-natured ribbing and signature funny nicknames like "Chicken Lips." We even had our own team motto: "We may not be the best team out there, but at least we eat good." It may not have been the most athletic motto, but we got a kick out of it. And, true to the motto, Cheese would always take us out for burgers, pizza, or crushed ice after every game.

I was not the most talented player on the team. In fact, I was quite possibly the worst. I didn't make a basket the entire season. Every once in a while Cheese would send me off to practice shots on my own while he talked to the rest of the team. I didn't know what they were meeting about, but then during one game they put their plan into effect: as soon as I made a basket, the whole team dog-piled on top of me in celebration. We ended up winning the game by two points, which made me feel like I had really made a difference in the game.

I got famous that year. I was only a fifth grader, but that didn't stop the local newspaper from running a three-page spread on me, and basketball was featured as one of my accomplishments. Boy, the directors from the youth basketball league must have been embarrassed. The story was picked up by other newspapers, *Boys' Life* (a Boy Scouts of America magazine), and TV stations all over the world, not to mention the *Associated Press* and CNN. Strangely enough, I did not hear a peep from the directors who had decided not to let me play basketball.

Journalists flew in from as far away as Korea and Germany to interview me. Camera crews followed me on my paper route and around school, and some of them even wanted to film how I went to the bathroom. I was pretty weirded out. Why did these people think my daily routine was noteworthy? I was just a kid. Sure, playing basketball was pretty cool, but pushing myself to school was just something that needed to be done. I realized not many of my classmates got up at the crack of dawn to deliver newspapers. I just wanted to be viewed as a normal kid. My mom told me that in other countries it was unheard of for a kid without legs to do the things I did on a daily basis. More than anything else, though, it was annoying. Not only were they following me around but I often had to stop and wait for them to get a better shot. I just wanted to do what I had always done. But, on the other hand, it was pretty cool to get put on TV. Many of my classmates thought it was cool I was being filmed and hung around in hopes of being interviewed themselves. It even prompted girls to talk to me. My family kept me grounded though. My siblings continued to make fun of me, and my parents made sure I continued to be respectful and not let the attention go to my head.

By the time I entered middle school, I was confident in who I was and about my potential. I had gone from being an insecure little boy to a self-assured, resilient, (slightly) bigger boy. I was going to show the world I could rise up and fly.

# CHAPTER 6
## THE NEW KACEY

*"I took the one less traveled by,*
*and that has made all the difference."*
*—Robert Frost, American poet*[7]

Middle school is tough for just about any kid. For me it provided a time to find out who I really was, and my path led straight to sports. This was not the easiest path for me. I was never going to be given a free ride, unless that free ride included sitting on the sidelines cheering for my teammates. Fighting an uphill battle every day molded me into the person I would be for the rest of my life. At times I felt like the Greek mythological figure Sisyphus, every day rolling a giant stone up the mountain only to have it roll back down. That is still a huge part of life. We cannot measure a task only by the outcome. We can and must measure the task by the battle fought along the way. Running a 5K is a minor accomplishment for some of us, but for others— an amputee veteran, a cancer survivor, the obese, or the newly disabled—it is a whole new lease on life. Everyone's journey takes a different road. I decided to choose a challenging one.

I WAS ONCE AGAIN CONFIDENT in myself. The one place I always felt like I belonged was on the playing field. As a consequence of this newfound confidence in sports, I was gaining a lot more muscle and using up more of the energy I was still stuffing into my face. I wasn't worried about my weight because I was starting to figure out who I was.

7 Robert Lee Frost, "The Road Not Taken," *Public Domain Poetry,* http://www.public-domain-poetry.com/robert-lee-frost/road-not-taken-1222.

In seventh grade I had a group of friends, mostly from church, whom I walked home with. My mom still made me wear my legs to school every day, so it was a lot harder to push my wheelchair because I had to carry my crutches, backpack, and fake legs. So instead I worked out a deal with my friends. I would carry their band instruments, and they would push my wheelchair. Then at the top of the big hill I pushed up to do my paper route, we would separate, and I would zoom down the hill to my house.

One day they did not show up after school. I sat around for a while wondering where they were—maybe they had a band meeting. With a shrug I pushed myself home. The next day they were there again.

"Hey, where were you guys yesterday?" I said, a little irritated I'd had to push home by myself.

"We're starting a sport, so we won't be able to walk home with you for a while," said Greg Nelson.

"What sport?" I asked. I was always looking for things to do and be a part of.

"Wrestling," Tyler Davison said.

"Really? Is it fun?" I asked.

"Oh yeah! It is," Greg replied. "But it's really hard, too."

Well, that sounded right up my alley—something challenging but fun. When I finally got out on the wrestling mat, I knew I had found my sport. I knew there was something special about wrestling. To begin with, there were no tryouts. You didn't have to earn your way onto the team. Anybody was welcome to come and see if they had what it took to be a wrestler. As long as your medical form was filled out and you paid your team fee, you could come and test your muscles against whoever was there. The team's coach was Mr. Mann. He had a large birthmark on his face that made me think he had been burned. I thought it made him look tough, like he had some awesome story of saving pygmy koalas while fighting forest fires in the Australian outback.

I loved the challenge wrestling presented. It is the hardest sport I know of. It combines every single bit of athleticism there is. Because of that I took to it with a drive I hadn't realized I had. I had to be fast to attack my opponent's legs before he could get me off balance. I had to have strength to flip him over and fight for control. I needed endurance to be able to last the entire match. Six minutes did not seem like a long time when I was playing basketball, but in wrestling six minutes is a lifetime. Many times my opponent and I would be exhausted near the end of a match, and the outcome would come down to who had the greater endurance. Skill is also a factor, of course. As wrestlers we are not a just a group of meatheads pounding away at each other. The smarter I could be on the wrestling mat, the better I would wrestle. I found that brute strength is not as important in wrestling as being strategic and outthinking your opponent.

One of the biggest problems for me in wrestling was that my coaches had never coached someone without legs. They had never had to worry about how to adapt moves to fit a different wrestling style. This caused me to have to adapt the moves on my own. Many times I would ask for help with a move, and the coach would come over to try and help me by getting down on their knees and trying to make it work. But being on your knees is not the same as not having legs. So I had to create my own moves.

The first few tries were pretty laughable. The first move I made up I called the "log roll." I would roll like a log . . . until my opponent pinned me. That's not how it was supposed to work. I was supposed to grab his leg and take him down when I rolled close enough to him, but I usually just got pinned. Another one involved me spinning while sitting upright. This brought similar results. Maybe I had watched too many World Wrestling Entertainment matches in which moves like that actually worked.

Another huge disadvantage for me was leverage. There are a lot of moves in wrestling that do not depend on strength alone. You need to be able to position your body so you can tip, turn, spin, or otherwise move your opponent into a position in which you can take them down and pin them to the mat. Without legs this required a good deal of adapting. One of the advantages I used to adapt was that my arms were the size of their legs. This came from all the time I spent walking around on my hands. The extra strength allowed me to muscle through many problems.

I also had to figure out how to adjust my body in order to turn my opponents to their back. In wrestling you are placed according to your weight. With half my body gone, I had a pretty sweet advantage on the weight scale. Despite not having the leverage of my legs, I did have the arm strength of a kid weighing 140 pounds, yet I weighed less than a hundred. One of the biggest advantages I had was that I was being taught how to wrestle kids with legs, but they weren't being taught how to wrestle a kid with no legs. This caused many wrestlers to become frustrated, some even running around the mat trying to figure out what to do.

My first match served as an important lesson. Within the first minute of the first round, I ended up on my back. Surprised at how fast I was put on my back, I fought from my back until the referee counted to five. Thinking that meant the match was over, I gave up and lay down on the mat only to learn that it is when both shoulders touched the mat that you are pinned. I was disappointed and a little embarrassed. I had a couple more matches that day, but I never made that mistake again.

That whole first year of wrestling was all about learning from my mistakes. Sometimes, for example, when you make up moves, they are stupid and don't work. And it is a good idea to learn all the rules.

The most important thing wrestling did for me, though, was show me I was tough. Each practice was more challenging than the last one, but no matter what workout or punishment our coach threw at us, I found I could take what was dished out and keep going strong. This was a major boost to my self-esteem.

I knew who I was. I was a wrestler. All the other junk that happens in middle school seemed to not matter as much. I was still eating a lot. But, hey, I love food. The difference now was that I was burning it off as fast as I could shove it in. That first year of wrestling I only won one match. It was an exhibition match—it didn't count toward the team score—and I won in overtime. Despite my lack of wins, I knew wrestling was going to be one of my favorite sports.

As soon as wrestling was over, I started looking for something else to do. I didn't want to just go home like I had before. I wanted to continue playing sports. I went to the office to find out what all was available. It came down to either track or baseball. I had already done baseball and was not super excited to sit in the outfield the entire game, but I liked pushing my wheelchair, so I decided to try out for track. It should be easy, I figured. You just went around a hard track as fast as you could until the race was over.

Immediately I found I enjoyed doing the distance events. They were the longest and the hardest. The longer I could compete, the happier I was. I was not satisfied with a 100-meter dash that lasted a few seconds. No, I wanted to see how long I could last. Not only did I enjoy it but I was also good at it. As my confidence grew, I began to make friends with my fellow distance runners. I was disappointed when the season ended because I would have to wait until school started again to continue sports.

The next school year started, and I was an eighth grader. I was on top of the world. I made it into concert choir, I took a drama class and found I really enjoyed acting, and I was thrilled for another year of wrestling. To prepare for wrestling, though, I had to maintain and even possibly improve my cardio. I figured the best way to do that was to join another sport during the off-season. I was feeling great about who I was and wanted to get even better at what I was doing.

The options for fall sports in middle school came down to two choices: cross country or football. I had played backyard football with my brother for most of my life, so I was comfortable with the idea. But I could also see how playing football had the potential to turn out like my baseball career: sitting on the sidelines not doing anything.

Cross country, on the other hand, was a running experience that did not involve paved roads, and in Oregon that meant a lot of mud and grass. The idea both intrigued and frightened me. Racing across grass and mud in a wheelchair? That would be a lot harder than sitting down in the grass and trying to tackle the guy with the football. Despite that, I knew I could do anything, so it seemed perfectly logical to try the more challenging sport. I had already made it through a year of wrestling, and as one of the greatest wrestlers of all time, Dan Gable, once said: "Once you wrestle, everything else in life is easy."[8]

8 Dan Gable, *A Wrestling Life: The Inspiring Stories of Dan Gable,* Iowa City, IA: University of Iowa Press, 2016.

My decision was also partially based on the individuality of the sport. I liked the idea of being out there on my own with no one else to rely on—just me and the course. I went to the main office, picked up the form for cross country, and took it home.

"Cross country?" Mom said when I handed her the permission slip.

"Yeah! I thought it would be fun," I said.

"Well, Kacey, cross country is not exactly going to be easy to do in a wheelchair," she said, mirroring the concerns I'd had earlier about being able to navigate the course.

"So what, Mom?" I said, firing back. Why was she giving me such a hard time about trying a new sport? "I can do anything. It might be hard, but I'll figure it out."

"Kacey, cross country is not just running around a track," she said, concern tinting her voice. "Cross country is up and down hills. It is over grass and mud. You have to go through the trees—"

"Mom!" I said, my voice raising in defiance. "I am not going to run into a tree! They're big and round; I'll go *around* the tree, not *through* it."

"Kacey, you know what I mean," she said, exasperated. "Let's wait until your dad gets home to make a final decision about this."

The rest of the afternoon I waited around the house for Dad to get home. I had never known my parents to believe I wasn't capable, and now they were saying running a race would be too much of a challenge for me? I thought that was strange. They had encouraged me to do baseball, basketball, go on campouts, and hike trails in the woods, and now they were telling me that cross country was going to be too hard. Why? I was very frustrated to one day be told I could do everything and now to be told not to do something because it was too hard. Whatever their reasons, I was going to show them I could do anything. They had trained me to never take no for an answer, and now they were going to get exactly what they had trained me for.

By the time my dad got home, I was in my bedroom reading a book. He came in and sat next to me on my bed.

"Kacey, your mom tells me you want to do cross country," he said in a serious voice. "Hey, bud, I don't know if it's such a good idea. It will be pretty muddy, and the grass will be hard to get through as well."

"Dad, do you think this is impossible for me to do?" I asked.

"Well, no," he said, looking directly into my eyes and placing a hand on each of my shoulders. "I just think it will be . . . *challenging*."

"Well, then, I want to do it!" I responded excitedly. "The harder it is, the more I want to do it."

"Okay, if you want to do it, we will let you, but if you start it, you have to finish it," Dad said.

"Sure, Dad," I said, rolling my eyes. Of course I had to finish it. My parents had been telling us this from the time we were little kids. We all knew the requirements for doing an activity. It didn't matter if you were good at it or if it got hard. You had to finish it.

I took my signed form and my $25 down to the athletic office. The next day at school as I was sitting in science class, I got called to the office, where they sat me down in front of a bunch of adults, all of whom looked at me with serious faces.

"Am I in trouble?" I asked.

The principal chuckled a little. "No, Kacey," he said. "This is about cross country."

"Oh! There's an interview process?" I asked nervously.

The guidance counselor leaned forward.

"We just wanted to talk to you for a minute about it," he said. "Kacey, why do you want to do cross country?"

"Uh . . . I thought it would be challenging and fun, maybe?" I said, laughing a little to try to lighten the mood.

The cross country coach spoke up. "Well, Kacey, cross country is quite challenging," he said. "There is grass and mud and—"

"Trees!" I spoke up, cutting him off. "My mom told me about the trees. Don't worry though. I will go *around* the trees, not *into* them. That would hurt. I would need an ax to go through them, and that wouldn't be safe to run with an ax, so I'll just, uh, go around the trees."

"That's fine, Kacey," said the counselor. "One last question: What are your goals for cross country?"

I didn't know there was homework. It seemed weird to have to lay out your goals before doing a sport. Was I supposed to do this in essay format?

"My goals are to, uh, have fun, get better times in the races, and, um, beat somebody," I said, hunching my shoulders and hoping they would accept my goals as good enough. "But if I don't, that's okay. I just want to have fun."

"Kacey, we recommend you don't do cross country," the principal said, glancing at the others around the table for confirmation.

My head went down in disappointment but just as suddenly came back up again.

"Can I play football?" I asked, not yet ready to throw in the towel on participating in fall sports. I waited nervously as they looked at each other with concern and consideration. I could tell when they made a silent decision.

And then they said yes! Cross country was apparently way too dangerous for me, but football was perfectly safe. Cross country meant facing down scary trees; football had pads and helmets. Cross country bad; football good. So football it was.

I was on the lightweight team. That meant we were all under 125 pounds. After a year of wrestling, I had dropped some of that extra weight from elementary school and weighed around 80 pounds. The coach gave me plenty of pads and a helmet and sent me out to play football.

I did enjoy playing football, except for the part where I had to sit on the sidelines. That was the thing I couldn't stand about team sports: unless you were the top guy, you were always sitting on the bench. I was not very good at tackling, so they put me on the front line, where I could do the most damage. And by "do the most damage," I mean sit there and wait for someone to run through the defensive line so I could grab them. I was pretty good at this job, especially because I was sitting on the ground. The running back would see this nice empty hole and try to run through it, but I would be sitting right there waiting to grab his ankles.

Our team didn't win a single game. Regardless of that, I had a great time running around in the soggy Oregon grass, proving there was nothing that could truly hold me back.

Not only was I growing more confident about my athletic prowess, but I was also beginning to explore what I could do in other areas of my life. My choir teacher had us try out for spots for an honor choir trip to Seattle to participate in a singing camp and concert. Well, of course, that sounded like fun for me. I tried out, and to my surprise I made it in the group as a bass. Our teacher made each of us a tape of all the songs, as well as the parts we would be singing. I spent hours poring over that tape, going over my parts time and time again. I often stayed up late to make sure I had my parts down perfectly.

A week later we had our first after-school practice together. There were two of us for each part. All of the other students who were going were known as the choir students; these were the ones who seemed to be naturally gifted singers. Most of them were also in jazz choir and were considered to be the best singers in school. Meanwhile, here I was, a nobody in the singing world of Whiteaker Middle School, but as we started our first practice, I realized that hardly anybody else knew the songs.

As the lesson progressed, the teacher looked around and saw what had happened. None of her superstar singers had bothered to listen to the tapes. In fact, from the look of things, it seemed as if many of them had not even looked at the sheet music. My music folder was beat up and ragged from numerous uses on a daily basis, whereas many others' folders looked as if they'd never been taken out of their backpacks. I felt like my persistence put me in a position to sing with the best kids in the school because I knew I could work harder than any of them.

The lessons continued, and we eventually made it to Seattle. The trip was a lot of fun. I loved cruising down the streets of Seattle, practicing with kids from all over the Pacific Northwest in a building that was older than my parents (I didn't know how that was possible. I mean, were there cathedrals when dinosaurs roamed the earth?). As a teenage boy I was pretty excited to meet all the girls who were there, and I made a lot of new friends.

On the first day, there was a call for solo tryouts. Once again, disregarding the fact that I couldn't sing as well as the others, I tried out for all of the solos I could. I didn't get a single one, of course, but the director made a point of thanking me for trying out anyway.

At the end of the week we sang in a beautiful old cathedral with soaring ceilings and stained-glass windows. My parents came up to listen to the music and were both very proud. My parents have always supported me, no matter what I've done. Whether it was a concert in Seattle or just sitting in the cold mud on the side of the football field, they were there.

Between choir and football, fall was a blast, but it was just a lead-up to what I was really looking forward to: wrestling. My first season had ended with only one mark in the win column, and I was ready for more.

My second season started off a lot better than the year before. Joining football had helped me get stronger and added some muscle to my small

---

MOST SCRAPPERS ARE NOT NATURALLY GIFTED, BUT THEY MORE THAN MAKE UP FOR IT BY REFUSING TO GIVE UP.

---

frame. I got moved up to the varsity wrestling team, which meant that not only was I the top guy in my weight class, but I was also up against tougher opponents.

During the previous summer I had gone to a couple of wrestling day camps and learned a lot. The greatest lesson was that it paid to be a scrapper. It's always tough to wrestle a scrapper because they just won't quit. Their head is always up, making it nearly impossible to put them in holds. Every time you take them down, they stand right back up. Most scrappers are not naturally gifted, nor are they the best technical wrestlers out there, but they more than make up for it by refusing to give up.

Well, I became a scrapper. Gone were the days when I would let my shoulders go to the mat because I thought the match was done. Gone were the times of misunderstanding the rules. Gone were the days when I would only win a nothing match in overtime. I was ready to do some damage.

I learned moves on my own. One such instance came at Parrish Middle School, where I was wrestling the varsity match against a similarly matched opponent. I slid under him to grab a leg. He sprawled out on top of me to try and get his leg away, but doing this put his arm in easy reach, so I grabbed his arm and lifted him onto my shoulders. Boy did I feel strong. I played it up for the crowd for a minute and then put him on the mat, staying on top of him to get my two takedown points. I later learned that move was called the Fireman's Carry.

By the time wrestling season was over, I had racked up a half-dozen varsity wins. I knew I would be a wrestler for a long time to come. I was not an insecure little kid; I was now a tough wrestler, and it showed off the mat as well.

One time I was in the bathroom at middle school when a group of kids came in and started bad-mouthing me.

"Hey, you guys know that kid in the wheelchair?" one voice said.

"Yeah, he's so lame," another responded.

"What do you think would happen if I pushed him out of his wheelchair?" a third voice said.

"Ha, ha, he'd probably just lay there with that dumb look on his face," the first voice replied.

"He is like the Michael Jordan of being super annoying!" the second voice said.

"If only he would roll himself off a cliff," the third voice said.

I was amazed. I could not believe this was actually happening. I thought this kind of thing only happened in the movies. They were making fun of me. I kept thinking they must be just playing around. Somehow they must have known I was in there and were just trying to play a joke on me. After a minute I realized they actually were trying to make fun of me. I guess I should have been offended or something, but instead I thought it was hilarious. This was even funnier than if they had been playing a joke on me. The question was what was I going to do about it? I was having trouble controlling my amusement as I tried to determine what to do.

I considered staying put until they left so they wouldn't be embarrassed. But I couldn't resist; I knew I was going to bust out a laugh any second, but right then, an even funnier idea came to mind. I needed to act fast before they left. I opened the door and wheeled out of the stall to wash my hands. As soon as I opened the door, they stopped talking. It was absolutely silent, except for the sound of my tires quietly squeaking on the tile floor. I couldn't see their faces, which was probably good because I would have laughed so hard. I pointedly ignored them as I finished washing my hands and rolled to the paper towels. As I dried my hands, I heard a voice behind me say, "We weren't talking about you, dude."

I turned around and looked at them for a second before smiling and rolling out the door. It was a picture-perfect exit. If there's ever a movie made about my life, this has got to be in it. I left them speechless and scared to ever badmouth somebody in the bathroom without at least first checking underneath the stalls. As soon as the door shut, I laughed my head off. Through the entire day I would find myself grinning and remember my favorite bathroom break ever.

I was on a roll as an athlete. I had laid some serious smackdown on the wrestling mat and conquered a brand-new sport. Now it was time to enjoy my second season of track. My times improved. The most momentous thing to happen, though, was receiving a racing chair. A local citizen had heard about me racing in my regular chair and decided to loan me his old racer he didn't use anymore. The racing chair is not like the typical wheelchair you see roaming the streets and malls of your local town. It is a three-wheeled, elongated piece of aluminum that's been adapted and changed over the years to lower friction and increase speed. These days it looks more like a personalized rocket on wheels or a one-man bobsled than your standard everyday wheelchair. It seems like it belongs more on a speedway than a jogging path.

With my racing chair, I was going faster as soon as I hit the track. The first race of the season I was speeding down the track, hitting better times than I ever had before. I enjoyed the freedom and speed the race chair gave me. In my regular chair I was fast, but in the race chair I was a lightning bolt.

With great grades and success in the athletic arena, I was ready for high school. I was even asked to speak to a class of fifth-grade graduates at my former elementary school about middle school. I told the kids classes were more difficult and there was a ton more homework. I also told them about the awesome electives like choir, band, cooking, sewing, drama, and wood shop. I loved talking to them. Both the elementary students and I were about to embark on a whole new journey in a whole new school, but first it was time for summer. Keith had already been planning on going to a basketball camp that summer. Feeling a little left out, I started looking for a camp I wanted to go to. I didn't want to go to a basketball camp; I had gone to wrestling day camps in the past, but what I really wanted was a challenge. As I looked around I saw a lot of different camps, most of them lasting only a couple of days. Then I saw something that lit the fire inside me: a two-week intensive wrestling camp.

The camp was located on the University of Oregon campus. It was more than going to a fun practice to learn some neat moves. This was a full-on, three-practices-a-day, wake-up-at-five-A.M. kind of camp. I was excited. I had been told about how hard high school wrestling would be compared to middle school wrestling, and I wanted to start off right. This camp was going to be harder than anything else I had ever done. Not only that but I would get to live on my own for two weeks.

The college wrestlers who were there with us drove us hard to show us just how far we could push ourselves. We had five workouts a day, consisting of one run early in the morning and another at night and three wrestling practices, for two weeks straight. It was awesome. We would hit them so hard that the only things we could do in our off time were eat and sleep. Each day pushed us to the brink of total exhaustion. At night my head would hit the pillow so hard I would be asleep before the pillow was no longer cold. Then, a few short hours later, we would be up early to go for a long run.

I was not in my prime yet, but I was getting stronger. I was getting better, and more than that, I was learning what it takes to truly be an elite athlete. Whether I was running steps in Autzen Stadium using my hands, pushing my chair running up the steepest hills near campus, or trying to take down a college wrestler on the mat, I was up for the challenge. I was not the best wrestler there, but I would not let anybody call me a quitter. There were times the college wrestlers told me I could sit out a workout. This made me laugh. I'd retort that *they* could take a break and I'd do their set.

I did experience quite the culture shock hanging around the other wrestlers. I was brought up in a very conservative household where there was no swearing, no vulgarity, and no bad movies. I experienced many things that made me cringe. My parents had raised me to not alter my values, regardless of the situations I was in. Even as the smallest and youngest kid at camp, I would nicely ask even the college wrestlers to not swear around me. I am sure they all thought I was a weird little kid, but for some reason they listened and tried not to swear around me. There was plenty of good-natured ribbing, but not a single one of them could find fault in my conviction.

There was only one workout on the last day of camp: a thirteen-mile loop around the city of Eugene that took us along the Willamette River and ended back at Hayward Field. Hayward is one of the world's best-known historic track-and-field stadiums in the country. It was exciting that we got to finish on the same track that had hosted some of the best athletes in the world.

I was not the fastest sprinter in the group, but what I lacked in acceleration I made up for with endurance. Within a mile of starting, I was out in front with only a couple of coaches ahead of me. The course wove for miles and miles along the lush path by the river, pushing my limits, but I kept going. I had come pretty far from that little boy fresh out of the hospital who could barely finish a mile.

I kept thinking there would come a time when I couldn't go any farther, but that time never came. In fact, I passed one of the coaches along the way. He was so surprised he thought I had cheated and taken a shortcut. Little did I know that would not be the last time I would cross the finish line at Hayward Field.

We finished the run with a few laps around the track. Before I was done, the coach I'd passed showed up and told me to do eight extra laps to make up for the shortcut he assumed I'd taken. I was shocked. I knew I had done the full thing and he was just sore because I had beaten him. I tried to argue with him, but the more we argued, the more laps we could get, so eventually I shut up and sped off around the track to do the extra laps. I was angry the coach hadn't believed me, but my anger disappeared as I raced around the curve and down the final straightway. No one else had even shown up by the time I was done. I had beat everyone else even with the extra laps. I had won, and I was determined to keep on winning. It was then and there I knew I would be a wrestling champion. I decided I would win state, and no one was going to stop me.

# CHAPTER 7
## LEARNING HOW TO BECOME GREAT

*"Sometimes I've believed as many as six impossible things before breakfast."*
*—Lewis Carroll*[9]

It has always been interesting to me how people classify what can and can't be done. There was a time when sports physicians, psychologists, and all of the people who supposedly knew all there was to know about human performance said it was impossible for anyone to run a four-minute mile. It took a bit of time, but it was done on May 6, 1954, by Sir Roger Bannister (himself a physician) on a cinder track in Oxford, England.[10]

What is it about our experiences that makes us think something is impossible? What is it about our lives that tells us we can't do something or makes us believe someone else can't do something? Is it just because we've never seen it happen so, therefore, it must be impossible? For me impossible is just something I haven't done yet.

Getting home from the two-week wrestling camp, I was fired up to become the best wrestler I could be, so I sought out more ways to train. A few times a week I would push my chair or ride my handcycle down to the high school to run stairs. I would spend an hour or so going up and down while the football team practiced on the field. I ran so many sets of stairs that there was a bright trail in the bleachers where my butt had passed over the

9 Lewis Carroll, *Through the Looking-glass*, New York: Dover Publications, Inc., 1999, 47.
10 John Bryant, 3:59.4: *The Quest to Break the 4 Minute Mile*, UK: Arrow Books Ltd, 2005.

same spot repeatedly. The only break I would take would be to do sit-ups or push-ups every five sets.

One day Keith came home and told me their football coach had used my workouts as an example to motivate the football players.

"You're too tired?" the coach would yell at them, shoving his finger in my direction. "That kid comes here every day, running up and down the stairs for longer than you run out here on a flat field, and *you're* too tired? Buck it up, Sally."

Ironically, when I was on a football team, I didn't get attention from the coaches. As my first year at McNary High School approached, I had a choice to make. Do I play football again? I knew what to expect. I would be on the sidelines for most of the game, wearing my pads and getting a cold butt sitting on the wet ground. The other option was to try again to join the cross-country team.

The day I went to the school to register for classes, one of my older friends who was on the cross-country team ran over and asked me if I was going to run with them. I was tentative and nervous. Was I going to be rejected like I had been in middle school? What were they going to tell me this time? I rolled into the athletic department, my heart beating a million miles an hour.

"Hey, I want to do cross country," I said in the calmest voice I could muster.

The secretary looked up from her work with a smile on her face.

"Okay. You will need to get the permission form signed and have a physical done," she said.

A little shocked and not quite ready to get my hopes up just yet, I told her they hadn't let me participate in middle school and asked if she was sure it would be okay.

"As long as the coach says it's good, then we don't have a problem with it," she said.

My heart leaped. I quickly got my physical and asked my mom to sign the form. She was no longer worried about it. She knew her stubborn redhead would find a way to make it happen. I was ready to take on this challenge I'd been told before wasn't a good idea for someone like me.

---

## IMPOSSIBLE IS JUST SOMETHING I HAVEN'T DONE . . . YET.

---

That year in cross country started out very much like my first year as a wrestler. I was slow, but it wasn't due to a lack of effort. Between wrestling camp and my preseason workout, I was ready to go. The problem was my chair was not. Have you ever tried to push a wheelchair or stroller over grass or skate across gravel? How about ride your bike uphill? Well, put all of that together and you can begin to understand the challenge of doing cross country in a wheelchair.

A regular everyday wheelchair has very small front tires, and mine were only about the size of an inline skate wheel. Any time there was the slightest unevenness in the ground, those tiny front wheels would try to dig in, bringing me to an abrupt halt or even ejecting me right out of my chair. I was slooooow. It took me forever to finish the courses. I was used to being fast. I would race up and down the halls all day long, but on a cross-country course that speed seemed to count for nothing.

It generally takes twenty to twenty-five minutes for an average person to finish a 5K cross-country race. I was more in the thirty- to thirty-five-minute range. Yet I improved in almost every race. I wasn't worried about winning. My first goal was simply to get better, but I *was* determined to do so. By the end of the season, I'd dropped my time by a few minutes, finishing at about twenty-eight minutes thirty seconds.

My second goal was to beat somebody. That first year I think the only people I beat were the people who dropped out of the race, at least for the first part of the season. By the end I was able to pass a couple of runners.

The most important part of taking on any sport, however, was my final goal: I wanted to have fun. This is such an important part of any activity because when you have fun you want to do it again. When you do it again, you want to do it better. Before you know it, you are on the road to getting good. And I always wanted to be better than the average runner.

One of the best races we did each year was called trask. Trask was pretty much a precursor to all those crazy mud runs. It was a 5K course that took runners over hills, through streams, and slogging through mud pits you'd sink into up to your knees (or, in my case, up to my chest). When I set out to tackle my first trask course in my freshman year, it was raining pretty hard, making everything extra muddy and slippery.

I started out thinking I'd be able to take my chair through some of the course. No course was great for wheelchairs, and I suspected this course would be that much harder to maneuver through, but I assumed I'd be able to figure it out once I got going. I had a friend on standby to take my chair if I couldn't go any farther.

Early on in the race we forded a stream. I jumped out of my chair to make the crossing while a teammate carried it to the other side. Hopping back in the chair, I continued to push up the course, but soon I realized my chair was not going anywhere. Rounding a corner in my chair, I saw the path slope downward. With all the grit I was able to manage, I pushed and shoved my chair through the mud. It got so muddy I eventually left my chair with a teammate and continued the rest of the way on my hands.

Near the end of the course was a valley we had to go down, and then we had to run across a stream at the bottom and head back up the other side. As I got to the top of the hill overlooking the drop-off, I was worried. The hill was steep and slick with mud. The trail had been thoroughly trashed. There was no vegetation anywhere along the main running part. The footprints illustrated that runners were sliding more than they were running. I knew that with one wrong move I'd be hurtling down the hill with no way to stop myself. I carefully inched my way down the slope, sliding my hands down the hill and trying to find anything that would serve as a handhold. It was too slick, though, and soon I was flying over the mud like a greased pig in a chute. I was very surprised when I reached the bottom of the hill in one piece, plunging into the stream. Landing in icy water over my head was a piece of cake compared to the death drop I had just survived.

The climb out of that valley was not as exciting, but it was much more painful. I was the last runner to come through. A lot of water from the rain and the swelling stream had washed out every foothold possible. I had to resort to climbing up the hill using every blackberry branch available on the side of the trail to pull myself up. For those of you unfamiliar with blackberry bushes, they are long vines that form giant bushes. Oh yeah, and they are covered with razor-sharp thorns. When I got to the finish line, there were not many people left to see me finish. Most people had gone home, and I was left with my ever-faithful teammates and, of course, my mom. Crossing the finish line was less like a victory and more like surviving a plane crash in the middle of nowhere. Exhausted and hurting, I crept over the line to the cheers of the McNary Celtic cross-country team.

After rinsing off the layers of mud, I found that not only was I bruised and sore, but I had a wealth of cuts, scrapes, and even a chunk missing from the palm of my right hand. Most sane people would take that as a sign to never attempt something like that again. But it gave me a taste for races that left me hurting, sore, and covered in mud.

Coaches normally recommend allowing a week between seasons to rest, but I was not about to take a week off. When the cross-country season was over, I immediately started wrestling again.

My high school wrestling coach was Tony Olliff, a short thick man with a military-style buzz cut. Before the season had even started, he had been told by school administrators that a kid without legs would be coming out for wrestling. He called a meeting before the season started to hand out permission forms and safety waivers. As soon as I came into the room, I saw there was no space to maneuver around the desks, so I hopped out of my chair and scooted across the tables to get to the papers. I could tell by the look on Coach Olliff's face that he knew I'd do just fine.

I hit the practice room ready to be a force on the wrestling mat. Being a new wrestler, I was not ready for varsity. Instead I participated in many novice meets, which gave me a ton of useful experience. Almost every week we would go to a small tournament, where I would pick up three to five matches.

Five days a week for two hours a day, Coach Olliff would walk around the wrestling room with a grim look on his face and bust out a random line as we were running around the room.

"Find a constituent roughly your stature."

"It's good to be up in the morning when everybody else is asleep."

"Show me a man with a strong neck, and I'll show you a man whose neck is strong."

While holding up headgear: "Repeat after me: I must be some freaking idiot to lose this."

"Three in a row, side by side by side."

"Last one on the bus has to feed the possum."

"Frolic. Frolic hard!"

And my favorite: "Never let anyone make fun of your shoes."

Coach Olliff's personality went a long way toward keeping me motivated, but when it came time to work with me one-on-one, Coach was at a loss.

"Hey, Coach, can you help me?" I asked one day as I sat in the corner of the wrestling room, trying to figure out the latest move.

"Yeah, Kacey, what's up?" said Olliff.

"I need some help figuring out how to do this move," I said.

Coach got down on his knees and demonstrated the move the way a person with their legs would do it.

"Okay, does that make sense?" he said once he was done.

"No," I said. "You're using your legs."

He sat back on his heels with a thoughtful look on his face. "You're right, Kacey. See if you can make it work," he said, patting me on the shoulder before walking off to help somebody else. I sat there for a second before getting back to work. I guessed I would figure it out on my own.

Despite the fact that he couldn't teach me every move, what Coach Olliff did teach me was even more valuable: the importance of grit. During a match, you often feel like you're fighting for your very survival at the hands of your opponent, and sometimes there is absolutely nothing you can do. Wrestling takes every part of your body and uses it to its full potential. In basketball you don't need to worry about a strong neck. In running, your grip strength isn't important. And who cares about endurance when you're playing golf? But in wrestling, you need every single bit of mental and physical stamina you can muster—speed, strength, endurance, technique, focus, determination, and a whole lot of grit—to overcome your opponent.

Olliff designed drills in which we would start with one person on his back with a partner's arms locked around his neck in a headlock. If he did not escape, he was punished with thirty push-ups, so we made darn sure we got out of there by any means necessary. For me it was more than a desire to avoid push-ups that fueled my fight; I did not want to lose. I soon found unique ways to get out of even the toughest holds. Instead of relying on leverage and body position, I used brute strength to shove my partner's face with both hands to free myself. Before long my practice partners dreaded going up against me.

When it came time for meets, I liked to start getting into my opponent's head before I even hit the mat, doing handstand push-ups or smacking my headgear. Then I'd follow it with a crushing handshake before the match started. As soon as the whistle blew, the fire inside me would roar to life, and I would attack their legs. I'd slam the mat as hard as I could to startle my opponents. Sometimes this move was so effective it would cause them to trip while backing up, at which point I would promptly take them down. I would throw move after move at them. When that didn't work, I would just use my arms to slowly bend them where I wanted them to go. I was never on the bottom for very long. I was a wrestler who never stopped moving. I made them work to keep me down. Sometimes during freshmen or novice tournaments, the freshmen I faced were the varsity wrestlers on opposing teams because they were the lightest on the team and sometimes the only ones who could fill the lighter weights. Despite my opponents being varsity, I was still able to win most of the matches. I ended the season with more than a hundred wins and only five or six losses.

A parent who was very concerned about my well-being asked Coach Olliff if he thought I would ever make it to districts. He gave her a sly grin and said that, with a little bit of luck, it just might be possible. He knew how driven I was. He knew I already had my eye on becoming a state champion. There was no doubt in his mind I was a winning member of the team.

Even though I had not made it to districts that season, I knew wrestling was the sport for me. I had learned very early on in life that the greatest rewards came from the greatest challenges, and there was not a more challenging sport for me than wrestling. It was also an individual sport. Whatever I did or did not accomplish would be up to me. I knew I could do the work necessary to win. I would rise or fall on my own merit.

Unfortunately, this would not be the case with track. Wrestling may have been the hardest sport physically, but track turned out to be the greatest challenge for me when it came to dealing with how others viewed a kid in a wheelchair.

Coming off my first year of high school wrestling, I was in great shape and ready to be fast on the track, but there were those who felt it wasn't fair that I be allowed to race with the runners. In cross country there was not the slightest outcry from a single coach or official, mainly due to the fact that I was not good enough to be a threat. I was very much in the that's-so-inspirational category rather than the holy-cow-he-is-fast category.

In cross country I had to overcome the challenge of going over terrain that was unfriendly to wheelchairs. But the hard rubber surface of the track allowed me to really take off. I started the season pushing in my everyday chair but soon received a new loaner racing chair from Kevin Hansen, a wheelchair racing coach who'd ended up in a chair after a skiing accident. Hansen understood what it was like to have others look at you like you were unable to do anything useful. When he got wind of this fast kid beating runners in a regular race chair, he decided to hook me up.

The first race of the season went well. I won both the 1500-meter and the 3000-meter. I was pretty stoked about my performance until the coach from the other team cried foul. The administration quickly looked up the rules. Apparently wheelchair racers' results could not count in a race with other runners. I was stunned. What did this mean for me? Would I be able to compete? Was I done being on the track team? I did not want to have to go play baseball. I wanted to do track. That meet the administration made the ruling that from then on my races would be counted as exhibition races. My times would not count for the team, and my races would be counted as totally separate events.

This was not what I wanted, but I was still able to race. I was scared what that meant though. Did it mean I would be put in my own special race every time? I was conflicted. I wanted to race, but what would I really be racing for if I had no one to compete with? I had a horrible sinking feeling that every race would go something like this: I would arrive at the start line, all by myself. *Ready! Set! BANG!!!* The gun would sound and off I go, all by myself. Everybody would stare at me circling the track on my own. I'd think, *Why are they all staring at me? Do they even know this is a real race? If I stopped right now, would anyone even care? Would anyone even notice?* Then the worst part of all: the finish line. As I would start into the last straightway, people would give the you-can-do-it claps. I would cross the line and feel less like an athlete than I did when I started.

I did not want to have to race by myself, but that is what happened anyway. Well, kind of. Apparently the rules state that if a wheelchair racer is put with the runners, then the wheelchair racer has to stay in the fourth lane. That means, to adjust the distance, I would start out in front of the rest of the pack. Luckily there were other people running on the track at the same time, so it became less of a solo race. I guessed it was better, but I still felt like less of an athlete. I had just come off a wrestling season in which every match I competed in was legitimate and I was considered to be a contributing member of the team. Now nothing I did counted. I was competing against myself. It was hard not to get down on myself when the rules told me I didn't matter. I had to dig deep for my inner stubbornness to help me overcome feelings of defeat. I could no longer care what others thought or what the "officials" decided. I couldn't change what they said, so instead I tried to become the best wheelchair athlete I could. I was going to work as hard as I did in the wrestling room. Many things might try to stop me, but I was not going to be one of them.

It felt to me like a lot of the things that were in place for adaptive athletes were more of a box to check off so school administrators could say they were letting us participate rather than an in-place strategy for helping us achieve athletic greatness. Worse than that was the feeling that I was out there as an "inspirational moment." I knew I was an incredible athlete.

---

## I WANTED TO MAKE SURE I WAS TREATED LIKE EVERYBODY ELSE.

---

During track season, I'd put in around three hours a day to make sure my body was in peak performance and could keep up with able-bodied kids my age. I was tough. I was strong. I could do anything any person could do. So it was degrading when the OSAA (Oregon School Activities Association) track administration acted like my athleticism was not the same as others' because I was in a wheelchair. My races didn't count at all. My wins didn't count; my points didn't count. I got the impression the officials felt like I should be grateful I got to be out there at all with other runners. But when I put hours of my life into being better each day, I wanted to be known for being a great athlete, not for being in a wheelchair.

Another area of my life I wanted to make sure I was treated like everybody else was in Scouts. I had been a part of Boy Scouts of America since I was eight years old. I enjoyed everything about it—learning new skills, going camping, and of course, making fires.

That summer we went to a scout camp that had horses. I was pretty excited because there was an overnight horse ride available and I could relive a bit of my childhood dream of becoming a bronc rider. We would ride a few miles, camp, and then ride back the next morning. I paid my money and showed up at the appointed time of departure. When I got there, they told me in no uncertain terms that I would not be allowed to go on the ride. I was mad and disappointed. Being a scout was all about being prepared, figuring out how to accomplish a goal, and never quitting. When I got home from scout camp, I went to my friend who had horses, and we took them for a ride down by the river. There was no reason I couldn't do it. When I rode, I just sat on the saddle and had to balance the entire time.

In our scout troop we would use the summertime for a big event. It was usually either scout camp or a high adventure, which is a week-long trip that takes scouts into the wilderness to pursue a goal. The first trip I did was a whitewater rafting trip. We loaded the boats up and proceeded to float down the river for four days, running the rapids and trying to see how wet we could get each other in the meantime. That was a blast, and at the end we were tired and ready for a good night's rest.

The next high-adventure excursion would be different. It was a fifty-mile hike requiring each of us to carry all the supplies we'd need for the entire week.

"What are we going to do about Kacey?" my dad asked the committee one night at the planning meeting. "You know he's going to want to do the hike."

"He can't hike the whole way, can he?" asked another leader.

"He'll try," my dad replied. "We need to come up with an option for him that will allow him to hike with assistance."

They started coming up with a plan for "allowing" me to join the hike. My dad had a lot of hunting experience and suggested an elk cart. An elk cart is a frame covered in cloth, with two wheels, used to haul a seven-hundred-pound elk out of the backcountry.

When I found out about the plan, I took it in stride. Well, not exactly in stride. I ignored them. There was no way I was going on a fifty-mile hiking trip only to let everybody else carry me the whole way. I made preparations like everybody else, gathering items from the required packing list.

The first day of the hike came, and we drove to the Santiam Trailhead. We got out of our cars and started getting our gear ready to go. Out of the trailer came the elk cart. It didn't look comfortable. The other young men had started hooking ropes onto the cart for the pull up the trail.

While they were doing this, I avoided the cart as much as I could.

"Kacey, it's time to hop in; we're ready to move out," Dad said.

"Dad, I don't want to ride in the cart," I said, pulling on my gloves. "I want to do this thing on my own."

My dad knew me well enough to know exactly what to say to get me into that stupid cart.

"Kacey, you need to let others serve you," he said with a serious look on his face.

What could I say to that? He had me. I made my way over to the cart and hopped in. It was as uncomfortable as it looked, with a bar running right down the middle. I had to sit on my pack so it was bearable enough to make it down the trail at all. It was made even more uncomfortable by the fact that I was being pulled by some of my best friends. They all took turns pulling it down the narrow trail. After about five miles we stopped for lunch.

"Hey, I'm going to start up the trail," I said after I was finished eating. "I'll hop back in when you guys catch up."

"Kacey," Dad said. "You have to have somebody with you. It's the buddy system."

"Well, then, you'd better hurry up," I retorted. "I'm going."

I started up the trail. He quickly donned his pack and headed after me. We walked the rest of the day like that. The cart eventually caught up with me, but by some stroke of luck, I was able to wave them past, and my dad let it slide.

That night I was pretty tired, but I went to bed satisfied I'd been able to do most of the hike on my own. The next morning I woke up pretty sore and tired, but after breakfast I grabbed one of my friends, and we started up the trail. We had a good hour lead on the rest of the troop and were able to make it a few miles before they caught up to us. We stopped for a bit and had lunch. Once again, in an effort to avoid getting in the cart and prove I could do it on my own, I left before everybody else. By the time we had set up camp that night, I had remained cart free.

That night I started to hear a few grumblings about the cart. It seems the cart wasn't all it was cracked up to be. It was becoming more and more difficult to pull. By the end of the first day the spokes were becoming loose and needed to be tightened every so often. By the second day the wheels were crooked and it was weaving all over the trail, which made it extremely hard to pull. I didn't feel too bad. I was no longer in the cart. The harder it was to pull the more likely they would ditch it at the halfway point. I hadn't wanted to bring it along in the first place.

That second night we decided that thing had to go. We would be hitting the halfway point, where we would come down to the road and meet up with a supply trailer. Not wanting my dad to have any excuses to put me in the cart that day, I made off extra early. Once again the cart passed me, and once again I continued my way up the trail. By the end of that day, I was so tired I didn't even have the energy to eat the pile of food the trailer had brought up. Still, I happily tossed the cart into the back of the trailer. Then I set up my tent and was out like a light.

Without the cart, I didn't have any way to carry my stuff. I knew I could do the hike, but doing it with a pack would be too much. Instead of killing myself trying to lug the pack, it followed the cart into the back of the trailer, minus anything important, which we divided up between different packs. I didn't need much. The tent was being packed by my tentmate and best friend, Chris Nelson. My sleeping bag was super compactable, taking very little room in my dad's pack. Aside from that I only needed gloves and food, which was dehydrated and was super light to haul around.

I was pretty relieved to be rid of the cart. Without the torture device to worry about, I focused solely on the hike. The only thing I had to worry about now was whether my pants and gloves would hold out. The pants held up, but the gloves became a mass of tattered leather.

I was getting more and more tired as each day went on. Every night I hit the sack worn out. Each day we would hike somewhere in the range of five to thirteen miles. The thirteen-mile day was Friday. I was bushed and ready to stop at mile ten, but we had a decision to make: camp at the edge of a mosquito-infested lake, or hike another three miles and be that much closer to our final destination. The leaders left it up to me. Even though I was beat, I knew if we could knock out three more miles, I would only have three left the final day. With a grunt of effort, I made the call to move on.

The next morning I grabbed a wrestling buddy of mine, and we were off. With the promise of the end being near, I booked it up the trail faster than I ever had before. The trail was bordered with plenty of ferns and grass. The early-morning dew brushed over my arms, chilling them and coating them with ice-cold water at every touch, but I didn't care. I was almost done. We burst through the trees onto a gravel road before anyone else had caught up to us, and I knew I was done. I lay down on the edge of the road, and it felt as comfortable as any mattress ever had. My body was done in, but my soul was triumphant. I had finished a hike even my dad thought was too hard for me to do on my own. I was able to do anything, even if that meant hiking fifty miles through the wilderness on my hands.

# CHAPTER 8
## SOPHOMORE YEAR

*"You just can't beat the person who never gives up."*
*—Babe Ruth, legendary baseball player*[11]

ONE OF THE GREATEST LESSONS we can be taught in life is how to learn from failure. We all fail from time to time. In fact, some of us do it on a regular basis. The important thing is to look at it as a learning opportunity. Thomas Edison was told he was too stupid to learn anything, Walt Disney was fired from a newspaper for having no original ideas, Elvis tried to join a vocal group and was told he "couldn't sing," and J. K. Rowling's *Harry Potter* was rejected twelve times from publishers.[12] Each one of these people persisted despite failures, which is a key part of the equation for success. The more we fail, the more we learn from our mistakes. Of course, there is a chance we may not learn, but that all depends on each individual. If we learn from our mistakes, we will be better in the future. If we decide we are losers and give up, then we'll be losers. I choose to not let my failures weigh me down. I choose to take each loss and use it to become better.

I STARTED OUT MY TENTH-GRADE year with cross country in the fall. I initially used my everyday wheelchair, but halfway through the season I

11 George Herman (Babe) Ruth, "Bat It Out!" in *The Rotarian*, July 1940, 14.
12 McGinty, Stephen (16 June 2003). "The J.K. Rowling Story." The Scotsman. Retrieved 9 April 2006 (https://www.scribd.com/document/245564470/J-K-Rowling), page 3; https://www.businessinsider.com/successful-people-who-failed-at-first-2014-3.

decided to try my racing wheelchair. Because of its thinner tires, I was worried it would not make it through some of the situations I had run into the previous year, like muddy grass, soft trails, and steep hills.

Cross country was very different from track. In track I could put my head down and plow ahead. On a cross-country course, I had to be vigilant of my surroundings. Was I on course? When was the next turn? Could I catch those runners ahead of me before we hit the grass?

After a trial run during practice, I gave my racing chair a shot. What a difference it made. I was no longer struggling through the simplest parts of the runs; I was now passing a few people. More and more, I saw myself as an actual athlete rather than a cripple in a wheelchair. My times jumped from thirtyish minutes to about twenty-five minutes. I looked at each race as an opportunity to improve and push myself further than I had before.

I was catching people. The first time it happened, I was surprised. I was used to passing the runners who had given up on the race, but this year I was passing some of the kids who kept trying. What I didn't know at the time was that that year was only a hint at how good I could be if I truly pushed myself toward the goal of being great.

That year in wrestling I was ready to earn my way to the state tournament. To make it to the district tournament, you need to be in one of the top two spots in your weight for your school. I knew I was not going to be the top guy at 103 pounds (that title was held by my teammate Ryan Stephenson, who was also gunning for the state championship that year). But I knew I would be able to earn the junior varsity spot. There were many times when, due to my strength, the coach would have me wrestle up a weight class. I wrestled 112-pound varsities. I did quite well, even though the kids were heavier than I was, only losing a handful of matches.

I continued to develop new moves to outwit my opponents. Since Coach Olliff wasn't able to adapt moves to my body, he focused on teaching me the principles of wrestling, namely strength training, situation drills, and cardio work, all of which gave me the foundation I needed to shape myself as a wrestler. One move I adapted from the single-leg takedown was a shot that fooled a lot of people. When the match started out, I would circle my opponent, making a few darting moves toward their legs to test their reactions. I'd then turn to expose my side or back to my opponent, who would let their guard down just for an instant.

In that heartbeat of time, using my left stub, I would launch myself sideways into their leg, snaking my python of an arm around their ankle and pulling myself in. From there I would use any number of strategies to get to work scoring points.

I don't remember my wins. I do remember my losses. There were not many. One of the losses was to one of the most inventive wrestlers I have ever faced, who was the future state champion. He had a way of getting down on one knee and positioning his other leg at a dangerous angle (dangerous for me, not him). Many wrestlers would try this move against me, thinking the lower they were to the ground the harder it would be for me to snag his leg, but very few were able to use it well. I was very good at grabbing any opening and taking the other wrestler down. Elis Rio knew how to do this, and he beat me in our one and only match. After that match I regularly made sure I sparred with the best wrestlers on our team. Because I'd been beat by Elis, I was never surprised by this wrestling tactic again.

My other loss at the 112-pound weight class was at the hands of a kid from Churchill High School who ended up taking a podium spot at state for the 125-pound class that year. Neither one of them were ahead by more than a couple of points by the time the final whistle blew.

I had a bit of a surprise in the middle of the wrestling season. It was 2002, and the Winter Olympics in Salt Lake City were gearing up. The Olympic torch was going to travel around the entire United States, and there was a chance we would get to see it because it was going right through Salem. What happened, though, was beyond what I ever thought would happen. I got a call one day telling me that my mom and I had been selected to be torchbearers as the torch passed its way through Salem. I was blown away. I would get to hold the Olympic flame. I would get to carry it down the street.

I found out it was my mom who had applied for me to receive this honor. What a shock for her, though, when the Olympic committee read her application and decided she was just as amazing and needed to run it as well.

As my mom and I were sitting on the bus waiting for the torch to be handed off, the committee asked me if I wanted to use a torch holder so I could push my chair with both hands. I said, "Heck no! I will do it by myself." My mom was dropped off first, and the van driver took me ahead to my drop-off point. He lowered me down the bus lift and onto the asphalt to wait for my mom. It wasn't long before I saw her coming fast down the road. There were two runners assigned to run alongside the torchbearers, and they were a good twenty feet behind my mom. When the group got to me, the runners were huffing and puffing from trying to keep up. My mom tilted her torch toward me to light mine.

I was a bit slower. I pushed my wheelchair using only my left hand and holding the torch with my right hand for the entire 0.2 miles of the route. The side runners became side walkers and caught their breath as I made my way down the road. What an experience it was to hold the flame that had been burning in the hearts of the world for many, many years. As I passed the torch on to the next participant, I was struck by how running such a small distance could be so monumental. It was less than a quarter of a mile, but it made such a lasting impact on me. The Olympics were a symbol to me of being a great athlete. I looked at the Olympic flame fading in the distance and knew I would do everything I could to make it to the state wrestling championships that year.

To get to the state championship, I needed to be one of the top four wrestlers at the district tournament. I felt pretty confident I would make it.

There was only one match at districts I remember. It was the final match, and it came down to me and my teammate Ryan. We knew there was nobody else in our district who could take us on. Ryan's advantage was his knowledge of how to wrestle me. It was a gridlocked match, with neither one of us able to gain the advantage over the other by the end of the third round. In overtime his experience and knowledge won out, and he was the one with his hand in the air. Of course I had wanted to win, but my goal had been to make it to the state tournament. Just one year prior I was sitting on the sideline watching my teammates mount the podium. This year I was no longer a bystander. Earning a place on that wooden platform just one spot from the top proved to me that my hard work had paid off. I was going to state.

The first time I entered the Veterans Memorial Coliseum in Portland, I was amazed at how huge it was. Up to that point I'd only seen wrestling tournaments with four to eight mats on the floor, but the coliseum easily held twelve. Not only that, but there were thousands of people sitting in the stands. I was a little stunned. I knew every eye was on me. Trying to put all of that out of my mind, I got ready for my first match.

Putting my headphones on, I scooted around, rolling my shoulders to loosen them up. Nerves were zinging through my body. Finding a quiet corner in the warm-up area, I bowed my head for a little chat with the man upstairs, just as I did before every match. Saying a prayer beforehand was my way to focus on what I needed to do my best.

When it was time, I hopped up into my chair. Rolling out through the tunnel that leads to the mats was exhilarating. As the tunnel opened up onto the floor of the coliseum, a sprawling display of noise and light sprung up before me. Whistles were being blown, and twenty-four wrestlers on twelve mats were going at it, fighting tooth and nail for their chance to be the next state champion. The mats were ringed by a fence to keep the crowd of coaches and wrestlers away from the mats. I attempted to tune all of this out and focus on one thing: my first opponent.

Hustling to my spot, I briefly nodded to Olliff, who was already waiting for me at the corner of the mat. He nodded back. Shutting out the overwhelming distractions was easier than I would have thought. Stripping out of my warmup clothes and buckling on my headgear, I scooted onto the center of the mat and did a backward somersault into a handstand followed by handstand pushups. This not only got me psyched up but was also a tactic meant to intimidate my opponent. I could see a glimmer of hesitation in my opponent's eyes as he toed his line. No wrestler worth his salt shows fear, but that doesn't mean we don't get a little nervous.

With the blast of a whistle, the match began. Even with the distractions from the lights and the sounds, I was able to focus enough to pull off a win. As my hand was raised in the air, I looked around in amazement. Not only was I at state, but I had actually won a match. It was incredible. I almost didn't even feel tired from the match. I was just excited to accomplish a win at state.

A bit tired but still pumped from winning, I went to take a break and rest my "feet" before my next match. About a half hour before I was due back on the mat, I made my way back down to the warm-up room to prep. I was no longer overwhelmed by the movement around me.

Coming out of the tunnel the second time, I didn't take time to look around. Within seconds of me getting to the line, the whistle blew. My opponent and I circled each other, looking for an opening. I found one and shot to snag his leg. Even though I had a good lock around his calf, I didn't realize I'd left him with an opening for a dynamite move. With one swift move of his arm, he threw me into a pancake, which is not as tasty as its namesake. It gets its name because you end up flat on your back counting lights. I was so startled by this quick turn of events that I barely put up a fight before the referee slapped the mat. It was one of the only times I had ever gotten pinned in my entire high school wrestling career, and it had happened at state. I was pretty embarrassed to have it happen in front of so many people. It felt like my spirit had been pancaked along with my body. I had one more chance to continue. If I lost one more time, I would be out.

"There are no more wimps at state," Olliff said to me as I left the mat feeling defeated. Not that anybody who made it to state was a wimp, but I understood his point. It was time to man up or go home. Nobody would be taking it easy on me, and nobody there was going to be an easy win.

Trudging my way up to the stands, I expected some sympathy from the one person who cared about me most—my mom. Instead she just looked at me and said, "Are you ready to start wrestling now?"

This shocked me. How could my mom say that? She was supposed to be supporting me, not telling me how bad I'd done. I already knew that. I sat for a few moments in silence, turned my anger away from her, and looked inside myself. She was right. There was something off. She saw that my performance in the first two matches was nowhere near the peak of my ability. She knew I had much more in the tank. I don't remember much about the next match, except that I won. Those few tough-love words from my mom had changed how I looked at myself and how I was wrestling that day. Winning that final match the first day meant I got to go on to the second day of the tournament.

Day two started early, with weigh-ins at six A.M. sharp. By the time the gym doors opened at eight A.M., I was already getting into the zone for my next, and possibly last, match of the tournament. A loss would put me out of the tournament, but a win would guarantee a place on the podium. Whatever the outcome, I would do my best. Coming out of the tunnel, I quickly took my place on the mat and was soon joined by my opponent. As the referee placed the whistle to his mouth, a grin spread across my face, and my prevailing thought was, *I love wrestling*.

The whistle blew, and the match was underway.

Each match can take a very different path. This one was no different. We battled back and forth through the first round, in which my opponent gained some points by taking me down. In the next round, I gained a point by escaping. But an escape only gets you one point, and I needed two to tie. He knew this and started to use a technique called stalling. The ref gave him a warning. On the second warning, I would be given a point. I pushed the pace, trying to either take him down or make him stall again. No matter how hard I wrestled, he made sure to avoid putting himself in a vulnerable spot. Despite my best efforts and my opponent's obvious stalling tactics, no stalling call was made. I lost. It was frustrating to be wrestling as hard as I could and still lose, not to someone faster, stronger, or smarter than I was, but to someone who chose not to wrestle.

I was disappointed. A feeling of loss settled over me as I made my way off the mat. I couldn't help feeling there was something wrong. I had fought so hard to get where I was to have my season end with a loss. On the other hand, I had won two matches at state. I really wanted to place, but I knew how far I had come from being that kid who lost every match to being one who was winning matches at a state meet. The biggest thing I learned at state was how much I didn't know. I knew there were things I needed to work on; the next year, I decided, I was not just going to get to state. I was going to be sitting on that podium.

I didn't have much time to sit around and wonder what would happen next wrestling season. It was time to focus on track. Once again I was racing against myself, looking to beat my own times, and I did. I was fast in the wheelchair-racing community, so when I competed against runners, I was far and away the fastest racer on the track. Many times I would even lap or double-lap runners. The rules were still annoying, but I was getting used to them. What really bugged me, though, was my inability to score points for the team. In wrestling, I had been a contributing member of the team. Now I was literally the least productive member.

While I fought to improve my personal times, Kevin Hansen fought for wheelchair racers to have a presence at the state track meet and was able to put together an exhibition 800-meter race. Because it was an exhibition, we would not be able to score points for our teams, but we would be able to have a race in the state track meet.

The race was on Saturday, but since it was a two-day meet, I got to hang out on Friday and watch the other athletes from my team compete. Later that night we went for pizza and afterward to an ice-cream parlor where there was a huge sundae called the Pigs Trough, which included two scoops of vanilla, two scoops of chocolate, two scoops of strawberry, two bananas, a pile of whipped cream, and all the toppings. I have never been one to back away from a challenge, so of course that is what I ordered. By the time I was done, I was rolling out of there in more ways than one, but I had finished it. At this time in my life, there was not even a thought in my mind about eating too much. I put it away like there was no tomorrow and proceeded to eat again an hour later. I loved food, and I didn't think I had to worry about my weight because I was burning off calories as fast as I was shoveling them in. I should have paid more attention to it though.

Even being one of the top athletes in the state across three sports, I was still carrying some extra fat. I had gained a reputation as someone who loves to eat. I was known by friends and family alike as the human garbage disposal. I was always the last one left eating at the dinner table, and if my mom made a casserole, I would finish it. If we were at a restaurant and someone did not finish their meal, I would finish it for them. Hot dogs were my staple. I would eat two to four at a time. This was not a big issue, because I was no longer sitting around playing video games. I was outside. I was wheeling to and from school and still doing my paper route. I was spending extra time working out two to three times per day.

Eating became part of who I was. I took it as a personal challenge to see how much I could eat. This habit stayed with me for years. Even at the peak of being unhealthy I would take on eating challenges because that's who I thought myself to be—the guy who could put it away. I was proud of it. Even as proud as I was of my eating prowess, the habits I was forming would eventually come back to bite me.

The next morning was bright and sunny. There were eight racers ready to burn our way down the track. For me the 800-meter is an intense race. I've always felt it was a two-lap sprint, and that is exactly what it felt like that day. As we prepared to start the race, I was cracking joke after joke. When I prepped for a wrestling match, I got serious, but in track it was the opposite. This was a party. I still loved the competition of the race, but the people I was racing against were my fellow wheelchair racers. I couldn't help but have fun. When the officials led us onto the track, I felt a similar sensation to the one I'd experienced when I'd stepped onto the mat during the wrestling state championship—all the people staring at me was a lot to

---

I FELT I WAS PART OF SOMETHING BIGGER.

---

wrap my head around. I was overwhelmed at the crowd around me. I felt like a fish in a bowl, with everybody just waiting to see what we would do. I took it all in for a minute before reining in my thoughts and offering a prayer of strength.

As we lined up for the start, my mouth shut down. There were no more jokes. I focused on the lines on the track. I was now facing my competition: the track and my own time. I might as well have been lining up against clones of myself. The noise of the crowd no longer mattered. The weather no longer mattered. All that mattered was the rubber in front of me and two full laps for the taking.

The gun fired, startling me into motion. My arms beat down on the hand rings, willing them to turn faster. By the end of the first curve, I had taken the lead. We started to pick up some serious speed down the backstretch. As we turned into the second corner, someone passed me. Ha! He'd moved too early, thinking he would be able to keep in front of me for the rest of the race, but we still had a whole lap to go.

Taking the back seat to him, I let him lead me across the start line and into the third turn. Sitting in his draft, I allowed my arms to relax. I knew as soon as we came out of the turn it would be time to use that break for more power to finish the race. As soon as we straightened out, I cranked up. Feeding off the burst of power from his draft, I sailed past him to retake first place. Rounding the final turn and facing the finish line, I could see his front wheel coming into sight in my periphery. It felt like someone had snuck up and poured cement into my arms. Despite the fatigue setting in, I dug past the pain and came up with a little bit more. It still wasn't enough to stop him from gaining. He just kept creeping up.

The finish line was drawing closer. *If I can just hold out until I cross it,* I thought to myself.

40 feet
30 feet
20 feet
10 feet

He was still behind me, and then my front wheel crossed the final white line.

Yes! I had done it. My fist shot into the air, claiming my victory. My exhaustion was quickly replaced with a surge of joy. What a battle for the finish line. I had fought for the victory and had won. I had won the state wheelchair-racing championship. I looked around me at the cheering crowd, all eyes staring down on us, on me. My chair slowed as I continued around the track. What a great way to finish off the year. Even though the victory was only in an exhibition race, it was still at the state track meet. I got lots of congratulations, but more than that, my parents were there to support me and cheer me on. I had always had their love as well as their unwavering commitment to me.

Being a part of the historic event, Oregon's first state wheelchair race, I felt I was part of something bigger than just the race. I was no longer racing just for myself and my own times. I was now racing to prove to the state that wheelchair racers were not cripples to be left out or put aside. We were athletes.

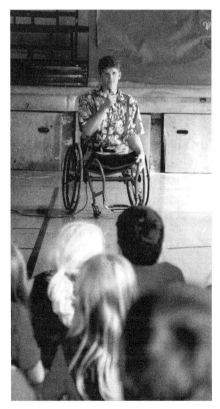

# CHAPTER 9
## JUNIOR YEAR

*"Once you've wrestled, everything else in life is easy."*
*—Dan Gable, Olympic gold medalist in wrestling*[13]

Wrestling was and probably always will be my favorite sport. I love it because it is the hardest thing I have ever done. Not just the matches but the practices as well. I would lie on the mat before practice, waiting with dread and excitement for practice to start because once it started, we did not stop for two brutal hours every single day. It was amazing. I knew the harder the challenge was, the greater the reward would be. But the reward was not winning. The reward was the ability to work harder than before.

As a junior I really started to intensify my training. More time training and more time studying drove me. I was leading my team in cross country, finishing most of the races near the front of the main group of runners. My times dropped from twenty-five minutes my sophomore year to about twenty minutes my junior year. I found the grass was no longer a hindrance. I not only knew how to push on the grass but was fast while doing it. I would take on each course with a single-minded determination to do the best I could. I was deep into the mentality of being a great wrestler; I knew what my goals were in regards to that, but I was beginning to find I was not satisfied with just being a great wrestler. I was going to be a great cross-country athlete as well. I got faster almost every race, and by the end

---

13 *A Wrestling Life*, 2016.

of the year, while I hadn't won a race yet, I knew I had that potential my senior year.

My junior year of school was the hardest. I challenged myself to rise up in athletics and in the classroom. I was an okay to good student most of the time, able to skate by because I would listen in class and do the homework without putting special effort into it. Junior year was different. I was taking classes like honors English, chemistry, French, and college algebra. They were the most challenging courses I'd taken to that point. The workload required just so I could maintain acceptable grades was significantly greater than I had previously had to manage. That is when I really had to work to maintain a proper balance in life. Sports were very important to me, but from a young age we had been taught by my parents that working hard was not just for sports. It was for all areas of life, including scholastics.

To be eligible for sports in the school system, you needed to maintain a 2.0 grade point average. That translates to a C-. In my family if there was even one C on a report card, it was grounds for a very serious discussion. This was more about how we thought about school than a punishment for dropping our grades. I once got a D in a math class. Rather than ground me or threaten me with taking away sports, my parents made sure I was doing everything I could to be successful in school. I understood that getting good grades in high school would mean creating good habits for the rest of my life.

---

WHILE I HADN'T WON A RACE YET, I KNEW
I HAD THAT POTENTIAL.

---

Wrestling in my junior year was even better than the year before. I was the varsity wrestler at 103 pounds, and I was laying the smackdown on my competition. It was finally my spot, and I wasn't going to let it go. I took every opportunity to perfect my best moves. My favorite was the cradle. Olliff didn't call it the cradle for me though. He called it the Kacey Crunch.

In a typical cradle, when you grab the leg and head, you use leverage to work the knee to the head. This was not so with the Kacey Crunch.

Instead of working the knee upward, I would use my extra strength to squeeze my opponent into a little ball and roll him onto his back. This was my favorite move because I was able to use my strength against the other 103-pounders. Every time I locked my hands together, I felt a rush as the anticipation of pinning my opponent settled in. There was still a chance for him to kick his way free, but with my arms locked up, it was a very small chance.

Other moves I loved involved using speed and strength. My favorite takedown was called the ball and chain. I would latch on to an opponent's leg, and as he reached down to pry me off, I grabbed his hand and pulled it down through his legs, prompting his entire body to come along for the ride. This ended with him lying flat on the mat and me earning two points. Even better, the ball and chain left my opponent in a perfect position for a cradle. After getting a good ball and chain, I would use my free hand to go head hunting. Grabbing the head and the knee, I would jam my head into his ribs, causing him to bend and allowing me to grip my hands together in a monkey lock that was rarely broken. He would soon be on his back, and my hand would be raised as the victor.

I only had one loss in the regular season that year, and like the year before, it was in overtime to the state favorite. I rolled my way through the district tournament, taking first place at the district meet and scoring myself a ticket to the state tournament. I ended up squaring off against a wrestler named Troy Baker in the quarterfinals. I had wrestled Troy once or twice in the past, and his biggest advantage against me was his ability to get behind me before I could stop him.

Going into the third round, we were tied. I was on the bottom, looking for a good chance to make an escape in order to earn some points. The whistle blew, and off we went. Bursting upward, I sprang back into Troy, throwing him off-balance. I then grabbed his arm and pulled it over my head, swinging my body out to the side, effectively getting out from under him. This gave me a point and the lead. Back and forth we went, with Troy trying to spin around behind me and me trying to grab his leg to prevent him from doing so. The third round was ticking down. With just ten seconds left on the clock, I pretty much figured the match was mine. I was going to the semifinals!

Right then he blocked my arm and spun around behind me, snatching two points. I had no time for any further thoughts. He had just moved ahead of me by one point. I had to do something before I lost. With eight seconds left, I swung my body to the side to make him drop his head on my shoulder. As quick as a sneeze, I reached up with both hands around his neck and pulled with every ounce of strength I had. I had used this move many times, and I knew it would work; the question was whether I had enough time to properly execute it. With five seconds left, I felt his body coming over my shoulder. I still had a chance. With three seconds to go, his back was on the mat. In the final second, the ref jumped in to see if my maneuvering would qualify as an escape.

The buzzer sounded. It was a no-go. I had just lost the match.

That was my last chance to make it to the state finals that season. Disappointed, I still had to wrestle to fight for my chance to place. Two wins later put me in a match for third place, but I lost my second match and ended up taking home a fourth-place medal.

In addition to confirming my belief in hard work, being on sports teams helped me become more comfortable in front of crowds. My love for presenting and speaking in front of groups continued to grow. When I was sixteen years old, I was invited to speak at a youth conference in Oregon. The person who asked me to speak worked for a big car dealership, and he knew what it took to give a good speech, so he came to my home and helped me write it. When I arrived at the event, youth were crammed into every crevice of a huge lodge. It seemed like they were even hanging from the rafters. I was nervous but also really excited to tell my story. Not only did I tell my story, but I also had a friend of mine put together a short video. When I had finished speaking, the room erupted in applause. I felt a sense of relief. I knew how difficult it was to entertain youth. I had just kept a room full of them interested for the entire hour I had spoken. Many of them came up to me afterward to let me know how much they had enjoyed it and how they had been inspired by my words. I was grateful to have had the opportunity to speak to them. To this day I have adults who were there as kids come up and tell me how much they enjoyed my presentation.

I decided to stay and hang out with the youth for the rest of the conference. That night we had a wrestling match: me against anyone else. It was pretty fun to be the center of attention.

After this experience I was even more determined to be a motivational speaker. I wanted to help others find value in the trials in their lives.

In high school there was a class that tried to help us decide what we wanted to be for the rest of our lives. Since I wanted to be a motivational speaker and a coach, my teacher found me a great person to job shadow. Mark Speckman was the head football coach at Willamette University and had been born without hands, so many of the things I had gone through he had as well. His parents were a lot like mine. They never told him he couldn't do things. Instead, they encouraged him to make the best of every situation. The word *can't* was not part of the vocabulary in his house. There was always a way to get things done. I was super impressed with him. He was doing what I wanted to do. He was a motivational speaker, but he was still involved with athletics. I now wanted to be him when I grew up.

Coming off a successful wrestling season, I was ready to do the same on the track. I was still considered to be in an exhibition race. But that year we were no longer limited to one race at the state track meet; that year there would be two. We were no longer a sideshow. We now had a foot in the door (not my foot, but you get the picture). I took this as permission to explode. I started to ramp up my efforts on the track. My times kept dropping, and I felt like there was no limit to how fast I could go.

I hit the state meet with a fury. We now had the 400-meter and the 1500-meter races. I lined up for the start of the 1500-meter. The gun fired, and I was off. My opponent from the previous year had graduated, but there were still a couple of racers who were tailing me as I sped around the track. As I rounded the corner from the last lap, my strap holding me in the chair broke, and I fell. I was confused. This had never happened before. This not only slowed me but also disoriented me, causing me to take second place in the 1500-meter, which was my best race. I was disappointed, but there was no time to feel sorry for myself. I put my gloves back on and got ready for the 400-meter. This time I was ready. I had duct-taped the buckle in place. There was no way it was going to snap on me again. I sped around the track, easily beating my fellow racers to the finish line. That meet was to be the first and only time I would earn anything but a gold medal at the state track meet.

The summer before I became a senior, I had a few incredible experiences. One was competing in the Adaptive Sports USA Junior Nationals in Connecticut, where dozens of wheelchair racers from across the nation come together to compete. I discovered something there that was extremely surprising: I was really fast. I knew I was fast racing against runners. What I hadn't yet realized was that I was just as competitive against the top high school wheelchair racers in the country. I was young and relatively new to racing with other wheelchair racers, so when I arrived, I was extremely nervous.

I did very well and kept up with the best in the country, even winning a couple of the races. What an amazing feeling to know I could hold my own against these great athletes. I was no longer the lone wolf zooming around the track, chasing my own times. I was now part of something bigger that would come to be a huge part of my life. Coming home from that trip, I knew wheelchair racing was not just going to be great my senior year; I was going to do it for the rest of my life. I was even approached by a coach from the University of Arizona about going to race for them. It was really cool to be asked, but I was still focused on being a great wrestler, and that meant I wanted to wrestle in college, not wheelchair race.

During the summer before my senior year, I decided to get a job that paid about $60 a week and required me to be "on the job" twenty-four hours a day, six days a week. I was a scout camp counselor or, more specifically, a waterfront counselor, taking care of the canoes and rowboats.

It was great fun making the kids swamp their canoes in fifty-degree water at good old Camp Cooper.

I loved being at camp. I loved working. The money really didn't matter as much as the experience did. I was happy to be doing something I loved as well as teaching others to improve themselves. It was one of the most idyllic jobs I have ever had, getting paid to spend all day in the woods enjoying time with friends and coworkers.

I really enjoyed teaching the kids not only to paddle the boats but also to think about what they were doing in the water. The lake was called Lake Hurl, which lends itself to all sorts of wonderful connotations, but it was actually named after a pair of brothers who helped found the camp. The other great thing about the lake was that it was glacier-fed, and it felt like it. It always hovered right around forty to fifty degrees. My first time jumping in felt like I had hopped into the middle of the Pacific Ocean.

I had come a long way from being the little kid fresh out of the hospital who didn't know how to swim. I had worked at it, learning what it would take for me to be effective in the water. There were very few pools in which I could touch the bottom, so I quickly had to learn to swim or stay in the kiddie pool for the rest of my life. Now, ten years later, I was a great swimmer.

Being the boat guy, I decided the campers needed to be ready for anything in the water. The first day of class we did one of the best requirements for the class. Well, okay, it was the most fun for me to watch. The students had to flip their canoes over and perform a water rescue. This involved not only being in the water but figuring out how to get your canoe right side up. I had a blast watching the scouts' teeth chatter as they tried to turn over a heavy canoe made of metal.

Since I was on the waterfront, I headed up something called a polar bear swim. For most places the polar bear swim just means waking up really early and going for a swim. But at Camp Cooper the polar bear swim was freezing cold. It was great fun to get a bunch of scouts, and sometimes scout leaders, down to the waterfront so we could all jump into the lake yelling a camp song at the top of our lungs.

Every week I would tell my canoe students that if all of them showed up for the swim, I would drive my wheelchair into the lake. Most weeks only one or two showed up. But there was one week when the whole class came to the polar bear swim. Well, that did it. I put a rope on the back of my chair and plunged into the lake. As the water closed over my head and my chair sank to the bottom of Lake Hurl, I realized it was *freaking cold*!

That was such a fun summer I almost didn't want it to end. Yet anytime I started thinking I didn't want to leave, I remembered what was waiting for me: my senior year. There was a lot left to finish. I had worked for years to become a state champion. Senior year was my chance.

# CHAPTER 10
## SENIOR YEAR

*"Strike while the iron is hot."*
*—Benjamin Franklin*[14]

One of the hardest and heaviest trees is called the ironwood. It lives in the desert, and the unrelenting sun and little water cause this tree to grow slowly, adding very little mass every year. It is one of the toughest trees known to man because it has fought the harsh desert elements and won. Woodworkers have to be careful when cutting ironwood due to the speed at which it will dull a blade.[15]

I have found it was not the big events that shaped my life but rather the small daily efforts. Distinguished musicians play every day; remarkable athletes practice constantly. To have a great life, we have to work daily at those things that will one day make us great. We may not see the results for years. But as we grow our rings, we will be stronger and a whole lot harder to cut down.

AFTER SUMMER CAMP WAS OVER, I began to train for my final year in cross country. I would get up early in the morning to go for a run and at night would once again wheel myself the mile or so to the high school, where I would run stairs for an hour. On some of the morning runs, I would go an

14 William Morgan, *Memoirs of the Life of the Rev. Richard Price*, London: Richard and Arthur Taylor, Printers, 1815, 96.
15 "Biological Survey of Ironwood Forest National Monument," Arizona-Senora Desert Museum, https://www. desertmuseum.org/programs/ifnm_ironwoodtree.php.

extra mile to pick up a fellow wrestler and cross-country runner. I did this six days a week, sometimes logging as many as twenty miles a day.

By the time cross-country camp came around, I was ready. We went to a nearby state park every day for a week and ran on beautiful forest paths under towering Oregon pine trees.

The first meet of the new cross-country season was on a new course that wove through trees and along dirt paths and diverted onto the road for a few hundred feet before weaving back into the trees. I was excited to take my brand-new wheelchair off-road. It was McNary blue and had already been nicknamed "The Blue Bullet." Even during warmups I knew this year was going to be different. I was not going to be just an "inspiration" anymore. I was going to be a legitimate threat. Being an inspiration is nice, but I put in a lot of work to compete with my peers. I did not want to be seen as someone who was disabled and trying but rather as a good athlete.

I started off slowly in the soft grass that kept me from maintaining a fast pace. The pack quickly ran past as I struggled to push my way across the soggy ground. We crossed the grass, running onto a path of hard-packed dirt. Immediately my speed jumped as my tires flowed smoothly down the trail. One by one the other runners fell behind. My hands hit the rims as if there was nothing else in the world. I marveled at what was happening. In the past my arms would feel weighed down as if slowly being filled with sand as the race went on, but not this time. My summertime conditioning had really paid off. I would not slow down for a measly 3.1 miles.

Nearing the finish line, I had only one runner ahead of me: Rob Schlegel from Crescent Valley. At the time Rob was the king of cross country in our district and the favorite to win the district title. We had raced together for years but had rarely spoken. As I crossed the finish line right after him, I shook his hand.

"Good job, Rob," I said. "It looks like I'll be trying to get you at districts."

The season quickly moved along, with meets one to two times a week, and I was doing quite well. I was finishing in the top ten. I even won a race or two. Then one day, Coach Anderson pulled me into his office. Being a senior and a leader of the team, I was in the coach's office a couple of times every week. I was prepared for him to ask me to help with the next meet or motivate the team or even plan a new run.

"Kacey," he said, gesturing for me to pull up to his desk. "The season has been going pretty well for you so far, hasn't it?"

"Yeah, I think so. I trained really hard this summer," I said, thinking I might be settling in for a pep talk about how far I'd come. "I think I have a chance at the district title."

"I think so too," he said, shuffling around some papers on his desk. "Hey, Kacey, when you pass the other runners, do you talk to them?"

"Sure," I replied. "I tell them I'm coming and they should move so I don't run over them."

"Do you ever run over their feet or hit them with your wheels?" he said, making direct eye contact with me.

"No, Coach; I'm really good about making sure I don't hit them," I said in a serious tone, beginning to feel a bit confused.

I had been doing the same thing for years. Why was this a big deal all of a sudden?

"Kacey, one of the coaches is concerned you are being rude to the runners as you pass," Coach said.

"You mean like calling them names or insulting their moms?" I said in an attempt to lighten up the situation.

This had to be a joke. Why would anyone take notice of me, much less care that I was warning people to move out of the way? For the last three years, nobody had cared about me, and *now*, after all the hard work I had put into getting stronger, faster, and learning how to kill it while going off-road, they were concerned about what I was saying to the other runners?

"Kacey, when you pass, just make sure you are being nice to the runners," Coach said. I didn't understand what he was asking me.

"So you mean instead of yelling, 'Move or I'll run over your toes!' I need to yell, 'Please move, or I'll run over your toes'?" I said.

"Um, yeah, pretty much," he replied.

"No problem, Coach," I said, rolling my eyes.

I guessed the price of becoming a better athlete was that now that I was a threat to win, the other coaches were coming after me. No one had ever seemed to care much about me when I was slow, but now that I was beating the better runners, the coaches were starting to worry.

One coach, whom I'll refer to as Coach Pounder, from a high school within our district, was such a pain that the ruling body eventually decided I would be unable to participate in the state cross-country meet, whether or not I had earned the right to be there. The reason cited was that the state course was not made for wheelchairs and was too difficult for me to navigate. Cross-country courses consist of running 3.1 miles on country across grass, mud, plants, and gravel and between trees. It's extremely difficult terrain for wheelchairs; I might have been the first wheelchair racer to attempt to do it. Therefore, no cross-country course is "designed" for wheelchairs. The ruling body's decision ticked me off. I had been racing for three years without anyone saying boo, but now that I was fast, suddenly the course was not designed for a wheelchair? It was the most ridiculous thing I had ever heard. I had never hurt myself or anybody else while I was racing. I had also proven I could destroy any course that came my way. But nothing my coach, the athletic director, or I said to defend our case changed the decision. I would not be allowed to race at state, and whatever place I took at districts would not bump someone else out of the spots for state.

I was fired up. They had limited me from going to the state tournament, but I would show them how disabled this little cripple was. I was going to win the district tournament.

When I arrived at the park for districts, I was told the course I had run for the last four years would have to be changed to ensure I steered clear of the runners in the more tricky portions of the race. I was pretty upset, not so much that they told me I needed to change the way I was racing but more because they had told me on the last day of my entire high school cross-country career. The driving force behind this was, of course, the coach who had complained about me before. Despite Coach Pounder's push to get me kicked out of the race, and for the change in the course, I pulled on my big boy pants and got ready for the race.

An even bigger force was about to rain down upon the coach who was attempting to stop my wheels from turning. Before the varsity boys' race started, my powerhouse of a mom found that hapless coach and chewed him up one side and down the other. Having been on the receiving end of her wrath a few times, I cringed at the thought of being a coach trying to encourage my runners while a parent on the opposite team yelled at me, but my mom absolutely rocks. I couldn't be more proud of her. When others were bowing to the demands of a bully, my mom was standing up and taking him to task.

The race started with a gunshot, and we were off down the grass field. Usually slower across the field than the rest, I poured on a burst of acceleration right off the bat, keeping up with the lead runners. Then we were across the first field and rounding the Willamette University football field. By the time we reached the first hill, I was well ahead, and I only fell a few places by the time I reached the top. Quickly regaining the lead, I sped off to tackle the rest of the course. Gravel, bark dust, grass, and hills tried to slow me down, but it wasn't until a half mile to go that I ran into the part of the course that would make or break me.

Coming out of the trees, I turned onto the last half of a soap box derby hill. After a few short yards, my old "friend" Rob passed me. I had expected to be passed at this point in the race—wheelchair racers have a more difficult time with hills than runners do—and two others from McKay passed me by the time I'd reached the top, where there was a paved path leading to a drop we called Suicide Hill.

Before I reached the drop, I had overtaken everybody but Rob. Arriving at the top of Suicide Hill, I risked a quick look up and saw Rob a good hundred yards in front of me. Usually this would spell disaster and defeat. But I had a friend called gravity, and he was on my side this time. Ducking my head back down, I slammed my push rims into greater speed, pounding them again and again as my chair rocketed down Suicide Hill. When I couldn't push anymore, I tucked down and watched the distance between me and my prey rapidly diminish. Flying by Rob, I knew I would soon slow and have to face the long stretch of grass leading to the finish line.

Rising from my crouch as my speed dropped, I pounded my fists into the rims once again, trying to maintain the speed I'd reached coming down the hill. I felt exhaustion creeping in. My nerves started to fail as thoughts of losing the race snuck into my brain. That nugget of fear had seeped into my mind. Was I going to lose? Pushing past the baseball field, I knew it would come down to the last stretch. Locking out thoughts of defeat and reaching deep down inside, I pulled the great redheaded beast out and fired it to life. My internal engine roared as I rounded the field. I stared down the stretch to the finish line and plowed into the grass, giving it all I had. Within moments I could hear the crowd shouting and cheering. I couldn't believe it. I was going to win the district title. I allowed myself a small smile. That was until I got close enough to hear what they were saying.

"Go, Rob!"

*Wait a minute! My name's not Rob!*

*Oh no!*

That's when I knew he was right behind me and gaining. With an effort borne more out of fear than willpower, I turned up the juice and with leaden arms continued to give all I had left in me. With every push, I got closer to the finish line. I imagined seeing Rob's feet overtaking my wheels. Not until my front wheel crossed the line did I raise my gloved hands above my head in victory.

My joy was short-lived. Not long after crossing the finish line, I was informed that Coach Pounder was once again trying to get me disqualified. His efforts to trip me up all year had failed, so he was determined to try one last ploy to stop me. He argued with the officials that I was wearing gloves and shorts (which could not be seen anyway when I was in my wheelchair) that were not standard school issue. I waited while the officials and coaches decided whether or not I had won the race or would be disqualified for something stupid. After an agonizing ten minutes, my coach told me the officials had turned Coach Pounder down flat. I had done it! I had just won a race meant only for runners. I was super stoked. I had done the impossible. I had overcome all objections to rise to the top.

It felt great to be the district champion and experience the payoff for countless hours of training. When I started, I had been the slowest, often finishing in last place. I could have easily given up the first time in middle school when I'd been told I was not able to compete, that it was too hard for "someone like me." But I had done it anyway. I'd accepted the challenge to become more than others thought I could be, more than even I thought I could be. I had no clue at the beginning that I would have any shot at being a district champion. Not only that, but I was probably the first cross-country champion in a wheelchair throughout the whole country. It was an honor to have gone as far as I did. I wasn't trying to be the best; I was just trying to do my own best, and I was glad I had never backed down when others were too afraid to allow me to give it a shot.

I did not have any time to sit around and think of that final season of my cross-country career, however. The Monday after districts I was in the wrestling room getting back into the best sport on the planet (in my humble opinion). Exhilarated with my cross-country success, I dove headfirst into the last wrestling season of high school. Coach Olliff had gotten a job offer closer to home at his own alma mater, Dallas High School, so we had a new wrestling coach, named Jason Ebbs, who came from one of the best wrestling schools in the state. I was sad to see Coach Olliff go, but I knew the skills and tools he had left with me would see me through until the state championship.

Every day after practice I stayed in the wrestling room, running up and down the floor, doing army crawls until I couldn't move. Some days I would be in the practice room for so long that most of the guys would be long gone from the locker room by the time I got out.

One of my favorite wrestlers was a man by the name of Dan Gable. He was one of the best wrestlers to have ever lived, only losing one match in his entire college career. The best story I ever heard about this amazing wrestler was how he had trained with the goal of working so hard he wouldn't be able to walk out of the practice room. He said he had never achieved it. Well, in that respect, I one-upped him. There was never a day when I was able walk out of the wrestling room; I usually scooted out.

Ever since I was a freshman, I had needed to lose a pound or two to make it into the 103-pound weight class. Coming into my senior season, I was 115 pounds. To be able to wrestle at 103 pounds, I needed to drop 12 pounds. This may seem like a lot, but in reality it was fairly simple to do. It just required me to stop eating like a garbage truck. By the time matches started, I was making weight.

A week after the season started, Coach Ebbs came up to me after practice. "Hey, Kacey, can we talk for a minute?" he asked.

"Sure, Coach. What's up?" I asked, slowing my wheelchair.

"I'm looking to change a few things up this year. One of the things I'm looking to do is have team captains. I've seen how you're working the new kids. They seem to look up to you and follow your lead. I would like you to be one of the team captains," he said, looking directly into my eyes.

"What would you need me to do?" I asked, surprised.

"I need someone who will be a perfect example of how to be a wrestler, not only in the wrestling room but also in school. Show these guys what it takes to be the best."

I agreed. Here was my chance to do just that. There were many times I didn't know what to do or how to get others to follow me, but the one thing I did know was how to work. I decided to lead by example and pull as many of the others along as I could.

The season came on fast, and before I knew it, I was at a preseason tournament going up against the one person I knew without a doubt I'd see in the state finals: Marty Eng. Marty and I had wrestled the previous year at state, and I had beat him. This year was no different. Our third matchup was at the North Bend Tournament. It was the most intense match to that point, but I barely won, with a final score of four to three. There was almost nobody else who could keep up with us, so we trained to beat each other.

The more he wrestled against me, the more he knew me and how to beat me. We both knew the next and final time we would meet would be at the Veterans Memorial Coliseum at the state tournament.

I knew I had every chance in the world of becoming a wrestling state champion. But there was one thing that frustrated me and made it hard to improve. I kept fighting the issue, but the harder I fought it, the worse it got. The problem was that I was winning. The best way to improve is to pinpoint your weak areas and hone your skills accordingly. I didn't have many weak areas. I was not having challenging matches. I pinned almost every wrestler I competed against my senior year. My tough matches were often still blowouts in my favor. I was the number one ranked wrestler at 103 pounds in the state of Oregon.

Since my opponents weren't challenging me in the way I needed, I decided to use each match to teach myself new moves, knowing that if I got into trouble, I could easily get out of it with plenty of time to win. It was in a match against an opponent from Cleveland High School that I came across a move I would use often and to great effect: the suicide cradle.

I was handling the match just fine until it came time for me to start my cradle. I locked my arm around his leg and then proceeded to grab his head. I tried again. Nothing. No matter what I did, that kid did not want to go into my cradle.

I backed off a bit and just lay on top of him to figure out what my next move was. At that point, the kid had had enough cradles. In an effort to escape once and for all, he came to his base (in wrestling, "coming to a base" or "basing up" means getting off your belly and onto your hands and knees).

I was still on top of him when he decided to base up, so I went up with him. Feeling like I was losing control, I looked around to see what I could grab. I already had his head, but I saw that as he'd come to his base, he'd brought his knee close to his head. I grabbed his leg, crushed him into the cradle, and tried to pull him onto his back.

Deciding that wasn't working but not wanting to lose the cradle, I went in the only other direction open to me: over the other side. This required

I do a headstand and pull him over the top of me, landing him in a cradle and allowing me to pin him in the next few seconds.

After the ref raised my hand in victory, I scooted over to my coach with a look of amazement on my face.

"Coach, what did I just do?" I said.

"That was a suicide cradle," Coach Ebbs said with a grin.

"Will you show me how to do it again?" I asked.

"Will do, McCallister," he said.

Coach Ebbs didn't have to struggle as much as Olliff had to coach me. After four years of experience, I'd already worked hard at conditioning and pushing myself toward creating my own unique wrestling style.

After that match, the suicide cradle was my go-to move. I already tried for the cradle nearly every match, but now I was upping my game.

By the time I got to state, I was undefeated (or would that be unde-*feet*-ed? *Ba-dum-tss*). Having won the district title, I was ready to face what I hoped would be my championship year.

The night before going to state, I was unable to sleep. I knew my first match was a bye (a bye in wrestling happens when there is no one for you to wrestle that round) and would be followed by a match with the number-three guy in the state. He was a scrappy kid from Woodburn I'd beaten at state the year before. I was confident but still a bit worried. My mind would not shut down enough for me to sleep, so I was up tossing and turning the whole night. I was still wired as we drove up to Portland the morning of the match.

When the match finally rolled around, I was tired and completely off my game, but I still gave it all I had. My opponent and I battled back and forth for three periods. When the third-round whistle sounded, we were tied. This sent us into overtime, which was where I knew I could beat him. I had the conditioning, and he didn't. The year before, I had worn him down before beating him with an escape followed by a takedown. Having him be able to go a full three rounds, each round being two minutes, was way more than anybody thought he would do, and he knew it as well. He was done. Before we even started the first overtime round, he went over to the garbage and dry-heaved. It was a simple matter after that to snag a leg and then take him down to win the match.

Because that was my only match of the day, I was able to relax. Later on at the hotel, my roommate and good friend, Danny Rung, said I was talking to him one second and the next I had rolled over and was snoring. I guess not sleeping the night before had really worn me out. I needed some major *Z*'s before taking on day two of the state tournament.

That second day, I woke up rested and ready to go. I got to the coliseum and weighed in without any problem. I was able to make my way past my next two opponents, which moved me on to the finals the following day.

That night I slept as well if not better than I had the night before. Danny had lost on day two and was out of the tournament, so our coach moved him to a different room so he could enjoy time with the team while I rested up.

Waking up on the third day, I reflected on how far I had come. I had started out as the little kid who won only a single match and had become a contender for the state championship.

Getting to the arena, I passed my last weigh-in of my high school career. The finals match was not until that evening, so I had time to enjoy watching a few matches, cruising around Portland, and eating. Oh yes, I could finally start eating again. I no longer had to cut down to a certain weight, but I couldn't just gorge because I still had the finals to get through.

The match that would determine whether I would realize my dream of being a state champion was against Marty Eng. At that point we had wrestled three times; he had learned how to wrestle me and had gotten better each time. We both knew we'd make it to state for the chance to claim a championship title. He would be the toughest opponent I had ever come across.

As soon as the match started, I knew I was in trouble. The instant the whistle sounded, he was spinning around me faster than I could anticipate, gaining the first two points. I was still confident. I knew I could control him now that I could grab him. He released me, giving me a point, but it set him up for another shot at a takedown. By the time the second period rolled around, he had gained the second takedown, and the score was four to one. I was frustrated. He was in control of the match, and I was fighting just to stay out of trouble. The second round allowed me to choose my position. I chose bottom, thus giving me the chance to escape and grab another point. Once the period started, I sprang into motion, snapping my hand out to grab his, but he moved as soon as I did and pulled his hand away. Back and forth we went, me trying to find an opening to escape and him foiling me at every turn. At one point I reached back to pull him over my head, but he pulled his head back, causing me to grab his head gear and costing me another point. The whistle blew to end round two.

The score was five to one, and my time was running out. I needed something big to get some points. I spun, grabbed, and fought for every inch, but to no avail. He pinned my chest to the mat and started running a bar. A bar is achieved by threading your arm between your opponent's arm and his back, giving you a ton of leverage to put him on his back. I was so surprised by his speed and strength that he got two back points before I got back to my base. The third round started with both of us up and the score seven to one.

I was in trouble. I needed to put him on his back now. The problem was he had already taken me down twice, and now he was positioned to do it again. I darted in and tried to snag his leg. He spun, attempting to get another takedown by getting behind me. I whipped my arm up, catching his leg and crushing it to my body. Now that I had his leg, I had a chance. He kicked back with the force of a mule. I barely held on, but this was my last chance to do what needed to be done. Pulling the leg in once again, I reached up, searching for his head. Having wrestled me a few times, he knew exactly what I was going for and stayed out of the way. Deciding it was not going to happen, I switched to the ball and chain, trying to pull the rest of his body down to get his head closer. As soon as I grabbed his arm, he tried to yank it away. I kept hold of it, but with him pulling away, I couldn't get his body to follow his arm.

Trying to surprise him, I let his arm go and went for a double leg takedown by driving my shoulders into his shins. Recovering quickly, he hit a sprawl, flinging his legs out behind him. He landed on my back, my face driving into the mat. That was the perfect position for him. All he had to do was wait out the time. I still had six points to make up before the whistle blew. Still holding his leg, I posted up, straining to bring the leg close to my body to once again try to put him in a cradle. Snaking my hand up, I tried once again to snag his head. He was ready for me, and I ended up flat on my face, holding his leg with only one hand.

He spun around, attempting to pick up two more points. As he did, his weight came off me enough to allow me to spring upright and wrap both arms around a leg. I quickly grabbed his head before he could pull it away. I had it, and now I could implement the Kacey Crunch. But I never got the chance.

The whistle blew. The match was over.

He won, and I took second place. I did not quite know how to feel; I was confused and numb. The goal I had worked so hard for four years to achieve had just come to nothing. As the loss set in, I quickly exited the main floor. Finding a quiet spot, I cried. I never cry. Even in the hospital with the nurses poking me repeatedly to find a vein, I hadn't cried. Even when it felt like there were watermelons coming out of my bleeding stubs while the doctors were scrubbing me clean, I hadn't cried. I had always been on a path to be tough, and crying just didn't fit into that plan. But that day, I cried. I cried because of all the hours I had put in, I cried for the years of pushing toward one goal just to fall short of reaching it. I cried for all the people who had supported me and had to watch me lose the last match of the sport I loved. After a few minutes I was done, and all that was left was a sense of loss. To this day that match was one of the biggest disappointments in my life, but I have no regrets because I did everything I absolutely could do to make sure I was the best I could be. In that match, though, Eng was better.

That was the end of my high school wrestling career. It hadn't ended how I'd wanted it to, but I was still a top-ranked wrestler in the state of

Oregon in 2004 and probably one of the best double amputees in the United States.

The loss did not lessen my appetite for great things. Track had already started, but before I jumped into it, I took a weeklong break. I needed to let my body and mind take a rest. I had let my grades slip a little and really needed to focus on getting them back up to where they needed to be.

By the end of that week I was getting antsy. I was ready to explode down the track the minute the first starting gun fired. I was ready to compete again. I was ready to feel the thrill of victory as I sped past runner after runner. I also got a little bit of a boost my senior year. I bought a pair of carbon-fiber wheels. The first day of practice I bolted those bad boys on and slowly started pushing around the track. They felt super smooth as I gained speed. There was no subtle flexing and they were lighter by far, but something strange happened as I picked up speed. I heard a noise, one I had never heard before. It was a constant *shuss, shuss, shuss*. I tilted my head, trying to locate where it was coming from. I just hoped it wasn't a flat tire. Then I realized it was my new wheels. It was like they were giving me my very own chant, a speed chant.

I started training with an intensity born of excitement. I was not motivated by fear or a desire to beat anybody. I was still competing against myself. I wanted to get a better time each meet. No runner could hold a candle to the times I was pulling down. I remember one meet in particular, I raced against a guy named Galen Rupp—one of the best runners in the country. I didn't know who he was at the time, but I found out after the race. The sun was out, and there was no wind—perfect conditions for a meet. From the time the gun was fired until I crossed the finish line, I was not challenged by a single runner. It was only later I learned I had just beat Galen Rupp, a state champion and future Olympian silver medalist.

Even as fast as I was, I still struggled with not being considered a legitimate track athlete since my races never counted toward my team's success, but by that point it hardly mattered anymore. I was still there fighting the good fight and proving to people that being in a wheelchair does not mean you have to give up on life. My best and favorite event was the 1500-meter. I pushed myself harder and harder each and every race. By the end of the season, I had whittled my time down to an impressive three minutes thirty seconds.

My 3000-meter time was solid all year. I didn't feel the hunger as much with that race. It was always near the end of every meet, and it just felt like everything was winding down. I loved it, but it became more a game of *how many times can I lap the lead runner* rather than how fast I could go. But one day I did something that amazed even me while it was happening.

It was a cool sunny day. We were hosting North Salem. I had already done well in the 1500-meter, not improving my time but coming very close. I lined up for the 3000-meter, ready to have a fun run. The gun fired, and I pounded my wheels, trying to get up to speed as fast as the runners. Before a dozen pushes, I was pulling ahead of the pack. This was normal. What wasn't normal was the pace I set for myself. When I hit the one-lap mark, I heard my time from the side of the track: sixty seconds. That was a pretty good pace even for me. I still had six and a half laps to go. By the fourth lap (about a mile), I was still holding a sixty-second pace. I was amazed and still feeling good. My arms were getting tired, but they kept pumping at the same pace. When I hit lap seven with the same pace, I couldn't believe what I was doing. I crossed the finish line thirty seconds later, with the exact time of seven minutes thirty seconds. I gave a whoop of excitement. What a rush. I had killed it! That was a race even Olympians would be proud of. I had just set a state track record for the 3000-meter.

The state track meet was an awesome place to showcase how far I had come. There were seven other wheelchair racers lined up. We filled the lanes. I was surrounded with fellow athletes. I was at the top of my game. First was the 400-meter race. From the instant the gun was fired to the time I crossed the finish line, I was in front, winning first place.

The 1500-meter was the last of my high school athletic career. As I sped down the final stretch, I soaked up the cheers, the thrill of the victory, and the excitement of being on Hayward Field, one of the most historic tracks in the nation. I was a champion. I crossed the finish line for the last time, with my fist in the air. Not only had I competed in two races at state but I had shown everybody that wheelchair racers are serious athletes who belong on the track. Through my career in high school track, I had set a record in almost every track event. Traveling home from the meet, I felt great. What an exciting year. I had done some impressive things, but now I had to figure out what to do with my future.

I knew I wanted to be a motivational speaker and continue as an athlete, but I wasn't quite sure I was on the path that helped me become both. I was a good student, but what really fired me up and got me going in the morning was sports, and sports would play a huge part in the decisions I would soon be making.

I knew when I turned nineteen I would be going on a mission for The Church of Jesus Christ of Latter-day Saints, but that was still a good ways off, and I had plenty of time to get some things taken care of before then. So the question was what to do in the meantime. Well, that was easy enough. I knew college was on the horizon, so why not get a year of it out of the way before the mission?

I sat down and made a list of what I wanted in a school. Priority number one: move away from home and see a different part of the country. Priority number two: wrestle. Priority number three: wheelchair racing. So I knew I wanted to move away, but where to? I looked at Southern Virginia University (SVU), where Keith went to school. They had a wrestling team, but it just didn't feel right. Utah Valley State College (UVSC, now Utah Valley University) was very appealing since they had a wrestling team, but once again it didn't feel like the route I was supposed to go. I really wanted to wrestle, but at the same time I needed to make sure it was the right place for me. Then there was the offer from the University of Arizona (U of A). They wanted me to join the wheelchair racing team. I was very conflicted about what to do. From a very early age I had been taught to pray, so I did, asking God where He wanted me to go. Where would be the best place for me to go before serving a mission? I did not get an answer right away. In fact, I prayed many times, trying to determine what I should do. For months I went back and forth between the colleges.

After visiting my brother in the fall, I thought SVU was where I wanted to go to school, but I soon realized it was not the right answer. With that option off the table, I concentrated on looking at UVSC. In March we took Keith to Utah to leave on his mission to Mexico. I visited UVSC to talk with the coach and check out the program. The coach was Cody Sanderson, the brother of legendary four-time NCAA wrestling champion Cael Sanderson. With a healthy dose of warning, he told me how hard college wrestling was going to be. There was no scholarship for me, and it would be difficult to earn a spot on the wrestling team. That made me want to do it that much more. I rolled out of there thinking UVSC would be a pretty awesome place to go to school. While I was thinking about it, I got a phone call.

"Kacey, this is Tyler Byers, head wheelchair track coach at U of A," he said. "We really want you to come down and race for us. We need more solid athletes like you. You would be one of the best racers we have down here, and I really think I could help you become one of the best racers in the country."

Coach Byers was clearly excited about the prospect of a potential elite racer on his team. Going to U of A might be a viable option. So I could either go to Arizona to race as an elite athlete or claw my way tooth and nail just to get a spot on the team at UVSC. I was not afraid of the prospect of earning a spot on a wrestling squad. I had done it before, and I could do it again. On the other hand, I was a really good wheelchair racer and felt there was a lot still ahead of me for that sport as well. It was a tough decision.

The answer came one day in a simple way. I was lying in the family room, reading and thinking about what I was going to do. I started to feel strongly I needed to go to Arizona. Within a matter of ten minutes, it was stronger than before. Right then my mom came in and told me she felt I needed to go to Arizona. She usually lets us figure stuff out on our own, but this time she practically told me to go to Arizona. We both knew God was guiding me. Just like that the decision was made. I was going to be a Wildcat.

About that time I got a call from a man representing a magazine, who wanted to do a story on me. To that point I had been featured in *Boys' Life* magazine and a fitness magazine called *Bigger Faster Stronger*. This magazine was different though, in that I had actually read it—I had read every issue for the last five plus years. It was called the *New Era*, a publication put out by The Church of Jesus Christ of Latter-day Saints and geared toward its young people. I was so stunned that I sat there for a few seconds not responding.

I reflected on the times throughout my life when I have been the subject of media attention, especially during high school. I would give the interviews, let them take pictures while I trained for my next event, and go about my day. One day, in the middle of my junior year, a man called me and said his name was Chad Hawkins. I immediately recognized the name. He was the author of some beautiful books featuring his paintings of temples of The Church of Jesus Christ of Latter-day Saints from around the world. At first I really didn't believe a prominent author would be calling me, but it soon became apparent he was who he said he was. He told me he was working on a new project called *Latter-day Heroes*. It would contain stories from members of the Church's past and present who had shown a hero's spirit. He asked if I would be willing to be in his book. Still not believing it completely, I agreed. He asked for some pictures, along with a request to call me again and interview my parents and me.

A few months went by with no word on the book or when it was going to come out. Right about the time I had stopped thinking about it, I received three signed copies in the mail. It was amazing! The pictures were absolutely beautiful, and it had *me* right there on the cover of the book alongside famous people such as the inventor of the television, Philo T. Farnsworth; and pro-baseball player Dale Murphy. What a humbling experience. I am still trying to live up to the ideals expected of a latter-day hero.

All this raced through my mind as I listened to the voice on the other end of the phone. I soon found out that someone from the *New Era* had gotten a copy of *Latter-day Heroes* and wanted to feature me in an article that would be seen by kids throughout the world. That was the greatest honor I could imagine.

---

I FELT LIKE NOTHING COULD GET IN MY WAY.

---

I was soon interviewed and photographed. That time, instead of putting it out of my mind, I eagerly waited for the article to come out in the June 2004 issue.

One night I went to a youth activity straight from track practice. I hadn't had time to go home, so I had not seen what had come in the mail that day. Rolling into the meeting room, I was immediately surrounded. My friends rushed to me with copies of the magazine, which had me on the cover. I had not told anybody about the article. I borrowed a copy from one of my friends and skimmed the pages.

This time I didn't get a signed copy; I was the one doing the signing. The article gave me a good bit of notoriety among Church members around me. That fame by itself did nothing, but if it could inspire others to better their lives, then it was worth something. Having said that, I thought it was pretty cool to be on the cover of a popular Church magazine. The June issue had come out just a month before I graduated high school, and it was an amazing end to an amazing year.

A few weeks later my senior class had an awards night. I won the "Run, Forrest, Run" award. I thought it was hilarious. I also was awarded "Boy Athlete of the Year" and "Boy of the Year." The latter two were voted on by the teachers at school. I was honored and humbled to be held in such high regard by the staff. Some people say their high school years were the best of their lives. For me, high school wasn't the capstone in my life, but it was a pretty big stepping stone along my journey. I was pretty much on top of the world and felt like nothing could get in my way. *Watch out world,* I thought. *Here I come.*

# CHAPTER 11
## ON MY OWN

*"After climbing a great hill,
one only finds that there are many more hills to climb."*
*—Nelson Mandela*[16]

The unknown is always before us, and it can be scary. But as we face our fears, we learn something new, and more often than not, we discover a new skill or talent we never would have discovered had we not taken the chance. Then, as we are improved by challenges, our minds are able to see the endless sea of possibilities waiting for us so that we can choose a path. Are we going to know what to do immediately? Probably not. Are we going to fail? Absolutely. That is part of facing life. For only in failure can we truly learn to live.

SOON AFTER GRADUATION I WAS hanging around the house when the phone rang. I scooted into my parents' room to answer. "Hello?"

"Hi, is this Kacey?" said a woman's voice on the other end.

"Yep, this is Kacey," I replied.

"Hi, my name is Lisa Sandstrom," she said. "You probably don't remember, but you and my daughter were friends in the hospital."

I was slightly confused. I had not been in a hospital since I was six years old. Could it really be someone from that long ago?

"From Primary Children's Hospital?" I asked skeptically.

"Yes! You knew my daughter as the little girl with the bloody braid on her head," she said.

---

16 *Long Walk to Freedom: The Autobiography of Nelson Mandela*, Back Bay Books, 1995.

A memory sparked as a vague image of a little girl named Cambria developed in my mind.

"I think I do remember her. Wasn't it due to a bike accident?" I said, trying to pull the pieces of the memory back together. "How did you find me?"

Excitedly she told me the story.

"I was in Deseret Book and saw the book *Latter-day Heroes*, and I remembered you from the hospital," she said. "I must have seemed crazy when I asked the clerk if she knew how to get a hold of you. Of course she didn't, so I just used directory assistance to find your family."

I was blown away. I leaned up against my parents' bed and held the phone with my shoulder. "That's amazing you found me after all these

---

ARE WE GOING TO FAIL? ABSOLUTELY.
THAT IS PART OF FACING LIFE. FOR ONLY IN FAILURE CAN WE
TRULY LEARN TO LIVE.

---

years!" I said. "Why did you even remember me?"

"Kacey, you might have saved my daughter's life," she said, her voice starting to crack. "She was very depressed and wasn't eating or progressing until you came into the room and told her to come and play. After that, she improved and soon was able to go home."

I was stunned that such a small action had made such an impact. I had just wanted to play. All Cambria had really needed at that moment was a friend. It was an incredible feeling to know I had made such a difference in somebody's life. After a few more minutes of chatting, Lisa asked if I would be willing to share my story of the accident, my life, and all the obstacles I had overcome at a conference for youth in Utah.

"Yeah, I would love to do that," I said without hesitation. I was always stunned at the effect my words could have over a group of people. I was excited for the opportunity, and since I had already been planning to go to Arizona to check out the U of A campus, it would be easy to stop and speak at the conference on my way back home.

After telling my mom the news, she started calling her family in Utah to let them know we were coming to visit. When her family heard of my speaking engagement, they jumped on the bandwagon, and I was soon booked for a half dozen firesides and youth conferences for their congregations.

We planned our intense trip to a tee. We would make a road trip with the whole family, except my dad, which would last for weeks and cover more than three thousand miles. The first leg would take my mom, my two younger siblings, and me from Oregon to the University of Arizona. After that we would be going to Junior Nationals in Mesa, Arizona. After pounding the track, I would head out on my first speaking circuit, including getting to see Cambria at her youth conference.

The biggest things I noticed as we got closer to Arizona was the heat and the landscape. The temperature just kept climbing, and the landscape just kept dying. It was like Wyoming, except instead of sagebrush there was nothing but dirt, cactus, and rocks. By the time we got to Tucson, the only thing left alive were cacti. The temperature never dipped below one hundred degrees, even at midnight.

The scorching heat could not dissuade me from my path though. I was super excited to be starting this new stage of my life. Signing up for classes and meeting the other racers got me even more revved up for my college experience. The only issue was finding a place to live. There were so many things to consider: price, location, furnished/unfurnished, distance from campus, to name a few. It was enough to drive me crazy. We finally spotted a winner among the "roommate wanted" postings at The Church of Jesus Christ of Latter-day Saint institute building, a kind of social hall slash rec center for students who are Church members that offers religion courses, dances, and talks from different speakers. With my housing set up, it was time for the next step on this summertime adventure.

This would be my third straight time going to Junior Nationals, but I felt like there was more on the line this time. This was my chance to show my new coach he was right to have recruited me. No pressure, right? I ended up winning first place in the 1500- and 800-meter races and setting a personal best in the 100-meter.

I also tried competing in weightlifting for the first time, and I didn't know what to expect. Fortunately the competition pool was not overly huge, and I won, lifting near my maximum of two hundred thirty pounds.

As soon as the events were over, we headed to Utah to meet up with the Sandstroms. The youth conference not only offered speeches but a lot of fun activities, and I wanted to be involved in all of it. One of the activities was a ropes course up in the woods. At one point on the course, we were supposed to climb a tree using U-bolts positioned about two feet away from each other. One of the bolts was stuck too far into the tree for me to reach. It wasn't a problem for those using their legs, because they could still use the U-bolt as a foothold, but I needed every handhold available. After a bit of trial and error, I discovered the tree had really deep bark, so rather than trying to climb up using the U-bolts, I wrapped my arms around the tree in a great big bear hug and proceeded to shimmy up the tree using the bark as handholds. It never occurred to me to just go back down. I just had to figure out a different way to do it, and as I have known my whole life, there is always a way. Later that night I spoke to the group, emphasizing the obstacles I'd faced with cross country and basketball when others had suggested I was not able to do the things I wanted to do and how I'd proved them wrong time and again.

When we got back to Oregon, I had spoken almost a dozen times in three weeks. That trip had been different than the others. That time I had been traveling to speak to people. Instead of speaking near my home at a friend's invitation, I was traveling to new places and seeing new things. Not only that, but I could see the impact I was having on thousands of lives. I loved it. There is no better feeling in the world than feeling like you've made a difference.

About a month later it was time to set off for that desert dream called college. My dad wanted to accompany me on the twenty-hour drive to Tucson; however, he didn't realize just how excited I was. We'd planned on leaving in the morning the following day, but I was so amped up I had the car all packed and ready to go as soon as he got home after a twelve-hour workday, at six thirty P.M.

"Come on, Dad, let's start driving tonight!" I said barely giving him a chance to come through the front door.

"No, Kacey, let's get a good night's sleep, and then we will be ready to go in the morning," he said with more than a hint of weariness.

Oblivious to how tired he was, I pressed the issue. "Come on; it'll be fine," I said. "I'll drive most of the way."

My dad was always the one who let us get hot dogs at football games and candy at the store, so it didn't take much for me to persuade him to leave that night. After he grabbed a shower and some food, we were on the road. We headed south, passing Salem and then Eugene. My enthusiasm didn't last as long as I had thought it would. After about two hours into the trip, I told my dad I was tired, so he traded places with me and drove for most of the night until he'd decided enough was enough and finally pulled over at a rest area so we could sleep.

To pass the time along the way, we listened to books. Some of my best memories are of listening to audiobooks on the long drives we took as a family during vacations. Anything by Louis L'Amour was always a popular choice.

When we weren't listening to books, Dad and I talked about whatever came to mind: college classes I was excited about, races I would be competing in, plans for my mission. My dad is a great listener. He has the unique ability to make a person feel like they are being heard and understood. There weren't many occasions when I had the chance to take a solo trip with my dad, and I took full advantage of having his undivided attention as we headed to Arizona.

At around ten the next morning, we stopped in Southern California. The instant we opened the door, we were struck in the face by a wall of air so hot it was like a physical blow. It was so intense both of us stopped in our tracks and gasped for air. I did not like the heat, but even this startling reminder of the desert conditions I'd be facing in Arizona didn't overshadow the excitement I felt about being out on my own. Despite the heat we rolled into Tucson without incident and found my new digs.

After getting settled in my new apartment, I took Dad to the airport.

I was finally free. I had a car so I could go where I wanted, I had my own space, and I didn't have to compete with any of my siblings. I'd never had my own room before, and now I was able to buy anything at the store and not worry about somebody else eating it. Most of all, my time was my own. I could sit around and read books all day long without anybody caring. I was free to figure out what I'd do with my time. I believe what we do when no one is around can truly show us who we are, and I was excited to be free to find out; no one was watching.

I lived four-and-a-half miles off campus, so instead of going home in between classes, I ended up spending a lot of time hanging out in the institute building.

It was a good thing I had a place to go where I could make the most of my study time because, as it turned out, school wasn't as easy as I thought it would be. Graduating from high school with a 3.87 GPA had given me the false impression I was a wiz in school. In high school all I'd had to do was sit in class and listen in order to successfully complete my assignments. But college required actual work. I had to put in some major hours outside of class just to keep up. It took me a while to figure out how to balance everything. I actually ended up failing my economics class, mostly because I constantly fell asleep during it, and it wasn't even an early class. Whether it was because I was exhausted from competing in two sports or just found it to be a really, really boring class, I am not sure.

When I wasn't hanging out at the institute building, I was at the adaptive recreation department, where the coaches for both wheelchair basketball and wheelchair racing kept their offices. While I was hanging out there, the wheelchair basketball coach approached me.

"Hey, Kacey, have you ever thought about playing basketball?" he said.

"Not really," I replied. "I was a wrestler in high school, and I can't shoot a ball very well."

"Well, do you want to give it a shot?" he said.

I was unsure about playing a sport I had never been particularly good at. I knew I couldn't shoot or dribble. I didn't understand plays or how the game was supposed to run. I knew the rules, of course, but I also knew how clumsy I would be trying it out for the first time since I was nine years old. But I figured this would be good for me. I would be learning a new skill.

"Sure, I guess I could try it out," I said.

"All right. We look forward to having you," he replied as he rolled away.

I showed up for the first day of practice in my everyday chair. The coach told me it would be really tough to do it from that chair, so he loaned me a basketball wheelchair, which did a few things for me. It sat me higher and had a fifth wheel in the back to prevent me from tipping over. It was strange sitting up so high. My hands almost didn't reach the push rims. But I soon got the hang of it and proceeded to blast up and down the floor, feeling the speed and handling of my new "shoes."

The coach was impressed by my skills . . . until he handed me a ball. My dribbling, passing, and shooting were probably the worst on the team, if not throughout the entire sport. During one game I remember staring down at my dribbling hand just so I wouldn't lose control of that bouncing orange ball (it's still embarrassing to think about). I also didn't have the experience for basketball strategy, so the coach and other players would yell directions at me from the sidelines.

I worked my ball-handling for hours every day, some days spending thirty minutes or more just throwing a ball against the wall to improve my passing and catching skills or dribbling the ball up and down the court. I knew I wasn't the best guy out there, but I also knew the power of repetition. Just like when I had put in long hours after wrestling practice, I knew the more time I spent working on my basketball skills, the better I'd become.

What I lacked in ball-handling skills, I made up for in speed. I had been in my wheelchair for twelve years, and I not only knew how to push but to push fast. It didn't hurt that I was the top speedster on the racing team. Within one or two practices I could keep up with the fastest players on my basketball team, not to mention I was really tall in my chair, which gave me the ability to block the ball. Blocking, stealing, and fast breaks (rapidly driving the ball across the court and into position to score so the other team's defense is outnumbered) were my bread and butter, and I earned the team a few points every game.

The best part of the year was a fundraising event called Lame for a Game, in which U of A's men's basketball players joined us in wheelchairs for a game. The night before the game we went down to the gym to help teach star basketball players how to play in a wheelchair. When I first got there, I saw a couple of the players from the men's team trying to play. They were holding the ball on their laps while pushing slowly toward the basket. They were laughing and acting like they had the wheelchair thing down. Chuckling to myself, I quickly hopped into my basketball chair and strapped up. With two pushes, I quickly gained some speed. As soon as I had a bit of momentum, I performed a simple but important technique called trunk twisting. When done right, this allows a player to move the wheelchair without needing to push the wheels. As I blazed toward them, they looked up to see me going three times as fast as them but without actually pushing my chair at all. Jokingly one of them shouted out, "Dude! That's unfair. You can't do that!" They soon found out wheelchair basketball was not an easy sport to master.

We wanted to make the game more exciting, so instead of the wheelchair basketball players creaming the able-bodied athletes, we had the teams mixed up, allowing us to interact and have some pretty interesting plays. Because it was a fundraiser and the people watching wanted to see some of the college guys play, the rules for the game allowed the U of A players to stand up once in a while to take a three-point shot. We were told we could not guard them in our wheelchairs when they got out of their chairs. Being a redhead as well as having to think outside the box my whole life caused me to look for a way around that rule. I had played basketball without a chair for years. As soon as the guy I was guarding got out of his chair to take a shot, I jumped out of mine to guard him. He didn't know what to do. He was so thrown off he had to pass the ball away. What a funny sight it must have been to see this 6'9" college basketball player guarded by a 3'1" double amputee. I had no chance of blocking his shot, but apparently the new situation was just too much for him to handle.

Later on in the game, I had another idea. Rolling up beside my teammate, future NBA player Hassan Adams, I told him my idea.

"Are you crazy?" he said, his face twisted with disbelief.

"No, it'll be awesome," I told him excitedly.

"Are we allowed to do it?" he asked.

"You guys are getting out of your chairs to run down the court to dunk the ball, so yeah, we can do it," I told him.

"All right, man. Let's do it," he said.

We kept playing for a few minutes, and then the time was right. I nodded to Adams and called for the ball. As soon as it hit my hands, I unstrapped myself. Then Adam's two huge hands wrapped around my body, hoisting me out of my chair, and ran down the court with me. We made it down the floor without resistance before he pushed me up to the basket for the slam dunk. It was an epic move. And the picture even made the front page of the paper the next day.

I loved playing wheelchair basketball. Not so much for the game but for the pure physical exertion that went along with it—charging up and down the floor chasing a runaway ball, working as a team to make a sweet play, beating the other team down the floor and blocking a shot. All of it was such a blast, and I loved feeling that rush. It was almost as good as the rush I felt while racing. As the basketball season progressed, so did the racing season. We were not hampered by snow or rain, so we were able to train all year long, often having practices at five A.M., well before the sun started baking the earth.

It was a pretty big shift for me to race other wheelchair racers. I had grown used to being the only one on the track and basically training to compete against myself. Now I was competing against a whole group of athletes who knew how to race in wheelchairs.

Our coach was Tyler Byers. Tyler was from the Pacific Northwest, so there were many times in the dry heat of Arizona when Tyler and I would find ourselves remembering the pouring rain with a touch of nostalgia. I loved being on his team. He had a quiet way about him that spoke of constant hard work. Tyler was on track to make it to the Paralympics. I looked up to him in a lot of ways. He was what I wanted to be as a wheelchair racer: fast and dedicated to the sport. Tyler helped me find a love for the long distances. In high school going around the track a few times seemed long enough, but now our practices were double to triple the distance. I couldn't have been happier. That was just what I wanted and needed. As a wrestler I was never satisfied with a practice that didn't leave me feeling exhausted, and Tyler's practices did not disappoint.

On Saturdays we would do a big run, usually in the range of twenty-plus miles, and we had a lot of different runs that really made practice interesting. Training can get boring if you are doing the same thing every day. With Tyler I never had this problem. All the runs had a certain charm and challenge to them. Some had a super steep hill. Others were a timed lap around a golf course, and some had a series of hills to tackle one after the other. One of my favorites was a seventeen-mile run along the river. Well, it wasn't really a river. It was actually a riverbed since there was no water in it. At one point in the run, there was a blind spot where the path crossed a road. If we wanted to take it at full speed, we could cross it in a snap, but we also risked a car running into us. I had learned my lesson about crossing roads blindly, so I took it a bit slower than some of the others. I wanted to be the best, but I couldn't do that from a hospital bed.

Other runs took us on trails all over town and out of town. Before training with Tyler, I never knew the true speed of a racing wheelchair. On a flat surface I could get going at twenty mph, but what I didn't realize was downhill I could really scream. During one marathon, as I sped down a hill, my odometer read 48.6 mph, which is just as scary as it sounds. In a racing chair the racer's face can be less than two feet from the ground, and the road is speeding past.

Tyler raced a lot more than I did since he raced on Sundays. The biggest drawback to my playing sports in college was my faith. That isn't to say my faith has anything against athletics, but I have a firm belief that Sunday is a day of rest. From a very early age, I was taught not to participate in athletics, go to the store, or do anything that would require others to work for us on Sundays. I believe Sundays are a day of worship and for family.

Many people questioned my decision, often telling me I had the potential to make it big. I could have raced a little on Sunday, but I had made a promise to God and to myself that I would honor the Sabbath day. Instead I looked for races, specifically marathons, held on other days.

The first marathon that I did was in Logan, Utah. We started at the top of a canyon. It was a chilly morning, and there were three or four other wheelchair racers in the race. The gun fired, and we were off, pushing down the canyon. Before long I was all by myself with only one person in front of me and the others a long way behind. As I flew down the canyon and around the corners, the sun started to find its way through the gaps in the hills. I should have been paying more attention to the road and less to the scenery because right about then a deer jumped out in front of me. He was as surprised to see me as I was to see him. Luckily he quickly darted away and I didn't need to move, as he was much faster than me; I can only guess what would have happened if we had collided.

Farther down the canyon, I took a corner too fast and ended up on two wheels. Putting my chair safely back on all three, I continued down the course with my heart pounding in my chest. Despite making a couple of wrong turns after missing some markers and almost hitting a kid on a bike, I crossed the finish line in second place. I thought it was pretty cool, it being my first marathon, although I was a little bummed when I heard the racer in first place had only been a minute ahead of me. If only I hadn't taken those wrong turns, I might have been able to catch up with him. Lesson learned: always know the course.

Later that year I qualified for the Boston Marathon, one of the most heralded of all marathons. Thousands of people run the Boston Marathon, and thirty wheelchair racers. Because the race requires a qualifying time, every runner who participates is a stellar athlete. I was pretty stoked not only to be racing in it but to be racing alongside Tyler and a teammate, Shirley Riley, and I knew I was able to push with the best of them.

Throughout the course of the race, Tyler and I would draft off of each other to make it easier on both of us. Because I was really good on the hills, I would pull away from him when climbing them, but he would always catch up on the back side. We were neck and neck until about halfway through the race. That was when we reached a hill where he wasn't able to catch me. In fact, he wasn't able to ever regain his position, and I ended up beating him to the finish line with a time of one hour forty-two seconds. I came in ninth place. It was a huge moment for me. The day had turned out great. The sun was shining, and I had a new medal around my neck.

I was pretty stoked to beat my coach, but he was not nearly as happy, especially considering I was the rookie who was always cracking jokes during races. He was so unhappy with the results he didn't speak to me much for the entire plane ride home. It didn't take him long to get over it, though, and soon we got back into our regular routine of battling it out for the top spot. Each time he would assign a run, I was right there, trying to beat him to the finish line.

As my college career progressed, my days filled up more and more. I would start out with a five A.M. racing practice and head back to the apartment to shower and get ready for classes. After classes I would go to wheelchair basketball practice, followed by some time in the gym hitting the weights. Sometimes we'd do a second racing workout in the evening.

Between my packed schedule and being out on my own, I found my diet fell into a very unhealthy pattern. I was extremely active, so I did not consider what I ate to be very important. As long as there was food in my stomach and energy in my body, I thought I was doing well. I lived on whatever was quick and convenient, which meant a Toaster Strudel (or four) in the morning, a stop at Panda Express or Jimmy John's for lunch, and then usually three hot dogs for dinner. If I went out with my friends, we'd hit the buffet and stuff ourselves until we could pop. That was how I had always eaten, and I saw no reason to change my habits.

Winter break rolled around as my first semester in college drew to a close. Except for failing my economics class, I did reasonably well, getting As and Bs in all my other classes. Not only had I put a ton of time into my athletics but I had also put a lot of time into my studies. I was tired and ready to go home.

I was starting to feel really homesick and couldn't wait to get back to Oregon. I missed seeing green grass and towering trees. I missed being around my family for the holidays. And I missed my mom. All I could think about the entire last week of the term was getting home for Christmas. While I was feeling super homesick, I got a call from someone in Salt Lake City asking me if I would like to speak at a New Year's Eve festival called First Night. My initial thought was that I just wanted to go home and spend time with my family, but after talking to my mom, she said it would be fine because we could take the whole family to the festival.

As I flew into Portland, it was wonderful to see the sea of green stretched out before me, with hills and trees as far as I could see. Over the years I'd gone away to scout camps, wrestling camps, and worked for months at a summer camp, but I'd never been truly homesick. I was happy to be home. It felt comfortable, and suddenly everything just felt right. I was where I was supposed to be.

I got home a few days before Christmas and enjoyed spending time with my family. Keith was the only one missing, still serving his mission in Mexico.

The Sunday after I got home I rolled into the church building and saw many of my friends who were still in high school.

Soon after Christmas was over, we loaded up the Suburban and headed off to Salt Lake City for First Night. It was a musical extravaganza, but since my musical abilities were not up to their high standard, I used a few other tricks to liven up the night.

The plan was for me to come out on stage doing a wheelie and then zoom down the ramp before doing a couple of other wheelchair tricks and come to a stop next to Charles Dahlquist, the Church's Young Men General President, who would introduce me. Right on cue, I burst out of the stage door and performed my tricks with flourish. By the time I came to a stop, the entire tabernacle was on its feet—my first standing ovation. I felt like I was in a giant roomful of friends and was pretty pumped. The crowd soon quieted down, and Brother Dahlquist and I had a Q&A. When I was done, there was another round of applause before I disappeared backstage. The rest of the festival was a blur, and I left there on a high. There was not much that could get better than that.

Spring semester of my freshman year went much more smoothly than my first semester at college. I'd learned the hard way how to better manage my schedule, and I started with a decision not to take any classes that would bore me. If I couldn't sit through an hour lecture on the subject, I probably wouldn't be motivated to attend. I also joined the choir. It not only provided me elective credits but was also a class I enjoyed. I was still not a great singer, but not being great has never stopped me from doing what I loved.

The hardest thing I found in college was the constant stream of papers required. I have never been big on writing, and I really struggled with it. I started college typing with one finger of one hand. I think by the end of that second term I was using one finger from both hands. Writing was a painful process for me, to say the least.

When summer rolled around, I was sad to leave my apartment, my new friends, and my athletics, but now I was ready to start the next challenge in my life.

When I got home I began to get ready for my mission. The first thing I needed to do was send in my application. For my entire life I was convinced I would be going on a mission. When I sat down for the interview with my Church leader, I had quite a shock.

"Kacey, I know you are ready and worthy to go on a mission, but it might not be possible for you," Bishop Nelson told me. I sat there for a moment, my heart dropping to my stomach.

"Bishop, there's nothing a missionary does that I can't," I said.

"Kacey, I was with you on the fifty-mile hike, and I know how capable you are," he said. "But the leadership in Salt Lake might not see what I see. The policy of the Church is that young men with disabilities can serve a service mission but are not required to serve a full-time mission. In a service mission you would be able to help out in the mission office."

"I don't want to go on a service mission," I said, trying not to panic. "I've made sure I can do what I need to. How do we make them see what I can do?" I wanted to serve a mission. I did not want to work in a mission office filing papers or sitting around all day typing on a computer. I wanted to be out on the streets bringing joy to others.

"Kacey, trust me, I am doing everything I can to make sure they know what you can do, but we will have to wait to see what they say," he said, trying to calm me down.

"Okay, Bishop," I said, trying to hold back my emotions. Disappointed, I finished the interview and left. What would it mean for me if I couldn't serve a mission? What if the only way I could serve was to be in an office somewhere? Would I be able to do that? What would the leadership say? Was there an appeals process? These questions rolled around in my head as I tried to make sense of what I was to do. Finally I decided I needed to trust that God had a plan for me. Peace settled over me. I still didn't know what was going to happen, but I did know God was looking out for me.

In the letter my bishop sent to Salt Lake was a story about that fifty-mile hike a few years before:

> At the age of fourteen, Kacey joined in a fifty-mile hike through the Jefferson Wilderness area in Oregon State. Although I had watched Kacey successfully tackle many challenges, I wondered whether he would be able to complete this long and difficult hike. Each morning

Kacey and his father would start out on the trail very early. Kacey walked in his usual fashion, utilizing his hands and torso. He was very careful never to slow the group or cause any distraction. The last night, after five days on the trail, before we all retired to our tents, I asked Kacey to offer the evening prayer for the group. His was a prayer I will not forget. His prayer reached to heaven and asked a blessing for those in our group struggling with pains long hikes can cause. I believe only his father and I knew Kacey's pain far exceeded that of any other. But Kacey had a cheery outlook for the entire hike. He was never a hindrance. Instead he lifted and inspired the rest of us.[17]

That summer I went to my third Junior Nationals, this time in Florida. Instead of the dry, blistering Arizona heat, which I had come to accept, I was competing in the sticky, humid Florida heat that never goes away, even with good AC. My little brother Kirt accompanied me under the guise of helping with my equipment. In all reality, he was there to hang out with me. We had a great time, but even though I was at the top of my game, my heart was not in the events. I was waiting for a call—a call I had been waiting for my whole life. A call to serve a mission. Finally, on the second day of competition, the call came. Well, kind of.

Usually a missionary gets his or her call in the mail and has a month or two to prepare for his or her mission. Mine was a different circumstance. When I got the call to serve, it was an actual phone call. The brethren who review missionary applications had been split when it came to approving mine. To serve a mission you need to be able to perform every function required of a missionary, with no special assistance. A mission is a time to serve God and His children. It is not for those who cannot take care of themselves. I had extremely strong recommendations from my local leaders vouching for my capabilities, but the leaders in Salt Lake weren't entirely convinced and decided to send me on a mini four-month mission. It would be a trial mission to see if I was able to complete the tasks required of a missionary. I would be considered a full-time missionary in every way and

---

17 From copy of the letter in author's possession.

would be expected to follow all the rules. I would not go to the Missionary Training Center (MTC). Instead, I would go directly to where I would be serving, forty minutes away from my home, in the town of Wilsonville.

The rest of Junior Nationals was a blur. I won a race or two and had a lot of fun hanging out with my brother. But I really couldn't wait to get home. I was going on a mission.

Within a week of getting home, I was off to prove I had what it took to be considered for a two-year proselytizing mission.

# CHAPTER 12
## ELDER McCALLISTER

*"I'll go where you want me to go, dear Lord, over mountain or plain or sea.*
*I'll say what you want me to say . . .; I'll be what you want me to be."*
—*Mary Brown*[18]

As a missionary you meet with anyone who might be interested in learning more about God and Jesus Christ, either by going door to door or by talking with people on the street. Missionaries are supposed to forget themselves and serve others. The best part about a mission is helping people have happier lives. There is no more rewarding experience than that. Missionaries pay their own way, receiving no compensation for their work; it is voluntary. It is difficult, sometimes monotonous work, but I wouldn't trade my experience as a missionary for anything.

LEAVING HOME FOR THE MISSION field was super exciting. I had been ready to leave ever since I had gotten home from college and had felt like I'd been playing the waiting game for three months. I had my suitcases packed, and now that I knew where I was going, I was ready too. My parents drove me down to the church where I met my companion. My parents and I had already made our goodbyes the night before, so with a hug from my mom and dad, I loaded my gear, and we were off to my new area. I was not sad to leave home. I knew one of two things would happen: I would either prove myself to be an able missionary, in which case I would see them again before I left for my two-year mission, or I'd be told I wouldn't serve a

---

18 "I'll Go Where You Want Me to Go," *Hymns*, no. 270.

two-year mission and be able to see them as much as I wanted over the next two years. I waved to them as we pulled away from the church building.

We got to the apartment and all but dumped my stuff inside before we were off and going. I barely got a tour of our apartment before we were back out working. We hopped onto our bikes and took off to spend the day visiting with people. Sometimes they were members of the Church, and sometimes they were not. We talked to people on the street or knocked on their doors. Every place we went we tried to share a message of joy and hope to help and strengthen the wonderful people we met. By the time we sat down to dinner with one of the members, I was starving. That night as I lay in bed I couldn't help but smile. Whatever was going to happen in the future didn't matter because right now I was a missionary.

Even though I had a lot of experience talking to people about my story, it was still a challenge for me to talk to random people about my beliefs. I am naturally an introvert. It takes a lot out of me to be the one to initiate a conversation. The mission pushed me to break out of my comfort zone and talk to people I would not normally approach, exposing me to new experiences I'd never encountered before.

After a couple of months, during one of our missionary meetings, my mission president, President Geisel, called me in for an interview.

"How have things been going, Elder McCallister?" he said, shaking my hand after I rolled into the room.

"They're great, President," I said, returning his firm grip with one of my own.

"Well, Elder, they sent you on this mini-mission to see if you would be able to serve full time," he said with a serious look on his face. "Do you feel you have been able to do all of the things that have been asked of you so far?"

"President," I said, meeting his gaze. "Back home I have a plaque on my wall with the scripture 1 Nephi 3:7, which says, 'I will go and do the things which the Lord hath commanded, for I know that the Lord giveth no commandment unto the children of men, save He shall prepare a way for

them that they may accomplish the thing which He commandeth them.'
If God says I need to be on a mission, there is a way for me to accomplish
a mission. There is nothing I can't do."

"I agree," he said with a grin on his face. "I am going to recommend to
the leaders in Salt Lake that you be assigned to a full-time mission."

I nodded. I was glad my mission president saw that I could do
everything that was required of me. I knew I could do it. But for my
mission president to see me in action and know it too meant a lot to me. I
left that meeting knowing that was it—the final hurdle. Either my mission
president's recommendation was going to send me on a full-time mission,
or I would be heading back home and returning to college. Now all I had
to do was once again wait on my mission call. I threw myself into the work,
making sure that, regardless of the outcome, I had done all I could in the
time I was given to serve.

A few weeks later we got back to the apartment to hear a message from
my family telling me my call had come in the mail. I shouted for joy upon
hearing my mom's voice relay the news. I immediately called my mission
president and got permission to contact my family. We made arrangements
for them to bring my call to me in Wilsonville, about an hour away from
home so we could open it together. The opening of the missionary letter
was a big moment. I had been dreaming about it for a long time. My only
wish was to be sent someplace cold, like Alaska or Switzerland, because I
get uncomfortable when the temperature goes above seventy-five degrees.

My nerves were all bunched up as I opened the letter and took out the
top sheet of paper.

"*Dear Elder McCallister,*" I read out loud. "*You are hereby called to serve
as a missionary of The Church of Jesus Christ of Latter-day Saints. You are
assigned to labor in the—*"

My mouth fell open. "*Arizona Tucson Mission.*" Dropping the paper,
I stared in stunned silence. I was going back to the land of the burning
sun. For a split second I was not sure how to feel. I had really wanted to
serve a foreign mission, to go someplace new, exotic, and cold. I knew

in my head that wherever I went would be where God needed me to go, but I was disappointed it was someplace I had already been. Then a new feeling came over me. I already knew where I was going. I knew the city, I knew some of the people, and I knew what awaited me. All feelings of disappointment fled as I considered what it would be like to return to the city as a missionary. A feeling of rightness and peace came over me, and I knew without a shadow of a doubt that that was where I was supposed to go. That was where Heavenly Father needed me to go to serve Him.

While I was busy processing my emotions, my family leaned in to try to see for themselves where I was going. Finally my mom told me I'd better read it out loud before she read it herself.

I took a deep breath and read the rest of the letter.

The room erupted in shouts of congratulations. Everybody was pretty excited to hear that I would be headed back to Arizona. They knew as well as I did that was where God wanted me to be. After a while the excitement died down, and with hugs and a few tears from Mom, my family filed out the door. As soon as they were gone, I called President Geisel to tell him the news.

"President! I'm going back to Arizona!" I practically yelled into the phone, still very excited by the news.

"Great, Elder McCallister!" he said. "I knew it would happen for you. When would you like to leave here?"

"Well, since we are having a transfer in three weeks, let's just do it then," I said. Every six weeks there was the potential for missionaries to be transferred to a different area and/or receive a new companion, so that seemed the right time to end my mini-mission.

Before I knew it I was home for Thanksgiving, and then, three weeks later, I was in the MTC in Provo, Utah.

For the next three weeks, I stayed with other missionaries in dorm-like quarters, living, eating, and going to classes. We were organized into groups (districts) of about twenty missionaries. In a district there are usually a few missionaries who are going to the same mission—not in my group though.

I was the only missionary in my district who was going to Arizona. That put a little distance between me and the rest of my group, but I didn't mind; I was only going to be there for the next three weeks, and then I would be in Arizona. The rest of the missionaries in my district were going to the California San Bernardino Mission.

After the first day in the training center, my group's senior advisors chose me to serve as our group's district leader. Our district quickly got to know each other, spending hours each day in classes, learning what it meant to be a missionary. We bonded over dumb jokes, wrestling, and hard work.

When Christmas rolled around, I got a care package from my family. In it was a pair of black socks with Christmas lights going all the way around them. I laughed out loud as I lifted them out of the box.

"That's cool! Are you going to wear them?" my companion asked.

I laughed at his comment, thinking he had made a great joke. I was always up for a good laugh about anything dealing with not having legs. He was more on the serious side, and I was glad to see he was comfortable enough around me to make jokes. He gave me a slightly strange look, but I thought nothing of it as we went to join the rest of the missionaries in our district. I showed them my new socks, which elicited chuckles all around. Again my companion asked if I was going to wear them.

"I guess," I said. "Where would I wear them? On my hands?"

"No, on your fee . . ." he said, trailing off as he looked down at where my feet should have been. "Never mind."

The room exploded into good-natured laughter. I laughed right along with them.

The MTC was a really good place to meet people. Because the *New Era* article had come out the previous year, a lot of people recognized me and came up to meet me. I also found there were a number of familiar faces from back home. One was a young woman whose name was Jennifer Sullivan. Jennifer had been two years ahead of me in high school and way out of my league, but that had never stopped me from admiring her from afar. She had run cross country for North Salem, so whenever we had had meets there, I'd made it a point to see if the cute older redhead was around. Her family was part of a different congregation of the same church I attended, so I had gotten the chance to dance with her at a youth dance a time or two. Those dances had lasted long enough for me to find out she shared my love of sports and my sense of humor. We were at the MTC together for a couple of weeks. I would see her every once in a while at the cafeteria as well as in the MTC choir we were both singing in.

Running into anyone from home was awesome, but to see the cute older girl I'd danced with was even more special. Missionaries are required to unplug from the world. That means no movies or TV, no phone calls to or from home, and no dating. But that didn't mean Jennifer and I couldn't keep in touch through the mail. We exchanged our mission addresses right before she went to Costa Rica.

After my three-week stay at the training center, I arrived in Arizona at the beginning of January, so it was very cool (around 80 degrees). I was sure I was going to die of heatstroke. Many missionaries go to different countries and learn different languages. I was going to learn how to deal with the heat. Granted, I'd made it through a year of college in Arizona, so I already had a pretty good idea of what I was in for, but being a missionary is a far cry from walking around campus and attending classes in air-conditioned buildings.

I remember the sun beating down on my head as I pushed my wheelchair down the street in the middle of a 120-degree summer day. When I would comment on the heat, people would shrug it off and say, "It's only a dry heat."

*Yeah, well, so is your oven,* I thought, especially when I had to get off my chair. If you've ever put your hands on a glass-top stove right after it has been turned off, you know what my hands went through every day.

Even when there's a breeze in Arizona, it does absolutely nothing to cool you down. If you've never experienced it, let me fill you in. Imagine you are in a dry sauna where you can't break a sweat because moisture evaporates off your skin too quickly. Then imagine a blow dryer set on high aimed directly at your face as you exit the sauna. Now you know what an Arizona breeze feels like. As missionaries we used to say that if you served in Arizona, you were going to heaven for spending two years in hell.

I did grow to love parts of Arizona, in particular the people there—they are very friendly—and the cacti. Maybe it was because I missed seeing greenery that I gravitated toward the cacti.

Having lived in Oregon, I thought I knew a lot about rain, but on my mission I learned even more. When it rains in Arizona the sky opens up as if a faucet has been turned on and the ground is flooded for a couple of hours. Then the faucet abruptly shuts off, and within an hour the ground is dry, the sky is clear, and the sun is beating down just as fiercely as it had been before it rained.

The weather wasn't the only challenge on the mission. My mission covered quite a bit of area, mainly in the southern part of Arizona, New Mexico, and the city of El Paso, Texas. Each new place brought a new set of people into my life as well as a new companion. Sometimes one of the missionaries I served with would initially be unsure of my capabilities, but I'd always show them there wasn't much that slowed me down. For the most part, I loved my companions. Some were goofy and some more serious, but the ones I enjoyed most were those who were not afraid of hard work.

Sometimes we would do actual physical work, and more often than that, we were on the go all day long. From the time we woke up in the morning until the time we went to bed, we were busy. We were actively teaching, finding people to teach, and providing service. There were not very many days on the mission when I did not go to bed completely exhausted. The mission is all about work, so when I was with a companion who wanted to work, time really flew by. When I was with a companion who overslept, dragged his feet, or disobeyed mission rules, it was a lot harder to deal with. We spent all day every day together, so we got to know each other pretty well. I became good friends with many of my companions.

As missionaries we would get several hours of one day off to do our laundry, clean the apartment, write letters to friends and family, and sometimes meet up with other missionaries to hang out or play a game of basketball.

In some areas we'd have a car, but in most cases, we would "walk and roll," or we would use our bikes. Because of the strain on my bike, it needed constant repairs. Twice I snapped a tube connecting the two main parts of the bike. When I was in El Paso, there were so many thorns and briars along the roadside that I would get flat tires almost daily, sometimes fixing all three of my tires in a single day. I was only in that area for one transfer period (six weeks) before transferring out, but man did I learn how to patch a tire in a hurry! It didn't take me long to figure out that I needed to keep a pump, extra tubes, and patch kits on me at all times.

I would run into people who were pretty shocked to see a missionary without legs. One time we visited a woman who hadn't been to church for a while to see if there was anything we could do to help them. When we rode up, there were a few people outside doing yard work. My companion walked toward them to inquire about the woman we were going to visit.

"Hi, are you Barbara?" he said.

"Yeah, that's me," she said, turning to look at us.

"How are you doing today?" he replied.

"Fine," she said abruptly, realizing we were missionaries.

About this time she noticed me sitting in the grass. I had just removed my helmet and was about to make my way over.

"Who is sitting down over there?" she said, her tone clearly implying she didn't have much respect for a missionary who would sit down on the job.

"Just me," I said, scooting toward her as I held out my hand. "I'm Elder McCallister."

Her whole body language changed. Her scowl was replaced with a smile.

"Well, it's nice to meet you," she said.

We started to visit her every week, and she was never rude to us again.

Our daily work would sometimes take us into the poorer areas of town. In my family we were taught from an early age that our bodies are our temples and that we should not to do drugs or drink alcohol or do anything else damaging to our bodies. Not surprisingly, spending time with drug addicts was something I'd never done before. They were some of the kindest people we met, inviting us into their homes for dinner and conversation even though they didn't have much food to spare. They treated us warmly because they knew what it was like to be judged based on what they appeared to be. I used to think negatively of addicts, but I now understand them better. Many of them have lived through tragedies that make mine pale in comparison.

It never ceases to amaze me how I was in the right place at the right time to help a person who needed to hear that someone else understood what it was like to lose a limb or two.

One day I got a call from a member of our local congregation, asking if I would be able to help a young man who'd just had the lower part of his left leg removed due to cancer. I was slightly stunned by the odds that I would be doing missionary work in this area at the exact time a local kid needed an extra boost.

"Yes, of course I'll come talk with him," I said.

Driving out to meet him, I wondered what I could say. I could barely remember my own accident, much less the trauma involved. This active teenager had just lost his leg. It would be a hard adjustment to make. But then I realized that was the whole point. I didn't recall much of the trauma I'd been through because I had gotten on with my life and had decided nothing was going to hold me back.

In the end, talking with the young man was not as awkward as I had anticipated. In fact, we ended up talking about video games and sports. I told him there was no sport I couldn't do, and there was no reason he couldn't do them as well. I doubt I changed the course of his life, but I hope I was able to help him in some small way.

Another time, a companion and I were knocking on doors when we met a lady who had only one leg. After we left, my companion turned to me and said, "That was the first person I have met on the mission who is missing a limb, and one day with you and we run into one." It was a testament to us both that God will put the right people in our paths at the right time.

While missionaries in foreign countries often find it hard to get enough food, we had the opposite problem: too much food. At the time I didn't think that was problem at all. In fact, I was pretty happy. I got to eat a full dinner every night, plus dessert. Once again I became known as the guy who could put it away. The only problem was I was no longer going to two to four practices a day. I was sitting around talking to people. Even when we rode our bikes or walked places, it was not enough exercise to offset the amount of food I was shoveling in. By the time I left the mission I weighed in at 180 pounds, a good fifty pounds heavier than when I'd begun. I still didn't consider that to be a huge issue. I figured I'd be home soon and get back into my workout routine, and the weight would drop off in no time.

That was, until the morning I woke up with an agonizing pain in my shoulder. It was so bad it took an enormous amount of effort just to lift myself onto my wheelchair. Going up and down all the stairs to our apartment with the added weight I'd put on had put a large amount of stress on my shoulders, causing them to wear down until I was unable to move from the pain. That whole day I lay in bed trying not to move, but my shoulder still throbbed.

By the next day it felt a lot better, but I knew I needed to see a doctor. When I went in, he recommended surgery to correct the swollen sac in my shoulder. Apparently surgery is often a death sentence for a missionary. I got a call the next day and was informed I would be going home so I could heal. I was devastated. Serving a mission is something I had wanted to do my entire life. I loved the feeling of having a great purpose every day, of waking up and working hard all day long. I loved meeting people and helping them have better lives. Now, because of some stupid injury, I was going home. I couldn't believe my body—a picture of health for the past twenty years of my life—would betray me in such a way. Not too long before, I could out-compete anybody. But now I felt like a cripple. I was limited in what I could do, which now was nothing.

I was given the details of when I would be leaving and quickly got off the phone. I had barely hung up before a flood of emotions overwhelmed me. I buried my face in a pillow and cried for the second time in as long as I could remember. I cried from the pain of my broken heart, I cried for the loss of being a missionary, I cried with the knowledge that I had contributed to my current state. I cried until I couldn't cry anymore.

---

UNDER THE PAIN AND THE LOSS, THERE WAS SOMETHING ELSE. THERE WAS A SENSE OF PEACE.

---

I had dreamed of being a missionary since I was a little kid, and because of my inability to control my eating habits, I was no longer able to serve in Arizona. And yet, under the pain and the loss, there was something else. There was a sense of peace. God was not only watching over me but had directed me where I had needed to go. In the weeks preceding these events, I had had a sense of peace—a feeling that God was pleased with who I was and what I had done on my mission. At the time, of course, I had thought I still had plenty of time left on my mission and was grateful for the comfort the feeling provided. As I sat at home recovering, I knew God was telling me something hard was coming but that He was giving me this challenge because he had greater things in mind. There was something else God was leading me toward, something that would come to bring me more joy than wrestling and mission work combined.

Family photo taken by Stephanie Farmer

# CHAPTER 13
## THE MAKING OF MY FAMILY

*"The strength of any nation is rooted within the walls of its homes."*
*—President Gordon B. Hinckley*[19]

The most fundamental unit of any society, community, or nation is the family. Some families are large, and others are quite small. There are families with a father, a mother, and children; families with a single parent; and families with adopted children. And of course there is everything in between and sideways. We get our views on life from how we grew up in our families. I grew up in a large family and knew how great it was to be surrounded by siblings. I learned how to share, do my chores, and even change a few diapers. Growing up in my home gave me a desire to create a family of my own. I wanted to be able to provide for, care for, and raise my own houseful of children.

WHEN I FIRST GOT HOME from my mission, my life revolved around recovery and healing. I spent my days going to different specialists to figure out how to get back on track with my health. One of the first options, as mentioned, was surgery. The doctors talked about the cutting, stretching, sewing, and the lying in bed that would need to be done in order for my shoulders to be back to somewhere under a hundred percent. I am not squeamish when it comes to surgery, but I didn't like the thought of something permanent being done to my body that wasn't entirely necessary, not to mention a recovery that would take at least six months. That would be six months

19 Gordon B. Hinckley, "Stand Strong against the Wiles of the World," *Ensign,* Nov. 1995.

of sitting around doing nothing. I would barely be able to push my chair, much less do anything else physical. I did not want to go down that road for something that would not bring me back to pre-injury status. The one thing I kept latching onto was how they'd never said I absolutely *needed* surgery.

I decided it would be better to get my weight under control and see if my shoulders would heal on their own. For the next few weeks, I didn't do much besides sit in front of the TV, giving my shoulders a long-overdue vacation. That was when I finally figured out how critical my diet was to the future of my health. I needed to change the way I ate. I just had no idea how to do it.

On my mission everyone we visited wanted to feed us, and they fed us well. Out of respect and politeness, I rarely turned down their offers. Before, I used to eat anything that was there; my teenage years before the mission had been an almost constant flow of athletics, so I figured I could eat whatever I wanted whenever I wanted without any repercussions. I was starting to realize that was not true. When I got back home, people like my wonderful mother constantly offered to make me food. I decided all I could do was start saying no more often, rewiring my brain so I could get a better understanding of how I needed to eat. I began to eat healthier.

What I realized was that by definition wheelchair users are stationary and hence we burn fewer calories. I still had the appetite of a full-bodied man but the nutritional requirements of a toddler.[20] This was going to be tough. I had never eaten so little in my entire life. In fact, except for during wrestling season, I had never restrained myself in quantity or quality, eating cake, hot dogs, pizza, or a whole pan of meatloaf whenever I wanted. I soon realized that despite my love of food, I wanted to be able to move myself around for the rest of my life and not be stuck in a motorized wheelchair. To do that, I had to eat less and start taking care of my shoulders.

It would take years of dieting, therapy, and exercise to get my shoulders back to normal. But in the meantime I was going on to the next phase of life by working, going school, and starting a family.

I've always loved being part of a large family. I was in middle school when my baby brother, Kyle, was born, so I was old enough to be a big

20 "Nutrition in Toddlers," https://www.aafp.org/afp/2006/1101/p1527.html.

help. Even changing diapers was not a chore for me but an opportunity to help out.

After my mission my goals included returning to college and starting a family. The first step toward accomplishing my final goal was to start dating.

I had not dated much in high school. I had only had one girlfriend, and most of the dates I had gone out on had just been with a large group of friends in which no one was pairing off. I had friends who were girls, but the thought of putting myself out there was always a challenge. I knew what I wanted though; I wanted a family. I knew I would eventually find the girl for me.

I started thinking about Jennifer Sullivan. Her bright smile and fiery hair flashed across my mind more than once. During the two years we'd been on our missions, we'd written a dozen or more letters, telling each other about the people we'd taught and the crazy things we'd encountered. We had seen each other as pen pals sharing in similar experiences from different parts of the world, but now I was starting to think we could be a little bit more than just pen pals. I decided to call her and ask her on a date. I was super nervous. I had only ever dated one girl, and we'd started by sitting by each other on the bus, so making my first "Will you go out with me?" call was a really big deal. My hands were shaking as I picked up the phone.

"Hey, Jen, this is Kacey McCallister," I said. "I was wondering if you'd like to hang out or something."

I know. What girl wouldn't be swept off her feet with an amazing line like that?

"Sure, that sounds fine." Little did I know she was freaking out a bit because she had also been thinking about me.

When I headed to her house, it didn't start all that well. I got lost. That was before GPS was a common thing, and I had to call her again just to figure out where I was. I did make it to her house, though I was a little late. We sat and talked while watching a movie. Her family was around, so I met them that first night. I didn't expect a bolt of lightning or a heavenly voice telling me she was the one, but there was a moment when I let go of her hand when we both felt a tingle. That sounds corny, and it was probably just static shock, but it caught our attention. Before I knew it we were seeing each other every chance we got. Then one day, after a midweek religion course, I walked her to her car. We stayed there and talked for twenty minutes before I took a chance by leaning in for a kiss. She didn't slap me or scream; she returned the kiss.

We quickly fell into a familiar pattern of dating, and it didn't take me

---

BUILDING A FAMILY TAKES DAILY WORKOUTS.

---

long before I knew without a doubt I wanted to ask her to marry me. I didn't talk to her dad about my plans. I knew if I talked to her dad, her dad would talk to her mom, and as much as I love her mom, she cannot keep a secret to save her life. So in my oh-so-sneaky way, I planned how I would propose.

The first thing I did was trick Jen into going ring shopping. How that did not give it away, I have no idea. I later learned she knew I was going to propose, but at the time, she was convinced we were nowhere near that point. Somehow I was able to call it a "What is your taste?" shopping trip rather than ring shopping. Since she's an athletic person, she wanted something low-profile that would be easy to take care of. Armed with this knowledge, I found a ring with a few small diamonds that was simple yet (as she always says) sparkly.

One of our regular dates was to go to Portland and stroll through the grounds of the temple there. Since we'd both just returned from our missions, we made it a priority to keep our focus on God (not to mention it was an inexpensive date we both enjoyed). The Portland Oregon Temple is the prettiest temple there is, in my opinion. It's set back into the trees far enough that you can't see the whole building from the street. From the interstate all you see are shining white spires rising up through the treetops. As you wind your way toward the temple, you pass beautiful homes surrounded by towering pine trees before entering the temple grounds, where you're greeted by the pristine white building. It is almost as if you've entered a hidden magical kingdom. You can barely see the outside world through the wall of trees, which stand like sentinels guarding this enchanted world. Everywhere you look is covered with flowers, trees, fountains, and footpaths, and right in the middle of it all is a shimmering reflecting pool.

Being there always fills me with a sense of reverence. It's easy to see why temples are the houses of the Lord.

What better setting to propose? Every time we'd gone to the temple, someone had stopped us to say how cute we were together and that we should get married.

After we walked out of the temple that beautiful summer day, I asked her if she wanted to walk around. We made our way to the lower end of the temple grounds, where the reflecting pool is, and it was absolutely gorgeous. As we sat on one of the stone benches next to the pool, Jen wound her arm around me. Normally I would have enjoyed every minute, but that time I jumped and grabbed her hand, which was on the side of my coat where I had stashed the ring.

"What you got in there? A gun?" she asked with a suspicious grin on her face.

I knew my time was up. It was now or never. The starting pistol had just fired, and I couldn't trip at the start line.

"No, I've got something else," I said.

Slipping the ring box from my pocket, I got down on one stub in front of her and said, "Jennifer, will you marry me?" Down there on one stub, I can only imagine I was the image of a dashing prince, but inside I was absolutely terrified. I really loved her. She was smart, beautiful, and she totally got my humor, even my endless no-leg jokes. Now if only she would speak.

Between my beaming smile, the temple in the background, and the sun igniting her hair so it glowed, it was a moment worthy of an epic social media post. I sat there, staring up at her with the open box, the ring shining up at her, and waited. And waited. And waited some more with the cold from the ground seeping into my skin. Time seemed to stretch on and on. For a minute? An hour? More? What in the world was going on? What was she waiting for? My mind raced over the possible answers. There was yes, and there was no. That was it. Only two. Maybe she wanted more time to think about it. *Just, please, let her say yes,* I thought. I felt like I'd been waiting for so long. I felt sure she was deciding the best way to tell me no without breaking my tender little heart in two.

After what seemed like a year, she finally said yes and leaned down to kiss me. My head just about exploded with relief. I mean, the kiss was pretty great too, but I was much more concerned with hearing that one little word that held an eternity of meaning—that one single word that would set me on a whole new path for the rest of my existence.

The rest of that day was kind of crazy. As we made the hour-long drive back home, I called her dad to ask for her hand. It wasn't a great move, but what was even worse was his reaction.

"Hi, Greg, this is Kacey," I said. "Can I marry your daughter?"

"Um, which one?" he replied. With two daughters married and another still in high school, only one of his daughters was currently eligible for marriage (but to be fair to him, having that many girls can be pretty rough on a dad).

"Jennifer," I answered nervously. Was he joking?

"Who is this?" he asked skeptically.

"Um, Kacey. I've kind of been dating your daughter for a while now," I said with worry in my voice.

"Oh! Okay," he said.

It turned out that Jennifer and her dad had already sat down and had a serious talk about me, during which Greg had told her, "He's a really good guy; don't let this one get away."

We set the date for four months from then—December of that same year.

Before leaving the mission field, I'd had the feeling I would not be returning to the U of A for school. After praying about it, I felt God was guiding me in a different direction. My brother had returned from his mission while I was away and was already going to school at BYU–Idaho. Jennifer was also planning to go to school there. I had visited the campus a few times for youth events and was excited by the possibility of attending school there as well. Unfortunately, I was too late to gain admittance for the next semester. Instead of sitting around the house while my fiancée went off to school, I decided to take some night classes and stay in the same apartment building as my brother.

I had a few things I had to figure out besides just night classes though. By the time Jen was headed back to school, my shoulders were still not feeling great. I had lost twenty pounds since coming home but still had a long way to go.

I also found a job through a relative at a flooring store. As I pulled up to Gunderson's Flooring, they were loading the truck for the day's work. When I hopped out of my car and plopped onto the ground, their jaws hit the floor.

"Um . . . we didn't know you were . . . ," Roy stammered as he tried to find a way to tell me I didn't have legs.

"It's okay," I said. "I can do absolutely anything you need me to do."

"Um . . . okay," he said. "Well, get in the truck; we're headed out to a job."

I hopped up into the cab. I could tell they were still very unsure of what I could do. As we drove to the work site, they told me what they expected me to be able to do. I nodded and tried to assure them I was up to the task. We arrived at the home where we'd be laying tile, and I got to work. It didn't take them long to realize I was true to my word. I enjoyed the manual labor of the job. By that time my shoulders had gotten a lot better and were to the point where they didn't hurt on a daily basis, and this type of job gave me a fairly low-impact type of work that was still active. I ended up working for them until I started going to school full-time.

The term went by quickly as Jen and I continued nurturing our relationship. Some interesting things happened as we prepared to get married. About a month after the start of the term, we were planning the wedding and honeymoon when we both got a feeling we needed to move the date. I was thinking the date was coming up quickly, so we could afford to push it back. However, as we thought and prayed about it, we felt we needed to move the date up, though it made little sense. If we moved it sooner, it would have to be during Thanksgiving break, and that would leave us no time for a honeymoon. We didn't know why we felt so strongly about this, but we decided to trust God to guide us. So we moved the date to Thanksgiving weekend. We continued to make preparations and decided to have our honeymoon during Christmas break. The days flew by, and soon it was time to go back home.

We traveled back to Oregon to be married in the same temple where I'd asked Jen for her hand. I picked her up the morning of the wedding, and we drove to the temple together. It was a cold day, the flowers were not in bloom, and all the leaves had fallen off the trees. The surroundings might have been slightly less than perfect, but Jen looked so beautiful I could barely take my eyes off her to watch the road. As we entered the doors to the temple, a deep and profound peace swept over me, and I knew this day was going to be something special.

Temple wedding ceremonies in The Church of Jesus Christ of Latter-day Saints are very simple. The bride and groom each wear modest white clothes, and sacred promises are made in front of family and a few friends. The room where the sealing ceremony takes place is a spotless white room lit from above by a glittering chandelier. Mirrors surround the spot where the couple kneels, facing each other; the mirrors reflect each other, creating a sense of infinity.

My wonderful parents were there, along with the rest of my family. As I entered the room, I couldn't help but think of the phenomenal example my parents had been to me. They had raised us to be independent, hardworking, respectful, and kind. For my entire life they had shown a powerful example of love and dedication. I was so happy to be there in that room with them and for them to be there to support me in marrying my beautiful Jen.

I could not wait to spend the rest of my life with this woman. The excitement I felt to just be near her filled me with joy. There is nothing better in this world to me than her smile, and I happily anticipated what the future would hold.

Later that night, at the reception, we saw many friends and family members we had not seen for a long time. I had grandparents who had come all the way from Idaho and Utah. Jen's grandma's health had been slowly deteriorating for some time and rarely left her house, but she was also able to come to the reception.

The next day we stuffed the wedding presents into my Yukon and drove the twelve hours back to Rexburg to start school on Monday. We had bought tickets for a Costa Rican cruise for our honeymoon during the next break. Being away from our families during Christmastime wasn't ideal, but what a cool trip to take. We would be going from Rexburg, Idaho, where it was negative twenty-five degrees, to a tropical cruise paradise, and we were really looking forward to it.

As soon as we got back to Rexburg, we started to feel like something was off with the honeymoon. Once again we felt we should change our plans. Trying to listen to the promptings we felt, we canceled the cruise. It wasn't until Christmas break that we would learn why it was so important for us to be available for Christmas.

When we went home for Christmas break, Jen's grandma was very ill. She had been living in a hospice care facility for a few weeks. She ended up passing away on our original wedding date. That date would also have had us in the middle of the ocean if we had kept our honeymoon trip as planned. Jen's grandma had been fading for a while, and we were grateful she had made it to our wedding.

Despite the sadness of that time, we decided to drop the news on our families anyway: we were expecting a baby. Not long after we made the announcement, Jen got really sick. We knew it had to be morning sickness, but it got so bad that on Christmas night we went to the emergency room. The doctor gave her fluids and sent her away with some pills that barely did anything. When we got back to Rexburg and Jen needed another round of fluids, the doctor there gave us some good medicine for nausea, but even with the medication Jen was sick all the time, throwing up after every meal. Just the idea of a bad smell would make Jen vomit. I was constantly brushing my teeth and putting on deodorant; I've never had better manners or hygiene in my life.

The medication barely took the edge off Jen's morning sickness, and we became well-versed in the world of constant nausea. Often I would make dinner. Jen would eat, thank me for the great food, and then go throw up. That put a huge strain on her body. She slept more and more and absorbed fewer nutrients. The one thing that seemed to stay down with any regularity was fruit. I was used to getting one to two bags of fruit at the grocery store per week, but when her nausea was really bad, I bought five to six bags. For two poor college students, this was pretty expensive, but it was what Jen could eat.

She was still managing to get to class, even though she had a hard time focusing. As we neared the end of the term (both for the pregnancy and for school), we decided to move back to Oregon to be closer to our parents. As soon as Jen's graduation ceremony was over, we were back on the road, driving toward greener pastures. Literally. We'd both sorely missed it.

We moved into an apartment in Monmouth, Oregon, so I could continue my studies at Western Oregon University. It was around this time I began to reconsider my chosen major. Since my dream had always been to become a motivational speaker, I was told I should become a communications major. After a while, though, I decided I really didn't like the direction it was taking me. Communications wasn't helping me be a better speaker, nor was it helping me learn how to motivate people.

One day Jen and I were talking about classes and potential careers, and I confessed I didn't feel the route I was taking was going to lead me where I wanted to go. But what should I study to be a motivational speaker?

"Why don't you become a teacher," Jen said.

"A teacher? Where did that come from?" I asked.

"You want to motivate youth, and you would love to coach," she said.

"Huh. Maybe," I said. I gave it some thought.

I didn't know that I wanted to teach, necessarily, but I did know I enjoyed mentoring youth, and the idea of being a coach was definitely appealing.

"What are your favorite classes?" she said.

"I liked my earth science classes," I said.

"There you go," Jen said, patting me on the back. "Be a science teacher."

I realized how fortunate I am to be married to someone smart enough to help me become what I wanted to be and supportive enough to help me realize my dreams.

By the time we got to Oregon, we had less than a month before the baby was due. We did all the right things in preparation for the birth. We took Lamaze classes, packed a bag to be ready when we needed to go to the hospital, counted the contractions, and memorized the quickest route to the hospital. Even with all that preparation, we were still not ready for the actual birth. The day before our daughter was born Jen was having contractions but was still able to walk around. She even went shopping with my sister. Later we were home relaxing, and Jen was becoming increasingly uncomfortable. We had already gone to the hospital once for false labor and really didn't want to do that again.

After a few hours Jen was having contractions five minutes apart. We decided that, false alarm or not, we were going to the hospital. I grabbed the bag and helped Jen out to the car. After hopping in, I cranked the key, and . . . nothing. It just clicked.

*No, no, no, not today!* I thought.

I tried again. Sputter . . . click. Again. Click, click, click. This was not happening. That was the most important day to have my car working, and it just kept clicking. I suggested we call a friend and have him take us to the hospital. Jen said we should try saying a prayer first. We bowed our heads and offered a fervent, desperate prayer. Then, with a little bit of hope, I cranked the key again. Vroom! It was working! God was definitely watching out for us. I quickly shifted the car into drive before the car could reconsider, and we were off. When we arrived at the hospital, the nurse took one look at Jen and sent us straight to the pre-birth room. The baby was coming.

But there was a problem, and Jen needed to have a C-section. After less than thirty minutes, I was brought back to meet our new baby girl. She was a very cute, wrinkly little ball with a huge mop of dark-brown hair on her head. With a little laugh the nurse pointed out three small sores on our baby's hands and wrists, indicating where she'd been sucking on them in the womb.

We'd had a bunch of names ready, but when we met our daughter, we knew she was going to be Anna. We were excited for that little bundle of energy to come into our lives. Even with the unexpected complications leading up to the C-section, Jen was in good spirits and barely let me hold Anna because she was so happy to have a little girl. I was overjoyed as well and didn't leave the hospital during the five days Jen had to stay. I slept on the floor next to the hospital bed so I could be close to her. We were starting our own little bunch of rug rats, and life was good.

Within the week we were back home and ready to learn what it took to be parents. Jen was finishing up her student teaching at a local high school, so I got to stay home and be Mr. Mom. I thought I would be ready for it. Hanging out with Anna all day proved me wrong. It was really hard at times. Anna did not want to take a bottle, so we built a relationship on screams and cries. I didn't do it for very long though. Soon Jen finished up her semester of student teaching, earning her degree in Spanish education. It was now my turn to work on a degree.

Soon after we moved to Monmouth, I looked up my old wrestling coach Tony Olliff, who was still coaching nearby at Dallas High School, and asked if he would mind if I came and helped out. He didn't mind at all, and I was thrilled to be back in Tony's wrestling room. Being on the coaching side of the mat was a whole different experience. Now I got to understand the *whys* of wrestling rather than just the *hows*.

Helping out in one of Olliff's wrestling rooms kept me a lot more involved than many other programs I have seen. While I would walk around and help kids with moves, it was more than that. Often I was on the mat with the wrestlers, providing a wrestling partner. The first year I helped out, the team won the district title. A few years later, when I was nearing my graduation from Western Oregon University, in 2012, Dallas won the state tournament. It was amazing to be a part of such a great wrestling program for so many years. Tony Olliff was awarded Coach of the Year that year and many since.

Eventually Tony asked if I would be willing to help LaCreole Middle School, with their wrestling program, and I jumped at the chance. The coach there was a kid younger than me named Austin Markee. He'd just graduated from high school and was going to school at Western Oregon University. Austin had been doing a great job teaching his team about strength and endurance. I really had a lot of fun learning how to coach middle schoolers as opposed to high schoolers. They were eager to learn and give it a hundred percent. Being a college student, coach, husband, and brand-new father was sometimes tough. I had to figure out where to fit practice in around my class schedule.

I finally got to a point where I was able to start student teaching. Typically student teachers are randomly assigned a mentor teacher to work with, but after asking around, I was allowed to pick my own. Of course, I chose Coach Tony Olliff. That was such a fun time. I was able to teach with him during the day and coach with him after school. I was still very wet behind the ears and had ideas about teaching that would make veteran teachers laugh. Tony was a great coach, not only in the wrestling room but also in the classroom. He taught me what it meant to be ready for class and how to handle a classroom full of hormonal teenagers.

Unfortunately, I was not able to continue with Tony for the remainder of my student teaching, so the next term I was moved to Talmadge Middle

School to student teach an eighth-grade science class. As wrestling season rolled around again, I decided to coach at Talmadge instead of at Dallas. I wanted to be able to interact with the athletes on a day-to-day basis in the hallways, not just at practice.

The Talmadge Middle School team had been led by the high school's wrestling coach for the last few years. I offered to take it over, allowing him to spend more time, energy, and focus on coaching the high schoolers. As I started as the head coach, I was excited to try out some of the coaching practices I had only witnessed up to that point.

I found success in being a head coach. I found I enjoyed coaching, and I was able to help them become one of the better teams in the area. What was more important than that, though, is I found I could motivate them to push themselves to be better. I was able to connect with the kids and help them improve as wrestlers and as people. Many of the kids had never had to push themselves to the extreme before, so there were many groans and complaints and even some tears at first, but what came out of those kids was something truly amazing.

I knew something those kids didn't. I knew each and every one of them had the heart of a fighter. The first few meets were fine. They did okay, but I knew they had more in them. I started to see a concerning trend. It seemed every match we lost we'd lost because the kids were giving up too easily and getting pinned. As one who hated getting pinned more than anything else, I cringed every time one of my kids went to his back. After a couple of meets, I decided to do something about it. Taking a page right out of the Olliff playbook, I started running them through situation drills to show them how to get off their backs.

The next meet came around, and I was excited to see if the drills had paid off. They hadn't worked. Once again the kids gave up and let themselves get pinned. So the next week we worked on it again. At the beginning of the meet, I gave them a little incentive to stay off their backs: every time one of their teammates got pinned, everybody would have to complete three suicide runs.

Suicide runs go by many different names: gassers, lines, sprints, waterfalls, wind sprints, shuttle runs, ladders, pyramid drills, or liners. But perhaps the true name should just be pain. When done right, regardless of the shape the runner is in, the drill will leave the runner puffing and gasping for breath.

The runner starts at one end of the room and sprints to a line about a quarter of the way across the room, returns to the starting point and sprints to the middle of the room and back, then to the three-quarter-length mark and back, and finally across the full length of the room and back. As the kids came back to the starting wall, they'd often slam themselves into the pad on the wall so they could turn quickly back in the other direction. Run. Slam! Run. Slam! Run. Slam! Run. Slam! We had done a few of these in practice, and my wrestlers knew they did not want to do a bunch of them.

With that incentive in their minds, I was excited to see the results of my brilliant coaching techniques, expecting to see these kids fighting tooth and nail to get off their backs. I was ready to show the kids what they could do when they put their minds to it. Well, that didn't happen at all, and we ended the meet with twenty pins scored on us. The next day we were looking at sixty suicides.

At the beginning of the next practice, I lined them up against the wall and said, "Some of you might think that just because you have earned a ridiculously high number of suicides, I am not going to make you run all of them. Well, I think you need to understand how much I want you to *not* get pinned. If you stay off your back, what can happen? *Anything!* You can score more points, you can pin your opponent, you can end up losing by points rather than getting pinned. But what happens when you get pinned? You're done. You can't come back from being pinned. I have tried to instill a bit of heart in you to help you get off your back. But if encouragement couldn't do it, maybe fear will. Run!"

They ran. A lot. Every five complete suicides or so I would give them a break for a minute or two. Halfway through the exercise I saw some of the kids start to crumble under the strain. But I knew they had more in them, and I needed to show them they did. So with thirty suicides to go, I started running with them. Man, do suicide runs suck! Part of being a good coach, though, is showing in addition to telling. I would not let a single kid give up. That day we did nothing but suicides. Eventually the practice ended, and they all limped down the stairs to the locker room and then home. I was nervous to see what would happen at the next meet. Had I pushed them too hard? Would some of them not show up? Would it work, or would they continue to get pinned?

What happened was amazing. They fought as if it was for their last breath to get off their backs. They clearly didn't want to run suicides anymore. But beyond that it created a pleasant side effect. They became a team. Before that they were a group of good friends that did a sport together. Now they were supporting, encouraging, and challenging each other to be better, to not give up, and to push until there was nothing left. Well, would you believe it? A miracle happened at the next meet. There were only two pins on us in the entire meet. The next day at practice they ran those suicides like it was free time. I was on top of the world watching these kids run those few drills. I had helped them accomplish something. I don't mean about them not getting pinned; that was cool and everything, but what I was super excited about was seeing the change in my wrestlers. They were a whole different team after seeing what they could do when they pushed past where they thought they could go. That was the miracle.

What was even better was it didn't stop there. The next meet was against a few schools, including LaCreole Middle School, where I'd previously coached. We had seen their team before, and up to that point it was a safe bet we'd lose. But that time was different. My team was wrestling really well, winning more than they were losing, rarely getting pinned, and scrapping for every point they got.

We got done with the meet and went home knowing they had wrestled their best. When I saw the results the next day, it blew me away. We had won the meet! We had beat LaCreole, one of the best middle school teams in the state! Boy, was Austin mad. I had worked with him for two years, and I knew how much pride he took in coaching the toughest team around. After that he put his team through the ringer. I saw a few of his wrestlers later on, and they complained about how hard he'd been pushing them because of the meet they had lost.

One day, a few weeks after the season started, I received a surprise when my most challenging student that year walked into the wrestling room wanting to join the team. She would disrupt class, walk out of the room while I was talking to her, encourage others to be disruptive, and was generally a pain in the butt. She really shocked me when she decided to start wrestling. I was not too worried because I knew who controlled the wrestling room. She couldn't cause disruptions there because of a little discipline tool I couldn't use in a classroom: suicide runs. She joined the team and wrestled for me the whole season. She didn't improve in class, but she did fine in the wrestling room.

Flash forward a few years, and I was in the gym lifting weights when who came over but this girl I had coached those years before.

"Mr. McCallister, I just wanted to say how sorry I am for how I acted in class all those times," she said a little sheepishly. "I wasn't nice to you, but I'm trying to be a better person now."

I couldn't have been happier. We talked for a bit about how life was going and what she was up to. I was impressed with what a nice young woman she had turned out to be.

And that is why I love teaching. Being able to help someone through tough times in life is worth the trouble they put you through. That was especially true with my own children.

Our own little girl was growing up. Anna was super smart and extremely active. People would ask us how she was doing, and we would tell them how energetic she was. They would respond by saying all kids are active, to which I would nod and think, *Yeah? Okay.* Then I would look around at other children her age, and they were able to sit still for at least ten seconds. They could walk down the hall without breaking into a run. They could make eye contact. That was not my beautiful little girl. Her mind went so fast she couldn't keep up. She could identify by name all the presidents on Mount Rushmore by the time she was eight months old and was reading chapter books by the time she hit preschool. Some would say she was like the Energizer Bunny, but that was not quite accurate. The Energizer Bunny slowly beats his drum and scoots around. Anna went at top speed as far as the day is long. She is full of energy, and I wouldn't trade her ever.

Our next addition to the family was bittersweet. Jen was twenty weeks pregnant and having severe stomach pain, so we visited the OB/GYN and were told Jen had a severe bladder infection. After six days of treating the infection, the pain was getting to be unbearable, and we were set to make an emergency run to the hospital. Jen was in so much pain she couldn't stand up straight and I had to dress her when we went to the hospital. We got to the emergency room, but we weren't safe yet. The staff didn't read the chart that said Jen was twenty weeks pregnant, and they had another emergency they had to life flight to Portland, so after six hours of waiting in the ER, the doctor came in and asked, "Do you know you are pregnant?" We had told the staff four times so far that day, but for some reason the nurses and doctors had not read the chart.

All the while Jen's pain continued to increase. An ultrasound was ordered, which revealed Jen needed emergency surgery. Things began to happen much quicker as doctors and nurses started rushing around the room to move Jen up to the operating room immediately. Jen and I said a rushed goodbye as the elevator doors began to close. I let go of her hand, and Jen said, "Tell Anna I love her." I wasn't sure if I would ever see my wife again.

I didn't know what was happening. I was told to go wait. Go wait? How was I supposed to go wait? Numbly I wheeled out the doors. As I was going out, a nurse told me it might be a while and I should go get something to eat. I got some food and found a place to watch TV. That's what waiting was, right? I stared blankly at the TV as the shows came on one after another without me really seeing them. I just kept thinking about

Jen and worrying about whether she was okay. It seemed to take forever. It couldn't be good news if it was taking this long for the hospital staff to get back to me.

It took three hours for the doctors to come back and update me. The doctor explained that as they were wheeling Jen into the operating room, she'd gone from bad to worse. Because of Jen's heart-shaped uterus, Anna had been situated on the side of the uterus that was fully developed. This new child, however, was situated on the other side, which was underdeveloped. The baby had been growing like a normal baby would, but the uterus was just too small. At twenty weeks the uterus had grown as much as it was going to grow. The baby, on the other hand, kept growing and pushing up against the uterine walls, eventually causing a leak. Jen's abdomen had filled with two liters of blood. Miraculously the baby had burst through the wall of the uterus just as they had entered the operating room. What a blessing it had happened when it did. The doctors were able to save Jen's life.

The next bit of news was the worst I had ever received. The baby did not make it. I was devastated. I had to balance my grief with the fact that my wife was still alive. My baby was dead, but my wife was alive. I held it together until the doctor left. I quickly made my way back to the room they had prepared for us and cried, and a nurse saw me. When she came in to talk to me, I cried some more. After a while I was all cried out. That was until they brought Jen into the room. They had not told her about the baby. When I told her, we broke down together.

We found out it had been a boy. He'd been too premature to breathe on his own. Even without the trauma of the delivery, he wouldn't have been able to make it. During the operation they'd had to perform a partial hysterectomy to remove the side of the uterus that was damaged. In a way, that baby made it safe for all our future children. We named him Samuel Aaron McCallister and buried him in a small plot close to home.

Up to that point I had only remembered crying twice in my life. I had cried after losing the state tournament, and I had cried when I'd been forced to return from my mission early. But losing Sam was the hardest loss yet. There were many times in the following weeks when I would feel the loss and find myself unable to stop sobbing. It was the same for Jen. Sometimes we would cry together and sometimes alone. It was a hard time for us, but we survived and moved on. Our relationship was strong. When I cried, she was there. Other times it was my turn to hold her until the tears dried. We were a family—me, Jen, and Anna. We all helped each other. Even Anna, with her infectious laugh and unlimited energy, helped cheer us up during that time.

As the months came and went, the pain lessened, and after about a year we decided it was time to try for another child. Now that I already had a girl, I was hoping for a boy. At twenty-one weeks we had the ultrasound appointment, and low and behold, a boy was on his way to us! I was pretty stoked at the idea of a little man running around. I was worried though. With Anna, the car wouldn't start. With Sam, Jen had almost died. It was not a good trend.

God must have figured we needed a break because this baby came into the world without a hitch. He was a little on the small side but as healthy as could be. Not only that, but he was a bona fide redhead. He needed a good Irish name to go along with all that red hair, so we named him Patrick. Not Pat. Always Patrick. I was pretty excited about his red hair. I had always been very proud of the fact that I was blessed with a fiery mop of hair, and I now had a kid with one as well.

Patrick complemented his big sister perfectly. He was quiet where she was talkative, and he was calm where she had the energy, but most importantly, they loved each other quite a bit. If there was one thing I would wish for my children, it was that they love each other, and they did. Still do. This is in large part because of their mom. She is the kindest person you will ever meet, especially when it comes to kids. If you want to make her mad, just try and be unfair or harmful to a child. Not even her child. Harm any child in any way and she will bring the hurt down on you. She loves kids. So do I.

Shortly before Patrick was born in the spring of 2011, I'd gotten a call from the Oregon chapter of the National Wrestling Hall of Fame. I had been selected as an inductee for the medal of courage. I was blown away. It had been seven years since I had wrestled, and I figured most people had all but forgotten about my performance in the state championship match. Now they wanted to induct me into the Hall of Fame. I was honored beyond belief.

At the induction ceremony were many of the people who had contributed to my success. Front and center was my family. My mom and dad had pushed me to never take no for an answer. Keith, who had always encouraged me to be my best, was there, and, of course, Tony Olliff was present. He'd taught me everything I needed to know about wrestling. As I sat there among the other inductees, I felt a sense of gratitude toward my family and coaches for all their efforts to help me become who I was.

As soon as I graduated from Western Oregon University, I started looking for a teaching position. At the time there were no full-time jobs available in the area. That meant substitute teaching. I enjoyed it. Of course, at the time I was looking for a full-time teaching position, but I still enjoyed getting to know the kids each day. Before too long, I got a long-term sub job, which was followed by a full-time teaching position at Willamina Middle School.

Throughout her life my wife has been drawn to the idea of helping people through foster care and/or adoption. When we were dating, she asked what my thoughts were on the subject. I hadn't really thought about it before that, but I had wanted to be supportive and said it sounded like a great idea.

As the years went by and we were starting to have kids of our own, the topic once again arose, and she asked if we could foster a child. I was a bit wary about it because I'd thought we would start fostering children when our kids were a bit older rather than when we were just starting our family. After many long talks, she wore me down, and we started the process of becoming foster parents. Soon after, we got our first foster child—a sweet little girl just three months old.

For us, being foster parents to this girl was the best possible situation. Her father was doing everything he needed to do to get her back, and we were blessed to be able to help out until he was ready. Just one week before we had our third child, she was able to go back to her dad. She was almost a year old, and it was the perfect time. That was our first and, to that point, only experience with foster-parenting.

While I was at Willamina Middle School, we had our third child, Jack. Anna was now six, and Patrick was three. Another boy had come into the family, and it was starting to look like having boys was the trend. Jen's family had had four girls and one boy, and my family had had four boys and one girl. It seemed like those McCallister boy genes were good and strong.

And Jack? Let me tell you, he is all boy. All my kids have shown they are pretty tough, but when it comes to shrugging off injuries, this kid does it in spades. All he needs is a kiss on the owie or a tickle in the right place, and he is off doing the exact same thing he was doing when he got the owie.

I have so much fun with my kids. I can't wait to see if any of them will like wrestling.

My family was growing, and I was getting healthier by the day. I was racing in marathons and track meets as often as I could. I even started training for the Paralympics, the Olympics for those who have a physical disability (not to be confused with the Special Olympics, which are geared toward mentally challenged athletes). To make it into Paralympic ranks, I would need to be much faster. I would need to train two to four hours a day. I taught at a school twenty-five miles from home, so instead of driving home, I would get a ride to school and then push my way home.

While I was teaching full-time, my speaking business and athletic pursuits started to take off. I would have people here and there ask me to speak at various events. I knew this was what I wanted to do, but I didn't yet know quite how to make it a business. Sometimes I would be gone for a week at a time, either giving a speech or competing in a race. I was stoked to be so busy, but it was not conducive to being a full-time teacher. So after a year and a half of teaching, I decided to hang up my teaching hat and go into the motivational speaking business full-time. Jen was concerned about making this leap. Teaching never pays super well, but it does pay. It is a consistent nine-to-five job that will always be there. With motivational speaking, money is a big wildcard; sometimes you work, and sometimes you don't. When you do work, you are gone for days at a time and not around for your family. But as always, Jen supported me and is and always has been my biggest fan.

I continued to train, sometimes going on two to three runs a day. I was getting close to achieving the times I would need to hit to make it into the Paralympics. I was on the road to go to Rio in 2016.

God probably laughs when mortals make plans, so I'm sure He was having a hoot while I was having dreams of Olympic glory and getting ready to begin my motivational speaking business, "Rise Up with Kacey." Even though I would have to put the business on hold for a bit, my next detour would change my life for the better.

# CHAPTER 14
## WELCOME, ALEX!

*"Do you want to do something beautiful for God?*
*There is a person who needs you. This is your chance."*
—Mother Teresa, Catholic Saint[21]

There are many challenges that occur when two people combine their lives together, and even more arise once kids come into the picture. I love my wife and children, but life is not always a party. Just like building muscles, building a family takes daily workouts. I have found that just spending time with my family is not enough. It must be quality time. It is almost never easy to put the work in, but for my family, it is always worth it.

WE HAVE A HABIT OF adding to our family when things are going too smoothly. Our youngest child, Jack, was one and a half. He wasn't quite hitting his terrible twos, but he was close. I had just resigned from a stressful job to pursue my speaking career, and life was starting to take on a more relaxed atmosphere. It was around that time I was asked to teach a midweek institute course. This is a nonpaid volunteer position that helps young people between the ages of eighteen and thirty gain spiritual fortification throughout their week. One of the lessons was about families. There was a question in the lesson that asked what we treasured most. I was teaching young adults, so I started to think about all the things they would consider important. Then I read the leader's answer. He said our treasures are the

21 "Something Beautiful for God," *The Salvation Army*, https://australiaone.info/2017/11/03/something-beautiful-for-god/.

things we spend our time and money on.[22] And even before I read the rest of the talk, I asked myself what I spent my time and money on. I concluded that I spent most of my time and money on my family. They truly were my greatest treasure. I began to realize the athletics I had held in such high esteem were not nearly as important as I thought they were. At the time, I was struggling to go from great papa athlete to elite para-athlete. I decided to put my dreams of Paralympic glory aside and focus on what really mattered: my family.

I made the mistake of mentioning this to my wife, and I guess she was feeling the adoption bug coming on because she was all over it like a little girl on a pony. So fast it made my head swim. She was spending nearly every spare minute on the computer, searching for a child to adopt. Eventually she found herself drawn to Ukrainian children. From there she figured out who it was who would become our child.

She said that from the moment she saw him she knew he belonged in our family. On the adoption website, his name was Ulysses, but later we would learn his real name was Stanislav, or Stasik for short. Stasik was a six-year-old little boy who was blind, had cerebral palsy, and had been abandoned at birth. Since Jen had made up her mind about Stasik, I was under the impression we were golden. That was when my wife suggested we should adopt two. I wasn't so sure we could manage adopting two children at once. We talked about it for weeks, with her wanting two and me wanting one. Eventually I realized she has supported me in all the crazy things I have done, all of which had taken much of her time and support, and I could have faith in her and support her in adopting two children. So we started the process to add another. We did end up getting a second child; however, it was from a more heavenly adoption process. It was about halfway through the adoption process that we discovered Jen was pregnant. We were told we would not be allowed to adopt two if we were expecting. We were disappointed, but at the same time, we knew it was meant to be.

The adoption paperwork took time, but after eight months it was finally completed and we were ready for the go-ahead. The crazy thing

---

22 F. Burton Howard, "A Question of Time," *New Era*, Jul. 2002.

about it was we could get called to go to Ukraine at any time, and that is exactly what happened. For weeks we had been practically sitting by the phone, waiting for the call. We were hoping it would come at the start of August, but instead we got the call two weeks early. When they call, you go. We had just six days to get ready to travel. With a flurry of excitement and the stress of taking our family halfway around the world, we were soon packed to go.

---

JUST SPENDING TIME WITH FAMILY IS NOT ENOUGH.
IT MUST BE QUALITY TIME.

---

Traveling with three kids under the age of eight and a pregnant wife was quite an ordeal. We flew out of Portland all the way to Amsterdam on a nine-hour plane ride and then hopped onto a four-hour plane ride to Kiev, the capital of Ukraine. The kids held up well with all of that traveling. But when we got to Kiev, only two of our three bags had made it. Losing a bag on a local flight is bad enough, but when it's your first time in a foreign country and after traveling for twenty-four hours, it was almost too much to bear.

Trying to sort out information in another language was a challenge, but as I would be repeatedly shown, the people of Ukraine are extremely kind. We got out of the airport and contacted our driver, who took us to get some food and then to our apartment. The ten-hour time difference was tough on the entire family. The kids wanted to be awake when we were trying to get to sleep.

The next day, after we had finished up the paperwork in the capital city, we traveled nine more hours down to Mykolaiv, the closest city to where Stasik lived at an orphanage for boys. Our first apartment had only one bedroom, big flowing curtains, and a bunch of glass stuff—glass plates, drinking glasses, and glass countertops. In other words, there were many things our children could break. We requested a different apartment almost immediately. The next one we got into was not as nice, but the kids had their own room, and there were fewer things they could break. The one thing lacking was the opportunity to go outside and get fresh air. There was a playground near the second apartment, but it was one we would only let our kids play on if we were ready for them to leave this world. There was a really nice park, but it was a good mile away, so for the most part the kids had to sit in the apartment all day long not doing anything.

The first time we met Stasik was not anything like I imagined it would be. I had imagined meeting him, and even though he would not understand us, he would feel our love and immediately we would all bond and he would somehow feel like he had always been part of our family. The clouds would part, the sun would shine, rainbows and unicorns would cover the sky, and everyone would be happy. But that is not what happened.

When we entered the orphanage, the caregivers took us to a small windowless room with a couch and a small end table, and they left without another word. We sat there for twenty minutes waiting to meet Stasik. When the door opened, he came into the room in a stroller that allowed him to lie mostly flat. The orphanage workers immediately picked him up out of stroller and put him in Jen's arms. Stasik did not feel the love. Instead he felt what any blind six-year-old kid would feel in that situation: stranger danger! He started screaming and flinging himself backward. He did not know us and didn't want to be placed in our care.

The staff didn't take him right away. Instead they let Jen hold him as best as she could for a few minutes before taking him back. They gave us a few days after meeting him to decide if we wanted to go through with the adoption. That night, as we lay in bed talking about the day and what had happened, Jen expressed her concern and disappointment that our first meeting had not been the love-filled gift we had been expecting. She wondered if we should go through with it. I held her and told her that day was not how the rest of life was going to be with him. Today we had seen a scared little boy who didn't know us—a boy who needed a good home, with us. I knew that, regardless of how the first day had gone, Jen was already in love with him and there was nothing that would truly scare her away from Stasik. We returned the following day with our decision.

We would proceed with the adoption. That day the visit was the complete opposite of the first. Stasik smiled throughout the visit. He even laughed a bit after listening to his new siblings' voices on a recording. We knew he was going to be a great fit for our family, and we visited him as often as we could. We decided to name him Alexander Stasik McCallister.

Alex has had many challenges in life. He was born prematurely. I mean, like, *really* prematurely, weighing only one pound at birth. Because of that, he suffered from hydrocephalus (a buildup of too much cerebrospinal fluid in the brain), blindness from detached retinas, cerebral palsy, and hip dysplasia (a condition in which the ball and socket joint are malformed). In Ukraine there is no health insurance, so every medical procedure is paid for out of pocket.

Because it's so expensive to raise a family in Ukraine, it's very unusual for a family to have more than one child. Alex's parents had already had a son, so when a second child was born with so many issues, their only choice was to relinquish their parental rights and give him over to the government. Alex was kept at the hospital for a few weeks after he was born, until he was able to be moved to an orphanage for infants. He lived there until he was four years old, at which point he was moved to the institution for boys with disabilities where he was living when we adopted him.

Because the orphanage is a thirty-minute drive from Mykolaiv, most of the staff has to commute to get there, and the pay is very poor, making it quite a challenge to entice qualified people to work there. The people who do work there are very kind and want the best for the children, but the orphanage is so understaffed that mealtime alone is a near-impossible feat. With almost twenty boys needing to be fed by hand, it takes quite some time to accomplish the task.

When it comes to personal interaction, the children do not get much. They are kept either in a bed or a stroller for the whole day. The one chance they have to mix it up is when they are rolled into the courtyard to soak up some sun (bear in mind, it's Ukraine, so it's freezing outside for nine months out of the year). Toys are nonexistent. The orphanage just doesn't have the money to provide things like that. When we first showed Alex toys, he had no clue what to do with them. He pushed them away. It took a couple of weeks for him to grab on to anything, including Jen and me. Interaction came slowly as we helped him recognize us and feel safe when we were there. He did not at all like to be held. He hated being restrained in any fashion, even if that meant just holding his hand or touching his hair. We were not prepared for such a reaction and had to take things very slowly. Our visits were two to three hours long, and often we would sit for the entire time gently touching his head or his hand. Sometimes all he would allow was for us to sit close to him while Jen and I talked.

Prior to arriving in Ukraine, I was under the impression that people in former Soviet countries were stern and walked around with blank expressions devoid of emotion. That was generally what I got in the States from passersby on the street or on a first meeting. But what I came to realize was the people of Ukraine are some of the nicest, kindest people you'll ever meet. More than once a notary would come downstairs to street level so I could sign papers if the building didn't have an elevator. I tried to emphasize that I could make it up the steps just fine, but they would have none of it.

After a week in the new apartment, we were able to send the papers to the government offices and wait for a court date. It was not a fun time for us. Jack, who was two years old at the time, developed a piercing scream when he didn't get his way. All the kids were cooped up for most of the day without any outlet.

Because it was the end of summer, many of the judges were out on vacation, so everything took much longer. When we were informed our court date was set for more than two weeks away, we had a decision to make. We could stay in the cramped little apartment, getting more and more stir crazy, or we could go home. We had already been in the country for almost two weeks, but leaving and coming back would mean another trip for Jen and me, not to mention spending more money and time away from the kids.

The day our court date was confirmed, Patrick was standing on a chair and fell onto the tile floor, landing on his face and biting through his lip. I was taking a nap when I suddenly heard Jen screaming my name. Jen is not a screamer, so I knew something was wrong. When I got to the scene, there was blood everywhere. Patrick had blood all over his face and down the front of his shirt. I jumped into action. Surprisingly this wasn't the first time Patrick had bit through his lip, so I knew he would be okay, but what scared me was the possibility of going to a hospital in Ukraine. Some hospitals would not even let parents stay with their children. After I got Patrick washed up and Jen calmed down, I assessed the damage. Patrick's teeth were fine, and there were no other injuries to his face, but this trauma convinced us it was time to go home.

My wife and I had ten days before we needed to return to Ukraine for court. Luckily my parents lived close by, so we left the kids with them and headed back overseas. Traveling was a good deal less stressful that time around since we didn't have to worry about the kids. We were able to enjoy a full day in Ukraine by ourselves, walking the streets and visiting with our son.

I have not spent much time in court, but our experience with the adoption was different from what I'd imagined it would be. There was a small jail cell with iron bars and locks on it on one side of the room and wooden benches and tables on the other side. The wooden benches were extremely uncomfortable for my wife, who was now almost eight months' pregnant and was having contractions throughout the court proceedings. We sat on the wooden benches waiting for the male judge and a two-person female jury to enter. The judge and jury sat at the front of the courtroom, asking questions to the members of the court, which included my wife and me, our adoption case worker, the social worker, the orphanage director, and the prosecutor.

In Ukraine it's pretty tough to be in a wheelchair. The sidewalks are terrible, and there are little to no services like ramps and elevators. This makes it difficult for those in wheelchairs to get out and lead a full life.

There I am considered disabled, and I was asking for the right to parent a child with disabilities. It is possible that there had never been any foreign adoptions from Ukraine from someone in a wheelchair, let alone someone without legs. Certainly I was a first for this judge.

We had no idea what the reaction would be from the court officials. Our interpreter did most everything for us. My one job was to read a prepared statement about our family, our home life, and how we planned to support and care for Alex. The prepared statement was then translated by the interpreter to the judge. We talked about our family and the opportunities he would have in our home. Then others had a chance to weigh in, telling the judge why they agreed or disagreed with the adoption. The social worker began by saying how important it was for kids to have families. She continued with saying I was as capable as, if not more than, Ukrainian men are, and after meeting me she never thought of me as being in a wheelchair.

Next, the director of the institution spoke about Alex's capabilities and emphasized he would never have the chance to improve if left at the orphanage. He was well aware of his institution's limitations and fully supported the adoption.

Lastly, the prosecutor spoke. He noticed in my biography that I had been playing sports since a few months after my accident with the semi-truck and then listed all the sports I have done. He said he felt I would be the perfect father for Alex, adding that I was an example to everyone in Ukraine. I imagine he was referring to the lack of integration of those with disabilities into Ukrainian society.

We waited for almost two hours for the judge and jury to make their decision. After what felt like forever, they reentered the courtroom to inform us our adoption was approved, and after the mandatory ten-day waiting period expired, we'd be the official parents of Alexander Stasik McCallister. Jen cried, and I saw a jury member wipe away tears. Afterward the jury members congratulated us. On August 25, 2016, one day after Ukraine's Independence Day, Alex was forever free, an orphan no more.

I got to spend another full day alone with Jen before she flew back home to get the kids ready for the start of school. I was staying for another two weeks to make sure no relatives came forward to claim Alex. We knew a relative trying to claim him was not a possibility, but the wait was still required by law.

After arriving home from her own thirty-hour trip (while eight months' pregnant), Jen was rear-ended driving home from the airport, prompting an ER visit (luckily everything was fine). The next day, she was getting the kids ready to start a new school year. Anna was going into third grade and Patrick into kindergarten. Everything seemed to be going fairly well, except that while I was still in Ukraine, Jen had come down with the flu badly enough to warrant another trip to the ER, where she received fluids. This was while she was taking care of three kids on her own. Fortunately, my parents were able to help out.

Challenges are life's way of helping us get ready for a new chapter in our lives. Sometimes they come one at a time; other times, though, they come as a flood, one plowing into the other before we even have time to clean up the mess from the previous challenge. During such a flood, it feels like there is no end in sight, but it does end, and we get through it.

This began probably one of the most frustrating and boring times in my life. I have always been extremely active and have prided myself on being able to get a good workout in as often as possible. While I was in Ukraine, though, it was a lot harder to do.

My days consisted of trips to the orphanage, during which I would stay with Alex for a few hours. It was hard at times to interact with him. He did not like being held, and even holding his hand upset him. I spent a lot of time rubbing his back and touching his hands to get him used to being around me. This was really hard for me. I went every day to a place where no one understood what I was saying and talked to a boy who not only didn't understand me but from whom the best reaction I could hope to get was for him to simply tolerate my presence. I was used to kids being shy around me and knew how to help kids warm up to the fact that I was a little different, but Alex would even push away the toys I had brought for him. In my mind I knew he would eventually warm up to me, but right then it was really hard to deal with. I eventually just spent the time listening to a book and rubbing his back.

After coming back from seeing Alex, the rest of the day was mine to do with as I pleased. My ability to go exploring was severely limited since I couldn't speak Ukrainian. And since the roads were pretty bad and the sidewalks even worse, exploring required a good deal of off-road wheeling. So aside from brief trips to the orphanage and visits to an open-air market three miles away, I stayed in the apartment doing practically nothing. I worked on some cross-stitching and puzzles I'd picked up. And I watched a ton of Netflix. Every time I see a commercial for *Sherlock*, I remember the many hours I spent in that lonely apartment on the other side of the world.

My favorite part of the day was dinnertime. Before we left for Ukraine, we'd talked to some people who said they had a hard time finding good food to eat in Ukraine. I don't know if it's just that I'm not that picky or that I genuinely love all food because that was not a problem for me. Between sitting around the apartment and stuffing myself with takeout, I started to gain weight. I couldn't even work out, except for running twenty feet inside the apartment.

The days went by, and I got more and more stir-crazy. After what felt like an eternity, the ten-day waiting period was over, and we were able to start the paperwork to bring Alex home. There were passports and medical checks and photos to sort out, all accomplished through a driver/interpreter. It was through this process that we learned how much Alex hates going to the doctor's office.

Before leaving for the States, Alex had to get checked out. The moment we entered the first doctor's office, Alex started flipping out, screaming and kicking for all he was worth. I sat with him, trying to hold him while he flailed and screamed the entire time. Since Alex is blind, he was likely reacting based on his memory of what a doctor's office sounds and smells like. Additionally, I don't know if it was because he was always restrained at the doctor's or if he was scared by strangers, but whatever it was, he knew where he was, and he didn't like it. Even when we got back home, he continued to have issues whenever we went to the doctor (he's better now, but it took a while for that to happen).

Traveling solo with Alex went so much better than I could have hoped for. When we drove to the train, he was happy and smiling. By the time we boarded, he was laughing. I had never heard him laugh that much before. It was a sleeper train, so I set Alex up on one of the beds, and he laughed and smiled for an hour until he finally got tired and drifted off to sleep. What I was really worried about was the nine-hour plane ride to Oregon. It was one thing for him to flip out on a train where we had our own compartment. It would be another matter entirely once we were sitting inches away from other people for nine hours.

When I told family and friends I was going to be taking Alex home, they asked me how I would make it through the airport with everything. I didn't have any issues handling it, but it was remarkable nonetheless. Even after checking the main luggage, I still had a backpack, Alex, a stroller, a five-foot-long tube with paintings inside, a blanket for the trip, and my own wheelchair. I made it all work by wearing the backpack on my back, placing the tube across the stroller, and shoving the blanket underneath the stroller. We cruised through the airports, and Alex did great in the stroller with his legs dangling off the front end and me pushing him through the halls. When we got on the plane, we were grateful to find that they had given us seats with an empty one next to us so Alex could lay down for the entire trip, thus saving all of us from hearing him scream for the whole flight. He had ridden in a car only twice in his life, so the trip to Oregon was a whirlwind of new sounds and experiences.

After another day of traveling, we arrived home on September 16. Our family didn't even get a few hours to take a break because not more than a day after we'd landed, the most stressful part of our lives began.

I was hoping to have some time to adjust to this new member in our family. We didn't get that time though. In fact, life had a bunch of other challenges in store for us.

With Anna mingling with other girls and, more importantly, other girls' hair, she got lice, and we had to deal with the fun of cleaning the house like we were prepping for surgery.

During the same time we were fighting off the head bugs, we were also fighting a battle with Alex. For the most part it seemed like he was enjoying our family, except for the fact that he wouldn't eat anything. At first he would eat a little bit here and there, but he slowly started refusing food. When Alex came home from Ukraine, he only weighed twenty-six pounds. In the orphanage he hadn't had a chance to develop a positive relationship with food. He couldn't see the food he was eating, and he didn't bond with the caregivers as they force-fed him every day. Food had always been traumatizing for him. Coming to America, he decided he wasn't going to eat, and for a malnourished six-year-old, that was a big problem. We figured the stress of the long journey combined with being in a new home had been too many changes that he had no control over happening too close together and that eating was the one thing he could control. One morning, Jen rushed Alex to the ER to see if we could get him set up on a feeding tube.

She spent all day and most of the night in the ER, followed by an ambulance ride up to the children's hospital in Portland, where Alex was kept for three days. I then drove to Portland to relieve Jen so she could go to an ultrasound appointment and hopefully be able to relax a little. I was more than happy to take my turn sitting in the hospital with my little guy. It would be challenging sitting there doing nothing all day, but I had made the sacrifice for him before, and I was happy to do it again. I ended up getting the better end of the trade with Jen.

The day we switched off, there was a massive windstorm, creating dangerous driving conditions. Jen had all of the kids in the car with her except for Alex. During her ultrasound, Jen had been lying on the bed as the tech diligently tried to do her job. Not only were there three kids in the tiny room full of sensitive medical equipment, but a two-year-old Jack decided that was the perfect time to start potty training. He removed his diaper and went right there. He then treated the exam room as a jungle gym before attempting his naked escape into the unsuspecting doctor's office. Anna, barely eight years old, now had the job of trying to wrangle a wiggly toddler down to the floor to put a diaper on him (something she had only ever done on dolls).

"Is that all?" you may ask.

Oh no, just wait; it gets better.

After the disaster of an ultrasound appointment was over, Jen and the kids stopped at a store to pick up a present for a cousin's birthday party later that evening. While getting out of the car, the kids decided to lock the car doors with the keys still inside—a seemingly minor annoyance until you add the fact that Jack, the recently diaper-less child, was still strapped into his car seat. Jen had to wait half an hour for the locksmith to come and free Jack from the car. Somehow they still made it to the birthday party.

That should be enough stress to last anyone for at least a year, but there was more in store for us. Later that week Alex came home with his brand-new feeding tube sticking out of his nose. The hospital had wanted to keep him over the weekend, but I had to leave for a job in Wyoming, and Jen could only be in so many places at one time, so we'd brought him home.

The next Tuesday, as I was waiting to board the airplane to Wyoming, I thought of all the crazy things we'd dealt with since Alex had come to our home. I had been hoping for a calm period so Alex could slide gently into our family's life. I was happy to put that recent series of stresses behind me and get ready for the next part.

*I sure am glad all the adoption stuff got done before the baby comes. Now we can just focus on the baby,* I thought to myself with a little laugh.

I didn't know how badly I had just jinxed us. Right before I had to turn off my phone, I saw a text from Jen: *Alex just pulled out his feeding tube.*

I sat in my seat, worrying about Jen for the next two hours, feeling helpless. As soon as we landed, I called her. She had called a nurse friend to come help. I relaxed a little now that I knew Jen had help. But it was a false hope. Later that day Alex pulled his feeding tube out for probably the fifth time. Jen was at her wits' end. She got my parents to watch the kids and drove Alex back to Portland, where they fitted him with a nose harness to prevent him from pulling the feeding tube out again. The feeding tube allowed us to feed Alex and bond with him without the stress and trauma of worrying about the tube getting pulled out.

The next morning Anna woke up sick and in major pain. Jen took her to urgent care, and it turned out Anna had an ear infection. By the time I got home from the airport around one on Friday morning, we were both extremely beat. It had just been one thing after another with little to no time to take a breath. We kept putting out the fires just to have another pop up. It had been less than a month since Alex had come home, and we were quickly realizing how crazy life was going to be.

We were scheduled to be at the hospital at seven A.M. the following Tuesday for Jen's C-section. So for the next few days we did absolutely nothing. Our brains had been so focused on putting out fires that we'd barely had time to start thinking about the baby. I didn't even end up getting the crib set up until after he was born.

The birth went off without a hitch. Declan was born the same way the other kids had been—small, but alert. Within the hour he was opening his eyes. We enjoyed a few hours of relative peace in the hospital before I was back home taking care of the other four monkeys. Because of the C-section, Jen spent a few extra days in the hospital to rest. We knew as soon as she got home there would be little quiet to be had. Having a new baby in the house would mean no sleep, no rest, and lots of cleaning. Oh, and there was a lot of crying, and not just from Declan, although he was the main culprit.

In keeping with the pattern of crisis we'd been establishing for the past month, the day after Jen came home from the hospital, the washer broke down and Patrick got a double ear infection. I had to just sit back and laugh . . . or cry . . . actually I think it was both. Not that there's anything funny about an ear infection, but at some point during our trials, we have to make a choice: we can let them beat us, or we can learn how to get through them. Sometimes that means laughing at all the ridiculous things that happen at once.

Life fell into a predictable routine after that (and by predictable I mean it was predictable that we got no sleep). I had to put my new business on hold to take care of the family. Usually Declan didn't let Jen sleep much, so she would need a few extra hours in the morning to catch up on some shut-eye. I tried to help by taking the baby during the night, but Declan refused to take a bottle, so Jen was needed to feed him during the night. I let her sleep as I got the kids off to school and cleaned the house. Then there was usually a doctor's appointment for either Alex, Declan, or Jen. Then, before we knew it, the older kids were home from school.

One day, after about six weeks of little to no sleep, I was sweeping the house, feeling like a zombie, when my high school lessons about good old Maslow's hierarchy crept into my sleep-deprived brain cells. Something about needs. I decided to Google him and found that he'd created a model for what people need in life. It looks like a pyramid, with the basic needs on the bottom and the higher needs on the top. I was on the very bottom. The most basic needs for life are air, water, food, shelter, and rest.[23] I had the first four, but I didn't have much rest. Neither Jen nor I were getting much of that.

The next morning I woke up to Jen crying. I quickly sat up. "Honey, what's wrong?" I said, worried.

"I'm just so tired I don't want to do it anymore," she said as tears ran down her face.

I pulled her close. "I know, honey. Is there anything I can do?" I asked.

She couldn't even speak as she laid her head against my chest.

"Why don't I take him at night," I offered. "He's old enough now that he'll survive the night without eating. And if he gets hungry enough, he'll take the formula."

"I can't sleep if I even hear him crying," she said with exhaustion in her voice.

---

23 Neel Burton, "Our Hierarchy of Needs," *Psychology Today*, posted May 23, 2012, https://www.psychology-today.com/us/blog/hide-and-seek/201205/our-hierarchy-needs.

"I know, hun. I'll figure it out. You don't worry about it; I'll take care of you," I said.

She was so tired she actually said yes. I didn't blame her at all. I had been looking for ways to help her out as she recovered from the C-section, and now I could. Even though I was also tired, I could take the baby and let Jen get some sleep.

Much to Declan's chagrin, I started taking care of him at night. I tried to take care of him from our bed, but Declan didn't like to sleep. I tried everything under the sun. I tried the let-him-cry-it-out method. Five hours later everybody in the house was cranky. I tried moving him across the house while he cried. This just made the sound echo more. Eventually I decided the couch was going to be my friend, so Jen and I had a forced trial separation, so to speak. This lasted for about a month. I didn't sleep much, but Jen finally got some rest. And wouldn't you know it? Sleep makes you happier, and as the saying goes, "A happy wife is a happy life."

After a few nights of the baby crying, I found a system to keep Declan quiet when I was worried he would wake Jen. I first put on a baby carrier and placed Declan in it. Then I would put on my hoodie and zip it up, creating a little warm, dark cocoon for Declan on my chest. I would then roll around the house or go clean the garage until he fell asleep. After that I would lie on the couch with him on my chest (not a great way for me to sleep, but it was better than listening to a crying baby).

Sometimes even this would not work, and I would take the fussy baby in his cocoon to my outside office, where I would let him cry up against my chest while I played video games. I would bounce him until he stopped crying. He would stare at me with his cute little blue eyes as if to say, "Feed me." More than a few nights I was up well past midnight waiting for him to fall asleep so I could go back inside and take a nap on the couch before the other kids got up.

Anna has always been an early riser (Jen blames my genetics). Before, it was merely annoying, but at a time when so little sleep is taking place, it became imperative she sleep later, so we made a rule that she couldn't come out of her room until six A.M. Any earlier than that and she'd have to return to her room until seven A.M. We even gave her a Kindle Fire that would unlock at five thirty A.M. Yes, that's right. We bribed our child.

After three months we were starting to come to grips with our new life and were even getting more sleep (not a lot, but more). Every once in a while, Jen and I would even get to go out on a date. It was fun to take the baby with us. People would come up to make goo-goo eyes at him.

"Oh, that's a really cute baby. How old is he?" they'd ask, often followed by, "Don't blink; they grow up too fast."

"We know; he's our fifth kid," we'd say in return.

They'd get a funny look as if they wanted to keep smiling but didn't know why. They were probably thinking:

*Do they have that many kids on purpose?*

*Weirdos!*

*That's probably contagious; I should run away!*

Whatever they thought, we knew they didn't know how much they were missing. Sure, parenting is a lot of work. In fact, it is the hardest thing to do in this world. There is nothing more challenging than being a parent. It is literally a twenty-four-seven job. But with the greatest challenges come the greatest rewards.

One of the biggest challenges Alex had was the simple act of sitting up. He hated it. He had spent the last six years of his life lying down, and now we were forcing him to sit up. He would try everything in his power to lie flat, flinging himself backward or scooting himself forward. Even in his new wheelchair he would slide as far against the seatbelt as he could so he could slouch as low as possible. Then one day all that changed.

Alex was sitting in his wheelchair, getting a feeding through the G-tube in his stomach. I was lying on the couch reading a book when I saw him moving. Glancing over at him, I saw that he had slid forward in his chair like he had done many times before. I thought nothing of it and started to turn back to my book. Then I saw something amazing. Alex put both of his hands on the chair and pushed himself backward so that instead of slipping down he was now sitting up. I couldn't believe it. He had never done anything like that before. Never had he appeared to want to sit up much less try to do so on his own. I put my book down and stared at him for a while. Then it happened again. His butt slid toward the end of the chair. Then, just as before, he put his hands on the seat and pushed himself back upright. I called for Jen, making sure to keep my voice quiet so as not to startle Alex. Jen came in and saw him once again push himself upright. We cheered together.

That small accomplishment led Alex to start exploring other areas as well. He began to play more actively with toys; things that made sound or had a different surface could entertain him for hours. We were also able to get him to a physical therapist. After a few weeks they made him some braces and taught him to stand. That was incredible as well. This little boy had gone from the supine position he'd been in his whole life to standing. We couldn't be happier. Who knows what else he will learn in the future?

Above all, adopting Alex has shown me how awesome Anna, Patrick, and Jack are. They love him without reservation. They refer to Alex as their giggle buddy because they know how to make him laugh. Jack acts like a big brother, even though he is five years younger than Alex. He helps feed him, change his diaper, and push the wheelchair, and he plays with him as he would any of his siblings.

Our family had really grown into what we had hoped it would be. We were all excited to have Alex in our wonderful family unit. There is no doubt in my mind that God picked Alex just for us. Yes, our lives are challenging and we never seem to have enough time or money, but that is because we are spending them on what we truly value: our family.

Photos taken by Aaron Tharp

# CHAPTER 15
## BECOMING A SPARTAN

*"What stands in the way becomes the way."*
—*Marcus Aurelius*[24]

I stared up at the flames that jumped higher than my head. People passed me, easily jumping over the fire to run through the finish line. The fire was the final obstacle in the most grueling race of my life. I scooted my exhausted body closer to the flames. I was covered in mud, bruised, blistered, and beaten down. Now I had to do something I had only seen done in movies and extreme challenges. I had to walk across fire.

The harder you have to try at something, the more value it has. Regardless of the reward, how much time, energy, and effort you put in defines what it is worth. If you receive the reward with no effort on your part, then it means next to nothing. It is when you have to push yourself that you gain something truly special. Often the reward doesn't even matter as much as the journey to get there. What does a chunk of metal matter after you've just finished your first marathon? By itself it means nothing. It is the hours of training and the miles of sweat and tears you've put in that make that medal a prized possession.

SOON AFTER I HAD DECIDED to put my family ahead of my athletic career, I discovered I couldn't stop being active. I still needed a reason to exercise

---

24 Alex Lickerman, "The Obstacle Is the Way" in *Psychology Today,* https://www.psychologytoday.com/us/blog/happiness-in-world/201405/the-obstacle-is-the-way.

and stay healthy; otherwise I would revert to my teenage eating habits, without the benefit of my teenage metabolism. The logical choice was to continue running marathons. I kept looking for opportunities where I could shoehorn in races between family and work obligations.

After a while marathons became pretty standard, if not boring. It was no longer a challenge to complete a race. It was only 26.2 miles. Even if I had not trained for a few months, I could still get out there and finish a marathon. I needed a new challenge—something that would spark my interest and push me past where I had been. I needed to feel like I was doing something that had never been done before. There were plenty of wheelchair races, and I still enjoyed them, but I needed a new challenge. I wasn't able to spend all day training to be the best wheelchair racer out there. I didn't have that kind of time. What I did have was grit. I knew how to figure out how to do things that at first glance seemed impossible for someone like me.

I started doing triathlons. I thought, okay, here is a race that's not just running. It's also swimming and biking. There was even the possibility of expanding into triathlons like the Ironman and the Ultra Ironman. Those should be right up my alley.

I started entering a number of smaller races that were exciting and earned me more shirts and medals, but I still found myself yearning for more. I realized what I really wanted to do was something crazy— something that would make me question if I really was tough enough.

One day while I was sitting at the computer searching for new races, I stumbled upon OCR (Obstacle Course Racing). The first one I saw was the Spartan Race. There were people climbing nets and ropes, carrying logs, and crawling under barbed wire. It looked like an absolute madhouse. My first thought was, "Holy cow, this is insane! I would never be able to do something like that."

As soon as that thought entered my head, another quickly booted it out. How awesome would it be to take on a military-style obstacle course? Jump over fire? I mean, come on! It's freaking fire! I could do that!

I got excited, and then the obsession just got worse until I knew without a shadow of a doubt I would be doing that race. When I excitedly shared the news with my wife, she looked at me like I had lost my mind, but she supported me in my new ambition. I signed up for a race an hour away, near Portland, and started prepping for a race I had no business entering. I didn't even know how to properly prepare. I *did* know I would have to use my hands for a good portion of the race, so I decided to train by walking on my hands for a few miles in a field. This didn't seem hard at all! It was nothing compared to a marathon or even a wrestling match. It gave me the false impression I was ready to take on the intensity of the Spartan course.

The first OCR I did was called the Spartan Sprint, which is the shortest of the Spartan Races. Since I'd already done trask in high school, I figured I would approach this race in the same way, with no gloves or extra protection for my stubs.

In the continual effort to put my family at the forefront of my life, I brought them along so they could suffer with me. Before starting my own race, I helped Anna and Patrick run the kids' race while Jen stood off to the side holding baby Jack. The kids' course was a mile's worth of scaled-down obstacles. They had to crawl under and through a tangle of ropes, splash down into mud pits, swing across some monkey bars, and climb over a cargo net. For their efforts, each was awarded a T-shirt and a medal. I loved seeing my kids involved with the same sport I was. I didn't have to worry about spending time away from them if they were there doing it with me. After they finished, it was my turn to race. Little did I know just how long this race would take me to complete. The sprint is a three- to five-mile run up and down hills with twenty-plus obstacles thrown in.

I'd brought my wheelchair thinking that, like in trask, I'd be able to take it over most of the course and pull it through the rest. But as I approached the starting line, something in the back of my mind told me the chair would not survive for very long on this course, so I left the chair with Jen. I scooted my way to the start.

Before you even get to the starting line of a Spartan Race, you have to jump a five-foot wall. Most runners just do a hop-skip and swing their leg over the top, but I had to reach up and haul myself up and over. I landed with a thud on the other side of the wall, to find myself in the middle of a sea of legs and bodies pressed closely together. One of the downsides to sitting on the ground is you have to try to avoid staring at a bunch of butts. Boy, was my face red. I ended up just staring at the ground.

I geared myself up for a starting gun, but that is not what I got. Instead a man with a microphone gave a few simple directions before starting a speech (I would find out later they do this at the start of every Spartan Race):

"Today you embark upon a quest like those of legends old. You will face unimaginable challenges and push thyself further than you ever thought possible, and to prepare you for that battle, I will ask you one very simple question, 'Who am I?' to which you shall respond, 'I AM A SPARTAN!'"

"Who am I?"

"I am a Spartan!" the crowd shouted back.

"We are honored by your courage and commitment to excellence, but know this—today your mind, body, and spirit will all be put to the ultimate test, for you chase glory on this day! Who am I?"

"I am a Spartan!" the crowd once again responded with enthusiasm, and I joined in.

"Look at the Spartans on your right and your left. You will draw strength from them as they will draw strength from you. You will NOT let them fail! Who am I?"

"I am a Spartan!"

The runners around me were growing restless as they knew his speech was coming to an end and were ready to race.

"By all that you hold dear on this good Earth, I bid you STAND, sons and daughters of Sparta! Stand and FIGHT! For today is the day that you rise to glory, not tomorrow, not next week. Right here, right now, in YOUR house, your HOME. Who am I?"

"I am a Spartan!"

"Who am I?"

"I am a Spartan!"

"Who am I?"

"I am a Spartan!!"

"Aroo! Aroo! Aroo! Go!"[25]

With that final yell, we charged the course. Wow! What a way to start such an epic race. Initially I was planning on starting with an easy walk to conserve my energy for later challenges down the course, but after that speech and rallying cry, I charged with the rest of the crowd down the trail. Of course, I didn't charge for long. After two hundred feet of a full-out sprint, I realized I could not maintain that pace. I slowed myself to a steady scoot. Steadfast in my plan to finish this course and not knowing what to expect, I took each obstacle as it came. I was the slowest participant out there. Every once in a while I found a few spots where I could go faster than others could. For instance, when it came time to crawl under barbed wire, climb nets and ropes, or crush the monkey bars, my smaller stature and muscular arms gave me an advantage.

The course was positioned around a huge hill, so most of the time we were either going up or down. I love hills. They are an amazing test of grit and determination. What better way to rise up than to tackle a huge hill head-on?

That first Spartan Race did more than take us up and down hills though. At one point, as we climbed up and down, we were required to carry a bucket of rocks with us. That first race was so tough that when someone offered to carry my bucket the rest of the way, I let them do it. Throughout my life I have done the exact opposite, even getting a bit prickly when someone asked if they could help. I had walked fifty miles on my hands during a scouting high adventure. I had done absolutely every workout my wrestling coach had asked everybody else to do. When it was time to do service of any sort, I was the first one to grab a shovel, rake, or hammer, ready to do everything I could to help. To let someone else help me was a testament to how difficult the Spartan Race was. But it was about more than oneself. It was about helping everyone finish. One of the greatest things about these races is the teamwork every person out there shows. Every person out there will help each other complete the race.

Another obstacle required us to carry a round sandbag weighing forty pounds over two hundred meters. I did not know how I was going to

---

25 Speech quoted with permission from Spartan Race, Inc.

manage it. I couldn't carry it in my arms. I finally figured out I could balance the bag on my neck and carefully scoot through that section of the course. It was not easy by any means. By the time I let the sandbag slide to the ground, my back, shoulders, and neck were cramped and sore.

My biggest challenge was facing a ten-foot wall. As resourceful as I am, I couldn't figure out a single scenario in which I'd be able to jump up and grab the edge. The wall was literally three times my height. I asked someone to boost me to the top so I could pull myself over and plop down to the ground on the other side. As hard as it is for me to admit, there are some things I just can't do . . . yet. I still think there must be a way to get up a sheer wall by myself; I just don't know how. I have never liked asking for help, but I have come to learn there is nothing wrong with doing so. When we ask for help, we not only improve ourselves, but we allow others to improve themselves as well. That being said, I still try to do everything on my own.

In the Spartan Races, if you cannot finish an obstacle, you are required to do thirty burpees (a push-up and then a jump straight up with arms parallel above the head), which in and of itself is a challenge for me. That did not stop me from taking the punishment though. Luckily I only had to take my licks on the spear throw. To modify my burpees, I dropped flat on my stomach and then pushed the rest of my body into the air. After that I swung my body under me and flung my arms in the air while giving a little hop with my butt. I am sure it looked kind of silly, but I found a way to accomplish every task, including the punishments.

The last obstacle of the day before the fire jump was the rope climb. To even get to the rope, I had to slide down a slope into a disgusting, murky, muddy water pit so deep I couldn't touch the bottom. I sat on the edge of the slope feeling dog-tired. I had not been prepared for the five-hour pounding I had just endured. There was no more energy left in my body.

Remember my smart decision not to wear gloves? Well, it turned out it wasn't the smartest move. My hands were tender and sore. Numerous scratches and blisters made each step painful. My butt, which had no more protection that a pair of sport shorts, was screaming in agony. Every muscle from my neck down was so depleted you would think they were too tired to be sore. But sore they were.

I had just walked four miles using only my arms, and now I was faced with climbing a rope hanging in the middle of a mud pool. I saw others jumping in, grabbing on to a rope with both hands, and attempting to jump out of the water only to splash back down and wade off to do burpees. Some bagged the whole thing altogether and waded straight to the burpee area. I could see the finish line a mere hundred yards away. It would be so easy to just be done. That wasn't me though. A flash of defiance and determination flowed through my weary body. Even though my muscles were tapped out, I was going to make it up that stupid rope.

I slid down the little incline into the water and swam over to the dangling rope. Reaching my arms up, I grabbed hold of the dripping cord with both hands. Summoning every last drop of will I had, I yanked myself out of the water. With little thought and as much speed as I could muster, I climbed the rope. Reach, grab, pull. Reach, grab, pull. Reach, grab, pull. Nothing else mattered at that point. The finish line was in sight, but all I was focused on was the bell at the top of the rope. All I had to do was hit it. I couldn't even hear my wife and kids shouting my name. They'd been waiting for me all day. Hand over hand, I flew to the top. Ringing the bell at the top was epic. I had just climbed an impossible rope after beating an impossible course. As I hit the bell, I bellowed at the top of my lungs, "I am a Spartan!"

It almost didn't matter when I crossed the finish line. I mean, the fire was out. It was the end of the day, and a thousand people had already jumped over it, dripping wet from the plunge under the ropes. I was disappointed. I had never jumped a fire before and wanted to give it a shot. All I had to do was hop over some wet logs to finish the race. But then I realized it *totally* mattered when I crossed the finish line. I had just finished the hardest race of my life. Never before had I worked out for five hours straight. Not even in a wrestling practice had I pushed my body to the point I didn't even want to take off my shirt because of how tired I was. It was incredible (and by *incredible* I mean I could barely move). I was wiped out. I had given everything I had to the race, and some of what I didn't have. I got the medal. I got the shirt. I had finished the race! For the first time in my life, I didn't care about how fast I'd finished; I only cared that I'd finished.

As Jen drove home, I sat in the passenger seat, uncomfortable, sore, bruised, and thinking about how this would be a great story to tell because it would be the last Spartan I was ever going to race. That thought lasted for about ten minutes. By the time the Ibuprofen kicked in, I had a new thought: If I'd just finished *that* race, what else could I accomplish? I wasn't even home from the race that had beat me into the ground and already I was thinking about the next one.

As soon as I got home, I hopped online to see which race I could enter next. To my delight I found there was not just one more level, but two— the Super and the Beast. Reading further, I saw that if you complete all three races in one year, you gain the Spartan Trifecta award. I knew I had found my next goal. I was going to complete the trifecta.

The next step was the Spartan Super. The Super was an eight- to ten-mile run with almost thirty obstacles. I wanted to do it. There was something happening in me that grew with every passing day—a need to go further and do more than I ever had before.

I found a Super that was taking place six months later near Seattle. I knew it was going to be hard. I had doubts about whether or not I would be able to do a race more than twice the length of my first Spartan. Yet that doubt did not stop me from moving forward. Instead of continuing to think in terms of whether I could do it, I started to think in terms of what the best way was for me to get it done. After I got done thinking, I got to work. My training became focused. I now knew what I was going to face and could work on improving in the areas I'd had trouble with. Mostly my training involved a lot of scooting and running a lot of stairs at a local stadium.

One day, as I was in the garage preparing to start a workout, my wife came out with a serious look on her face.

"Kacey, I know you're excited about this race," she said.

"Yeah, I love a challenge," I responded. "I can't wait to take this on!"

"Do you remember the last race you did?" she said, looking straight into my eyes. "It was only four miles, but by the end you could barely move. This race is going to be double that."

"I know, but I finished it," I said, meeting her gaze. "I want to see if I can finish a harder one." Was she trying to get me to cancel this race? I knew she cared about me. Could she see how important this was?

"You're crazy," she replied. "Kacey, this is going to be insanely hard. This might kill you."

"Hun, you're exaggerating," I said with a smile I hoped was confident and encouraging. "It might hurt pretty badly, but it is not going to kill me."

"Well, if you come back broken, don't come crying to me," she said with sigh.

"Jen, I'm a man," I retorted. "There will be no crying."

My wonderful wife, who loved me, was just trying to look out for me, and I am so grateful for her. There have been many times in our lives when I have wanted to do some new crazy race or event, and she has always been there to help me think through the consequences and whether I would be okay. She has never thought I couldn't do something, but she does worry about me getting hurt.

Preparing for the Super would not be like when I was training for the Paralympics. I could no longer take hours away from my family to train every day. I had to be more judicious about my free time. I could no longer waste time on activities such as video games or movies. I needed to become more than I had been before.

There was also a cost to racing, and the money I was making was not my own. I had a growing family to take care of. Every dollar I spent on a race was one more not going to my kids. Race entry, travel, and equipment would need to be purchased. I was brought up to be frugal. We did not spend too much money on things we didn't need. I could no longer afford the little things I thought were "deserved." There could be no more fast food or junk food just because and no more wasting money at the hardware store. I had to figure out how to pay for my races.

And to keep doing them, I would have to work on more than just my strength. I would need to train my mind and my body. I needed to change how I trained. I couldn't simply scoot around anymore. I needed to be lifting, pulling, and carrying heavy objects. I got a big tire from my dad's garage and started slinging that around our backyard. I also got a heavy wheel from him that I hooked up to a chain and began pulling in circles along our fence line. I also started looking at how to protect myself, testing out different gloves that would better protect my knuckles. My dad recommended I use mechanics' gloves because they have ribbing over the fingers, and they worked like a charm. Protecting my butt was a different matter.

Over the years people had helped me make different types of boots to protect my rear. My mom had made a cloth sack for me while I was hiking with my scout troop. When I was on my mission, a member of the Church had made me a hard leather shell to save my slacks and protect me from the blazing-hot ground of Arizona. I used both of these ideas as a blueprint to make my own boot for Spartan Races.

I did some research and found that my best bet for durability and for staying as dry as possible was marine vinyl. This sturdy material seemed like a good fit, so using the mad sewing skills my sweet mom had taught me all those years ago, I whipped together a boot for my booty. Armed with my new gear, I was ready to take on the Super. I knew it would be hard, but I also knew I could rock that thing.

Since the race was in Seattle, Jen decided to stay home and take care of the kids while I went and beat myself up. I knew the course would take a while to finish, so I made sure I was in one of the first groups in the morning. Scaling the starting wall with my new gloves and boot, I felt ready to take on the course. Once again the starter pumped us up with the now-familiar Spartan speech, and before I knew it, I was yelling, "AROO!"

It was a wet course—much wetter than the first. There were many places where the entire path was a bog of squishy, sucking mud, and I'd find myself sinking into the stuff up to my elbows. That was not the only unique challenge this course offered. At one point racers were required to run down a pebbled shore next to a river. As I was scooting along, I felt something squish under my hand. Assuming it was just some weird plant or a patch of mud, I didn't even look down to investigate. I just kept on going. After a few more feet, though, I saw what had caused the squish. There were dead fish everywhere. The bank was so thick with them I ended up giving up on trying to avoid them and just ran straight over them. It wasn't as stinky as you'd think it would be, but man, was it gross!

One of the hardest parts of the course was a monstrous hill. Remember how I said I love the challenge of hills? This hill took it to another level. This hill was intense. It vaguely reminded me of that last hill on the trask course in high school. But instead of flying down into a muddy river, I had to climb up with ice-cold trickles of water running past me. This hill was *huge*. Not only that but it was covered in mud. Not the light coating that made you slip but the sucking kind of muck that drained your strength with every step. The only way to get up that thing was to use the racers around you to form a series of human chains to pull yourself up. Ropes had been placed at various points, but the mud was so bad the ropes were getting sucked under, so you might be able to use the rope for about five feet before reaching for a friendly hand.

I was never on my own, because everybody was part of the Spartan team. I needed help up the ten-foot walls, and once again I got some help from somebody on the wall brigade. As I ran the race, my wife's voice echoed in my head, *This is going to be really hard. Are you sure you want to do this?*

The Super was a lot like my life, compressed into eight hours. Many times I would get to an obstacle in life that nearly defeated me just by the thought of having to face it. Like in life, though, there is always a way to get through. Sometimes it is with the helping hand of a friend or family member, but sometimes we don't even have that. Some obstacles are ours, and we have to endure them seemingly alone. Life can totally suck, but that doesn't mean we have to hate it. The Super Spartan had parts that truly and utterly sucked, but I was loving it.

When I got to the bucket carry, I was already tired, sore, and in desperate need of a nap. Of course, my reluctance to start the carry didn't stop my body from continuing forward. I grabbed the bucket and started shoveling in rocks. My brain kept telling me I had filled the bucket enough, but something else deeper inside kept telling my brain to shut up. I didn't stop filling the bucket until the rocks were a good inch above the required carry height.

Pushing forward, I looked up the hill we needed to climb. It seemed like it was even steeper than the mud hill. How was I ever going to make it up? I slid, scooched, and pulled the bucket inches at a time, trying not to look ahead to what I still had to ascend. I knew if I realized how much farther I had to go, it would be that much harder to finish, so I focused on the here and now—scoot, pull, scoot, lift, scoot, pull, scoot, lift—moving

---

I WANTED TO HELP OTHERS FIGHT THROUGH THEIR OWN
CHALLENGES AND GAIN THEIR OWN VICTORIES.

---

that bucket of rocks again and again and again. As I got halfway up the hill, I felt I could not move another inch. It had already taken me fifteen minutes to move that far, and I still had a long way to go. Right at the moment when I began to feel defeat creeping in, a man squatted down next to me and said, "Brother, I know you don't need the help, but I would be honored if you would let me help you the rest of the way."

Relief flooded over me. I gladly accepted and let him carry the bucket the rest of the way.

In later races I would end up doing the bucket carry by myself, but that day when I had needed the help, someone was there to lend a hand. I made it through the rest of the race on my own, once again missing the spear throw and having to do my adapted burpees.

As I neared the finish line, my eyes caught sight of the fire, its sparks jumping high into the air. In my first Spartan there was just a pile of damp logs. This time I would get to do the fire jump. All I needed to do was get through that, and I was done—one last obstacle to overcome before getting my medal. I felt the heat on my face. Not the comfortable warmth from a fireplace on a cold day, but a blistering, threatening heat. I wasn't backing down. With only a second's hesitation, I purposefully scooted toward the burning logs. I took a moment to figure out where I could place my hands among the glowing coals, and then I swung my body on top of and then through the burning wall of fire. I felt the heat wrap around my body and singe my exposed arm hair as I swept through the flame and landed with a thud on the other side. I was wiped out.

I looked up at the faces of the crowd looking back at me. What were they thinking? A desire to inspire rose up in me, and I let out one last bellow: "I am a Spartan!" I wanted to do more than overcome my own trials and obstacles. I wanted to help others to do the same—to fight through their own challenges and gain their own victories.

Photos taken by Aaron Tharp

# CHAPTER 16
## THE TRIFECTA

*"The only use of an obstacle is to be overcome. All that an obstacle does with brave men is not to frighten them, but to challenge them."*
*—Woodrow Wilson, 28th President of the United States*[26]

Sometimes I feel a sense of hopelessness, a sense that all my work and all my efforts have been wasted. I realize many people feel like this at times. Sometimes it might feel like it's too hard to go on. This is part of life. There are going to be times that are difficult beyond belief, when it feels like there is no way you can continue on. But the fact of the matter is there is always a way. It might be hard, it might make us cringe with the thought of another day fighting through the tough times, but there is always a way. No matter what, we have to keep pushing through and rising up.

TRYING TO GAIN THE TRIFECTA, I found out how far I could push myself. It turned out to pretty darn far.

As the saying goes, "Life is what happens to us while we're busy making other plans."[27] The 2016 year came and went as we adopted Alex and had baby Declan. It took Jen and me months before we'd slept enough to start thinking about the future, much less for me to find time for training. To get the Trifecta the next year, I would have to be ready to do another Super in April, just four months after Declan was born. We were still not getting a lot of sleep, but I knew if I didn't do it in April, I might not get the chance for another year.

26 "The New York Times Current History: The European War," vol. XVIII, Jan.–Mar., 1919, 211.

27 Allen Saunders, "Quotable Quotes" in *Reader's Digest,* Jan. 1957, 32.

At the start of 2017, things were looking different. The baby was sleeping through the night . . . ish, and Alex was in school. Jen and I talked and decided I should go for it. I should try and get the Trifecta. My plan was to do the Super in April, the Sprint in August, and the Beast in September.

The Super was once again in Seattle. I had already done the race twice, so I knew what to expect. A buddy of mine was also a double amputee, and I invited him to do the race with me. We had both competed in wrestling and track. I had beat him in our one wrestling match together, but he had beat all of my track records. With the spirit of a warrior, he accepted the challenge.

After the starting shout, we were off. That year's course was particularly muddy. The rain had been pouring the entire winter and spring, and the ground was super soggy. At certain points on the course, the water was so high that areas that had been clear the previous year were now completely submerged. In other parts the mud was so deep that my arms would sink so the mud was all the way up past my elbows, and my butt would get sucked in too.

When we came upon the gravel pits, we scooted onto a section that was almost like quicksand. Everybody who hit the area had to pull themselves along by crawling on their stomachs. As this mud bog of a race progressed, my buddy grew heavy with fatigue. He had not been ready for this race, but being a wrestler, he'd figured he was up for anything I was. Near mile six was the sandbag carry. For us there was no carrying to it. The bags were not only forty pounds apiece, but you had to take two of them. Unable to carry them on my shoulders or walk while holding them in my hands, I decided to drag them through the mud and up many hills. It was quite the slog. That obstacle alone took me and my buddy nearly an hour to complete. One of the hills was so steep and slick with mud we had to form a chain with other people on the course to drag our bags up the hill.

Soon after finishing that obstacle, my buddy started slowing down. He was digging deep into the pain cave and was at that point where he'd pushed himself so far for so long his body started rejecting even the thought of continuing on. Deciding I had punished him enough, we called it quits, and the race director gave us a lift back to the start. We didn't get a medal or a shirt for trying; it didn't matter that we had pushed ourselves as hard as we could that day. The race was not only about going hard; it was about finishing. It might seem harsh, but that was part of the challenge. What we did gain, though, was the journey. We had completed most of an eight-mile Spartan Race, and anyone who's done a Spartan knows that's a major achievement.

I wasn't done striving for my Trifecta though. I still needed to find a way to make it happen. I found another Super in Eden, Utah, a couple of weeks before the Sprint in Portland, and after discussing it with Jen, we decided it was now or never if I was going to achieve my Trifecta goal.

The Utah race was hot. I was used to racing in the freezing rain and the sucking mud of the Pacific Northwest, not the blistering heat.

Most of the race required me to climb a ski slope. Every step forward in the blazing sun was not only draining me physically but also zapping my water supply. By the time I had made it to the bucket carry, I had depleted my hydration pack and was hitting a wall. But I knew I could complete the bucket carry by myself. Halfway through the course and with the temperature hitting ninety-five degrees, I decided to rest for a minute.

My head was pounding. Not only was my hydration pack empty but so was my body. There was not enough water in me to produce sweat. My skin was bone dry. I started to feel nauseous. How could I have been so stupid? Not only had I not filled my pack up at the last station but I hadn't brought anything to replace my electrolytes. I knew I needed to get done with the bucket obstacle so I could get to the water at the end of the challenge. I was almost dry-heaving from the nausea when once again God and my fellow Spartans were there to help me. A man who had already finished his carry came up the hill and offered to carry my bucket. I was already at the top of the hill, and while I appreciated his offer, I told him I was going to finish it myself. He asked if there was anything else he could do for me. My first thought was, "I got this; I can do it on my own," but then I remembered the Spartan Race is a team sport, so I asked him if I could have some of his water. Without a second of hesitation, he emptied his hydration pack into mine. Then, with a nod, he was off. I called a parched "thank-you" as he left before greedily sucking down as much water as I could without getting sick. The water tasted different, and I realized it had a mix of electrolytes in there as well. My headache began to subside, and I started sweating.

Nearing the end of the carry, I realized I had made another mistake. I had not worn sunglasses, and my eyes were in as much pain as my body was. I tried to use my headband to protect my eyes, but I was unable to see where I was going. Once again God sent someone to help me. A man offered me his sunglasses and told me to keep them. It was only later I realized they were prescription polarized sunglasses with a bifocal for reading. That bucket carry might have been the hardest obstacle I have ever faced, but there was always someone there to help me when I most needed it. I was no longer the guy who needed help with the bucket, but that didn't mean I didn't need help. I had prepared myself to not accept help to prove that no matter the challenge, I would accomplish it. But life has a funny way of teaching us. I had to learn how to accept help. Even after conquering the bucket brigade, I still needed help from my fellow Spartans.

I finished the race by once again jumping the flames and getting my medal. A couple of weeks later, I did the same at the Sprint. I no longer struggled with the Sprint. The race that had beaten me down had now become child's play. Now I just had to face the Beast.

The Beast was what I had been preparing for all year. Heck, that was what I had been working toward for the past *three* years. It would be the ultimate race for me. Never before had I faced a challenge like the one now before me. I was looking at a thirteen-mile slog up and down hills through the mud (it was in Seattle at the same location as the Super, so I knew there would be mud). Thirteen miles on the road doesn't even take me an hour, but thirteen miles on a Spartan course equates to around one mile per hour.

Even starting with the competitive group at eight thirty A.M., I wouldn't be finishing until nine thirty at night. Frankly that scared me a little. I didn't know how my body was going to react to being out there all day long. I knew I was going to have a huge issue with energy intake. For the Supers, I would load up on protein and carbs right before the race, hit the nutrition station hard, and finish the race on what was left in the tank. That was not an option for this race. There would not be enough nutrition stands for the amount of energy I would be expending. I had to constantly be putting energy back into my body.

I also didn't know how my gloves were going to hold up. In every race up to that point they had slowly shredded as I'd progressed through the course. By the end of the Super, most of my gloves were hanging on by threads, literally. My boot was also going to be challenged to face five more miles than ever before. Anything could happen in an extra five miles.

Knowing the Beast would be harder than anything I had done before, I invited my friend and business manager, David Bacio, up with me to take video and pictures as well as haul extra gear for me. We drove up the night before so we would be right there come morning.

That night, as we camped out in a van in a church parking lot, I mentally catalogued every possible thing I would need to make sure I survived this challenge. Doubts crept in from all sides, exposing cracks in my armor, finding my weaknesses and faults like water through a wall, bringing them to the forefront of my mind to be replayed over and over again. *I didn't train enough. Why didn't I eat healthier? I wasted so much time doing stupid things. Am I wasting my time out here doing this race? Am I really helping anybody by being out here? Am I being selfish by taking time away from my family to do this? What if I can't finish? What if I just can't go any farther?*

I lay there in a hammock I'd strung up in the middle of my van, tossing and turning, wasting the precious energy I knew I'd need for the race but powerless to stop the thoughts that rolled through my brain like waves on the ocean. As thoughts crashed against the walls of my head, I began to think about who I really was and how far I'd come. I was Kacey freaking McCallister! I had come so close to winning the wrestling state championship. I had completed four Super Spartans on my butt. I was a dedicated husband and father. I did my best to live up to everything God asked of me. No matter how many doubts rushed in, they had no merit and held no power over me. I was going to finish the race. There was no other option. It might take me all day. It might be dark by the time I finished. But I *would* finish.

Turning my pillow to the cool side, I plopped my head down and sought refuge in sleep, finally at peace with the knowledge that the next day I would accomplish something never done before. I would become the first athlete in history to earn a Spartan Trifecta entirely on his hands.

I was up as soon as the sun popped up above the trees. Flooded with nervous excitement, I drove down to the field where the starting line of the Spartan race was located. As we drove up, I saw the main area spread out before me like a playground. Obstacles were scattered here and there, and I pointed out some of my favorites to David as we passed.

"Oh, there's the bender," I called out as the inverted metal ladder appeared off to the side of the road. "That's one of my favorites."

The A-frame cargo net, the rope climb, the spear throw, the Hercules hoist, and the multi-rig were also visible as we found a spot to park near the entrance to the arena.

As soon as the car stopped, my mind started to run through my pre-race prep routine. I started by offering a prayer to my Heavenly Father asking for help, strength, and the wisdom to know what to do with my water and energy blocks. I knew He was listening because there had never been a time in my life when He hadn't. Ending my prayer, I slipped on my race shirt, spandex shorts, and boot. I also checked the hydration pack for energy blocks, protein bars, and my Rise Up bracelets to hand out on the course, before slinging on the pack. After making sure David was ready to go, I hopped into my chair and made my way to the race.

I love arriving at a race early and soaking in the energy from men and women of all talents and abilities ready to take on an obstacle course others think is a little bit nuts. The weather was going to be perfect for racing—a mild sixty-degree day with no rain. Cruising over to the start line to watch the athletes line up, I still had one last thing to take care of, and that was to fill up my hydration pack.

Water. Water is one of the most important things on the course, and, as I'd found out in Utah, if I didn't have enough of it, I would suffer at the very moment I would most need my strength.

---

NO MATTER WHAT,
WE HAVE TO KEEP PUSHING THROUGH AND RISING UP.

---

There was a water station near the start line, so I scooted over to it to fill up my hydration pack. *Oh no.* Something was wrong. Something was very wrong. I looked down with dread and saw water pouring through my pack and onto the rocks as if it wasn't even passing through the bag at all. I searched for the leak, hoping there was just a loose connection. My heart dropped. It wasn't a loose connection. It was a hole that went right through the bag at the bottom. I had fifteen minutes before the race started. I had no idea how the hole had gotten there, but that was a trivial point right then. I had to figure out what I was going to do. There was no way I could race without water.

David was standing right next to me and sprang into action, running back to the car for water bottles. It wasn't the best solution, but it was all we had, and I was thankful for his quick thinking. I stuffed the bottles into my pack and made my way over to the start line to warm up. Watching the elite men and women start the race, I knew I was in the right place. I knew I was doing something important, even if it was only important to me.

My adrenaline was pumping, and I was ready to go. At eight thirty A.M. sharp, I hopped the wall along with a herd of fellow athletes. It was on. My brain zeroed in on the start, and I was no longer thinking about my water situation. There was nothing I could do about it now. I would have to figure it out on the course. Now there was only one thing left to do: race. I heard the end of the speech.

"Stand and FIGHT! For today is the day that you rise to glory, not tomorrow, not next week. Right here, right now, in YOUR house, Seattle, your HOME. Who am I?"

"I am a Spartan!"

"Who am I?"

"I am a Spartan!"

"Who am I?"

"I am a Spartan!"

"AROO! AROO! AROO! GO!"[28]

I sprinted for the first fifty feet, enjoying the feel of adrenaline coursing through my body and the power it gave my arms. It felt like I could go forever. That was good. I would need every last drop before the day was done.

After the initial sprint, I slowed down to a quick scoot, a pace I hoped to be able to maintain mile after mile. In the past it had taken me about an hour to cover a mile. I was determined to shave off some of that time by maintaining two miles an hour while on the flat parts of the race in hopes of finishing before dark.

The first path led us near the water, where we came to our first obstacle, the low crawl, which is exactly what it sounds like. There are ropes strung across the gravel shoreline that you have to crawl under. That was perfect for me. All I needed to do was duck my head to make it under the low wires. That was one point in the race where I would actually be passing people. Taking a little bit too much pleasure from it, I shouted encouragement to the people I was passing.

"Just pretend you don't have legs; then it's really easy!" I called out, drawing laughs and groans. "Here watch me," I said. "Just like this!"

My joy was short-lived though. I was going around and over the bushes and stumps that lined the riverbank until I misjudged one, and it hit me right in the stub. Getting hit on the stub is almost the most debilitating thing that can happen to me aside from a direct hit to other sensitive areas.

28 Speech quoted with permission from Spartan Race, Inc.

When that piece of wood tagged my stub, it felt as if a lightning bolt had shot right through my body all the way up to my brain. My back arched as I went rigid as a board. I couldn't cry out or even reach down to cradle my aching stub. My whole body spasmed, and I went down flat. The closest thing I can think of to describe the feeling is the sensation you get when you hit your funny bone, except multiply that by fifty and attach that sensation to the rest of your body.

I lay facedown in the gravel, writhing in agony for the better part of a minute. Within seconds of my fall, people stopped to offer help. I explained through gritted teeth that though I was in debilitating pain, it would pass and there was nothing that could be done until it did. With concerned looks they left me grimacing in the gravel. A mile into the race, and I was already facedown it the dirt.

*Is this what I'm in for?* I thought to myself.

The doubts were back and looking for a fissure I'd left open, but I remained resolute. The pain would pass eventually, and lying on the ground was not going to help. Pushing myself off the ground, I moved forward, not stopping to brush myself off. One step. Then two. After about ten steps, the pain had retreated into the back of my brainstem. In another fifty steps it was gone altogether. Oh yeah. I was back up to speed and getting this thing done.

The next obstacle was the rolling mud. There were three pits filled with ice-cold, muddy water. Without a moment of hesitation I splashed into the water. It was so cold it made me gasp. I stroked my way over to the other side as quickly as I could and tried to drag myself out of the water, but the far side of the pits were not only steep but muddy. But before I could even think to ask for help, a hand reached down to pull me out of the water. That hand was attached to another, and with that human chain binding us together as athletes, we all made it to the top of the mud-slicked wall.

The third pit had a wall that forced you to go under the water to get past it. That was really hard for a lot of people, and I understand why. Putting your head and body under muddy water and then swimming under a wall without any chance of seeing what's down there can be absolutely terrifying. Splashing into the water, I swam to the wall and plunged beneath it before I could think about it too much. Stroking down under the wall, I pulled myself into the murky depths. On my way back to the surface my busted hydration pack got caught on the edge of the wall. I panicked for the briefest of instances, imagining what it would be like to get stuck underwater. But then I regrouped and stroked downward to pull the bag free. I later learned this is a tough obstacle for many people because you are required to put your whole head under cold, murky water. But the Spartan Race is not about physical danger—it's about facing and overcoming the dangers you perceive in your head that create roadblocks.

The next few obstacles were easy. The bender was basically inverted monkey bars that I was able to fly up and over, followed by traditional monkey bars. The hardest part of conquering these was getting to the first handhold. I would either have to climb up the side of the obstacle or get a boost from a nearby racer if climbing up was not an option. Usually there was someone close by to give me a boost. I was nearing the four-mile mark and feeling good. Up to that point my time was solid. I had been keeping a pace of about a mile every half hour. I had nine miles to go.

Right after mile four came the twister. The twister has a rotating shaft running the length of the obstacle. Along the shaft are offset handles, and every time you grab one, the bar spins. If you do it right (and quickly enough), the bar spins toward you so another handle is easily within your grasp. If you don't, you're left dangling by one arm, trying to figure out a way to get the next handle to spin back toward you. It's monkey bars on steroids.

This was the one that had beat me just a couple months earlier in Utah. I had been climbing the ski slope, and didn't have much left in me by the time I'd gotten to the twister. Getting two-thirds of the way across, my grip had given out, and I'd dropped the eight feet to the ground. I'd laid there for a second before going over and taking the thirty-burpee punishment.

I knew I couldn't let it get the best of me this time. Climbing the side of the structure, I latched on to the first handhold and grabbed the next, facing backward. I went as fast as I could, grabbing one after another after another. Before I knew it, my head was inches from the bell. I attempted to head-butt it and missed by about an inch. I didn't care though. I was so happy to finish I laughed along with my fellow Spartans and reached out with a hand to ring the bell.

Next came the long hike. The hardest part of any of these races for me is the walking. It is not difficult in and of itself, but the energy required to walk on your hands is exponential when compared to using your legs. Our bodies are astounding machines, designed with efficiency in mind. In normal conditions, to take a step, all you have to do is shift weight to one leg, swing the other forward, and repeat. It is something so basic even a one-year-old can figure it out. Swinging your arms forward to scoot is a similar process; however, legs are made for absorbing the full body weight. Arms are not.

The five-mile hike would take me through the woods, over gravel pits, up a logging road, and down a treacherous rockslide. I was feeling good, but the race was starting to take a toll. I had been trying to eat something every hour, but I could feel the calorie deficit creeping up on me. I started to split my time between an easy stroll and a fast-paced scoot.

Coming out of the gravel pits around mile marker six, I came upon the zig-zag wall, which is a series of walls bolted together that veer alternatively right and left. The racers have to move across each wall horizontally in order to get to the next. Screwed to each wall are slanted two-by-fours measuring about six inches long, which make it difficult to get a good grip or plant one's feet effectively. Racers are also not allowed to touch the ground or grab the top of the wall to help themselves along. I only had the top set of holds to work with, so I knew I'd need to be hoisted up to the blocks and then would need additional help to maintain my position. Before I got on the wall, I looked for someone who was struggling. I wanted to offer my help before asking for it. I found someone fighting to get around a corner, so I helped guide his foot to the next block and supported him until he finished. He rang the bell and avoided the burpee tax.

Going back to the start of the zig-zag wall, I found a willing helper to give me a boost to the first handhold. My fellow Spartan also kept pressure on my back, giving me some extra traction to stick to the wall. I made my way across the blocks, eventually hitting the bell. No burpees for me either.

I was now at the halfway point. I was tired, but there would be no stopping. As I scooted past the halfway point, I remembered where I was nine years before. I had just had my first kid, and Jen and I had been playing kickball with some friends. I could barely make it to first base because of how far I had let my body go. My shoulders had hurt too badly for me to continue, and I'd had to sit to the side for the rest of the game. It had been then that I'd made the decision I would not let myself continue along that path, that I would lose weight and get stronger. I'd made the decision to be there for my wife and my kids. Now I was not only getting in shape but doing one of the most grueling races there was. The thought of how far I'd come caused the worry over how tired I was to fade into the background.

As I was trudging through the woods, something happened that had never happened before, something that could have stopped my run short of the finish line. My boot ripped. I had made many boots, and most of them had developed a little hole or even a split seam. But that day the bottom caught on a stick, and with a resounding *riiiiip* the entire bottom tore out of my boot. That, more than anything else, had the power to stop me cold. I didn't have an extra boot and still had five miles to go. I knew the flimsy athletic shorts I was wearing under the boot wouldn't hold up for the rest of the race. Before I let that thought fester for too long, however, I remembered David was standing by and could get me my jeans. When I reached the top of the hill, David was there waiting. He took one look at my boot and raced down the hill to grab my pants from the car as I continued on.

I only had four more miles to go—just the length of a Spartan Sprint left. My boot was ripped and my body worn-out, but I was still alive and kicking. The next part of the course had some of the best obstacles, obstacles I lived for. Overcoming every obstacle is exciting, but these I crushed.

First up was the inverted wall climb; it's always a favorite because it relies on all arm strength. Basically I had to scale a wall that was propped up and tilted toward me. To get to the top, I have to fling my body upward to grab the upper edge. Doing this, I am hanging by one hand, cliffhanger style. After that I have to push, claw, and pull myself over the hanging edge to slide down the other side.

Another one was done. Every obstacle I finish on my own gives me that much more power. Every time I figure out how to do something on my own I become stronger because I know I can do it from then on.

The next obstacle took me down a hill to the vertical cargo net, which was followed by the rope climb. I was slightly worried about the rope climb. The rope ascends up to a horizontal frame sixteen feet above the ground. The last two rope climbs had proven to be quite a challenge for me due to the fact that the bottom of the ropes had been covered in mud from people's legs. But as I started to pull myself up the rope this time, I knew I would have no problem getting to the top. My arms forgot about the miles they had just done, and I was soon at the bell. But once I'd rung it, I had a problem. My hands and arms remembered they were tired. Halfway down I couldn't keep a good grip on the rope and started to slide faster and faster. As the rope slid through my hands, I felt them burn. Three feet from the ground I couldn't hold on anymore. I let go and dropped heavily to the hay bales sitting under the ropes. As I hit the hay, I felt the burning pain in my fingers from the brand-new rope burn on my right hand. On the list of pains it was third after my butt and arms. I took a moment to process the pain, but as my body began dealing with it, I put it into a back corner of my brain and let my arms do what they had been doing all day: they took me to the next obstacle.

I hustled over to the next challenge, the multi-rig. They were monkey bars for adults. Getting across requires you to swing from rings, bars attached to chains, ropes, and even suspended baseballs. At the end, instead of the regular bell, there was a wooden frame to climb over. Normally this obstacle would excite me. It would be a new challenge that would allow me to swing across like an American Ninja Warrior, but now my hand was on fire and my whole body was worn out. Some people would skip right over it, but I couldn't do that. I had to do every obstacle. Steeling myself against the pain in my hand, I climbed up to the first handhold and started my way across.

I don't know what it is about the swinging obstacles, but I absolutely love them. As soon as I started, I forgot the pain in my hand and started to enjoy the thrill of swinging through the air. What was even more exciting was the rush of being able to do such a crazy obstacle when I was so tired. As I neared the end, I grabbed onto the hanging baseball, on top of which were the bolts holding it to the rope. The bolt dug into my hand directly on the site of the rope burn, and I almost lost my grip. The excitement from the moments before left me in a rush, and I found myself thinking about quitting just to make the pain stop. But I really don't know how to quit, so I continued on. I came to the last handhold and stared hard at the frame. I didn't want to miss the frame. If I missed, I might lose my momentum and be stranded in the middle of the obstacle. So I slammed my body into it, latching on and going up and over.

I had gone about nine and a half miles so far, and that was the end of the enjoyable part of the course. What was coming next would knock me onto my rear. It was the obstacle that had kicked my butt time and time again. The bucket brigade. No race was complete until the bucket brigade was done.

Luckily David showed up right then to hand me my jeans. I ditched the now-tattered bootie and pulled on my jeans. In a strange way, it was comfortable. My stub could move now that it was not crammed into the boot. The jeans being made of cotton also breathed, cooling me off. The downside was now I could feel every single rock and bump on the ground. The pant legs also dragged behind, causing a cloud of dust to follow me as I pulled myself up the hill and toward the brigade. I saw the pile of rocks sitting there, seeming to stare me in the face as I came over the crest of the hill. Knowing the trial that awaited me, I wasted no time. I grabbed a bucket and began filling it. A five-gallon bucket weighs eighty to a hundred pounds when filled with rocks. I can lift the bucket with no problem. Carrying the bucket was the issue. I scooted forward, moved the bucket, and scooted again. It was a painstakingly slow process, one in which I would move only around twenty feet per minute.

We went up a hill then along its crest, went back down, up another, and back down. It was a mind game of the toughest kind, challenging the racers to overcome the repetition of going back up the hill a second time. But it was not going to break me. I was locked in. The soreness and exhaustion taking over my body and mind were there, but it didn't matter. The only thing that mattered was getting to the end of the bucket brigade, which lasted a quarter of a mile that seemed to stretch on for eternity. It took me an hour to finally finish, and I dumped the bucket back into the bin, happy to be rid of it. I still had more than three miles to go, but it didn't seem as bad now that the bucket brigade was behind me.

That was until I hit the sandbag carry at mile ten. The sandbag weighed somewhere in the neighborhood of seventy pounds. That was more than half my bodyweight. I dragged a bag out of the bin and draped it across my right shoulder like a dead body trying to pull me down. Despite the temptation to drop it and use it as a pillow, I took a step forward. Despite the extra seventy pounds of weight to support, my arms held up, step after step. When I could no longer stand the pain on my shoulder, I allowed the bag to drop down into the dust.

No sweat dripped from my face. I was too dehydrated. I felt the layer of salt crusting my eyelids as I fumbled to open a water bottle. I didn't know when I would see the next water station, and with only two water bottles, I had less than half the carrying capacity I would have had with the hydration pack. I could only drink enough to keep me going but not enough to feel hydrated.

I again heaved the sandbag back onto my shoulder. It felt like it had gained ten pounds. I was heading downhill and hated every step because every step down meant I had that many steps to go back up. But go up I did. Nothing would stop me from finishing that carry. When I finished, I hauled the bag into the bin, and it landed with a satisfying thud. Taking a minute to catch my breath, I took another sip of water before I was off to do what I had come to hate the most: scoot.

I had been on the course for eight hours, and I was tired. I was now less than three miles from the finish line, but it seemed much longer than that. I was heading into an area of dense woods where the only sound I could hear was the dragging of my pants on the dirt. The dust flew up after every step, flowing along with me as I tried to outpace it. I could only do it for so long until exhaustion caught up with me and forced me to take a break. When I stopped, the suffocating dust overcame me, forcing me to hold my breath or get a lungful of dirt. Even if I could hold my breath and save my lungs, I could not stop the dirt from getting into my nose and coating my mouth. I didn't dare use too much of my water to wet my throat. If I drained my supply, I would really be in trouble.

By that point in the race, there were not many people passing me, so I scooted along the path on my own. Being alone in nature is usually a great pleasure, but that day I was worn out and beaten. Every part of my body hurt, and I could only focus on one thing: I must finish the race. I had entered the pain cave. In the pain cave nothing mattered except finishing the race. How to move my body forward was all my brain could think of. Usually I was more than happy to talk with people on the course, but when I was deep in the pain cave, I couldn't do anything more than put one hand in front of the other. I was locked in so far I couldn't be sure of anything anymore—I kept forgetting what mile was next. It didn't really matter. I had to get to the end. A few people passed me, but I was going so slow at that point it barely registered.

Until they came along. A mother and her daughter came up from behind me when I was so far into my pain cave I was about to blackout.

"Hey, do you need anything? Water?" the mother asked me.

I tried to remember exactly what my water situation was but couldn't recall how much I had left. I did know I needed some. Pulling out one of my now very crumpled and beaten water bottles, I drained the remaining water before she filled it back up. With some reassuring words I barely heard, they took off down the path.

I sank even lower. Self-pity was rearing its ugly head, and its timing couldn't have been worse. I was hurting badly. I had gone about ten and a half miles and my body hurt, but more than that, my mind was shutting down. It took me a while to realize how much trouble I was in. I needed to start going faster or I might stop. I knew if I dropped flat on the trail right then that someone would eventually find me and take care of me. But I was scared to death of quitting. I needed something to get me moving. I needed to finish. In that moment I realized I needed some adrenaline. But there was absolutely nobody around me. Nobody to yell encouraging words to keep me going.

I tried to encourage myself by telling myself how amazing I was, but it fell flat. All day long people had been telling me what a good job I was doing. I couldn't believe a word of it anymore. Then I started to get mad. I got mad at everybody who gave lame excuses for not living their lives to the fullest. I got mad that I was out there killing myself and some people thought it was enough to sit around playing video games all day. That got me moving. I picked up my pace, and after a couple hundred feet, my brain started to work a little more logically. Maybe there was more oxygen getting in, or maybe some last dregs of adrenaline were pumping through my veins. I was moving at a good pace and chewing up some ground. I realized it probably wasn't fair to get mad at people I didn't even know. It was then that I started looking inward.

I rarely ever criticize anybody because I don't want them to judge me and my many faults. But that day of the race I did criticize someone. That someone was me. I can't remember all the things I yelled at myself that day. I yelled at myself over every niggling doubt and insecurity I have. I know my shortcomings better than anyone. I let it all loose, yelling at myself inside my head for being such an idiot sometimes. I don't recommend self-deprecation. I believe we should look every day for ways to build ourselves up. But my inner dialogue did something that praise couldn't give me right then. It got me mad. Really mad. As mad as I had been just moments before at people I thought were lazy, I was ten times angrier at myself for not being able to control myself and become better than I was. I even thought of my spiritual shortcomings. Had I done all God wanted me to do? Was I being a faithful servant? In the darkest corner of my soul, I cried out for forgiveness for my weaknesses.

Suddenly I had a powerhouse of adrenaline flowing through my body. I didn't feel great, but I had the ability to charge ahead. I dug and clawed and punched my way out of the pain cave. Step after step I tore down the course. Coming around a bend, I saw the mom and daughter from earlier. They had come back to bring me some more water.

"Wow! I thought you would be way back there," she said, the surprise evident in her voice.

"I found a little extra adrenaline," I said, trying to figure out why I was seeing her again. Had she already finished? No, that couldn't be right. She had come back for me?

"You're almost to the next water station," she said.

"Good. I need it," I said with relief. She *had* come back for me. I was going to be okay. I was going to make it.

True to this woman's word, we soon broke out of the trees, and on the far side of two obstacles was the water station. I didn't even mind the barbwire crawl or the slip-wall climb because water was waiting for me. When I arrived at the water station, I was told I had a little more than a mile to go. I thanked the mother and daughter for all they had done and watched as they ran off into the woods. As I started to follow after them, a lady came jogging across the field, calling for me to wait. With tears in her eyes, she knelt down, and taking my face in her hands, thanked me for my courage and bravery. Slightly stunned and more than a little dazed from the last part of the race, I thanked her. Before I knew it she was jogging back across the field and hopping into a waiting car. It didn't even feel real. She was there and gone before I had a chance to process the encounter.

By that time another runner had caught up with me. He had injured his knee and was hobbling along at about my pace. We both needed some company and decided to walk together. By the time we broke out of the last patch of trees, we had been joined by another group as well as the sweeper. The sweeper is the person responsible for making sure the course is clear before they shut down for the night. As we came out of the trees, I could see it was starting to get dark. I knew the sun had started to go down, but now I could tell night was coming on.

I had been on the course for around ten hours at that point, and I was dehydrated and exhausted mentally and physically, but with only three more obstacles in front of me, I knew I was close. The first obstacle was the spear throw. To avoid the burpees, you have to stick your spear into a bale of hay twenty feet away and four feet off the ground. I had never been able to make the throw. With my arms as dead as they were, I knew there was little chance I could muster enough strength to make it stick. But I pulled my arm back and launched it as hard as I could. It crashed into the dirt far to one side of the hay. I hated doing burpees, but I had known they were coming. I quickly knocked out all thirty and continued on to the next obstacle: the Hercules hoist.

In this obstacle you have to raise a one hundred fifty–pound sandbag thirty feet into the air. Removing my pack, I quickly wedged myself under the guardrail to gain a bit of leverage and pulled down on the rope, pulling hand over hand over hand. About three quarters of the way up, my gloves started to slip, so I wrapped the rope around my wrist and continued to pull. My arms were dead. I couldn't get them to grab onto the rope any harder than they already were. As soon as I couldn't pull anymore, my wounded running mate hopped in, and we pulled the bag up together. Then I hopped onto his rope, and together we pulled his up as well.

The last obstacle was a piece of cake (that would have been awesome if to get to the end you actually had to eat a piece of cake). The last obstacle was the Olympus, which was basically a slanted horizontal wall with holes, chains, and climbing grips. All I had to do was make it to the other side. Hitting the bell, I landed with a thump. I could see the finish line. I didn't even bother putting my gloves back on. Instead I shoved them into my bag and planted my hands on the wonderfully cool grass, sprinting to the finish line. Or I *would* have sprinted to the finish line. My actual pace was more of a measured plodding. All the volunteers and slower runners had gathered around me at the end. Ten hours and forty minutes after beginning the race and thirteen miles and thirty obstacles later, I planted my butt squarely on the finish line and held my arms high in victory.

"I am a Spartan! I am a Spartan! I am a Spartan! Aroo! Aroo! Aroo!"

I had done it. I had completed the thing that couldn't be done. Nobody had done it for me. I had taken my punishments with the rest of the racers and finished the course. I had earned my Trifecta. I was excited, sure; this was what I had been fighting for. More than that, though, I had faced some pretty ugly parts of myself. I had felt myself slip deep into the land of exhaustion—so far, in fact, that I'd had to face my worst fear. Not the fear of failure but the fear of quitting. All those years of trying to prove I could do absolutely anything, and there I was inches from the edge of a cliff I never wanted to see. I had peered over the edge into what had appeared to be cool relief from soreness and pain but in fact was a sick tar pit of despair. If I had stopped, the pain would have stopped, but if I had quit just that once, I might never have made it out again. But I had not quit. Even during the worst of the course, when I was so far gone, I had not quit. God had sent me two angels who had cared about me enough to see me to the next aid station. I had stared that ugly Beast right in the eye and punched it in the nose. I had not quit. And I never will. Aroo!

Now it is time for you. You can't give up. You have been gifted this time on earth to do something amazing. You can't sit there feeling sorry for yourself. There is nobody who can live your life for you. It has to be you.

Sure, it is hard. It would not be worth it if it was not hard. Life is supposed to make us better. But how can we get better if we never go through pain?

Life is amazing! Pushing ourselves to be better every day is what we need to help ourselves achieve true greatness.

Now, go out there, and rise up! Aroo!

Photos taken by Aaron Tharp

# EPILOGUE

*"The important thing is this:*
*to be ready at any moment to sacrifice what you are for what you could become."*
—*Charles du Bos, French critic*[29]

So HERE I AM. I have accomplished some pretty incredible things. I have been inducted into the National Wrestling Hall of Fame, I've shared my life story with millions, I've written a book, and I've followed my parents' examples by building a wonderful family based on the belief system they taught me and which I hold dear.

As I look back on my life and everything I've experienced so far, I can't help but thank God for the path He has led me down. Sure, I had the will and drive to persevere in the face of sometimes overwhelming obstacles, but He was the one who put those experiences in place for me so I could become who I am. He laid the path for me to follow and gave me a family who taught me to have faith and to love God and all men.

Many times life is like a path with an infinite number of side roads. Every little choice can lead us down a slightly different road. We never know how a single decision can set a whole chain of events into motion.

For me, it's happened time and again, and I have never regretted changing my route when God has guided me toward new destinations. Let me share how one small path has had large consequences throughout my life.

---

29 This quote is translated from the original French, "premier tressaillement vital; surtout il s'agit à tout moment de sacrifier ce que nous sommes à ce que nous pouvons devenir." (Charles du Bos, *Approximations III*, 1922, 129.)

As I was preparing for the Paralympics, I was training so hard that I burned out. My body couldn't keep up with the pace of my training. I saw my times fall, and trying to counter this, I trained harder. It didn't help, and I missed my chance at making the Paralympic team. This caused me to look at my life and where I was heading, which prompted the decision to focus on my family. During that time, I found I could do things other than marathons and track events. I started looking for different races to enter.

One day I was sitting on a plane, and the guy next to me mentioned he worked for Spartan Races. That planted the seed in my mind and led me to completing my first Spartan run. Because of that first one, I did more until eventually I finished the Trifecta. Because of that Trifecta, millions have heard my story through social media and have found the motivation to try a little harder each day. What I do is no longer just about me. It is about what God can do through me. God has blessed my life so many times. I am grateful He is using me now to bless others.

So what happens next? That's a very good question and one I am still figuring out. At thirty-two years of age, I have won marathons; competed in more than a dozen obstacle course racing events; and have adopted a child from Ukraine, a country I had never considered visiting. Now I can't imagine having never gone there to meet the sweet boy who joined our family. I want to find out what else I can do. I am definitely not stopping with just one Trifecta, and I don't have any plans to stop pushing myself toward new challenges and adventures.

# ACKNOWLEDGMENTS

THIS BOOK TOOK YEARS TO write, but it has taken more than thirty years to create. Many people have made me who I am today: First and foremost, my parents. You taught me to do things on my own, most of the time by forcing me to do things I didn't want to do. Mom, you made me wear my fake legs even when I hated them, and Dad, you showed me what it was to be tough. I am constantly attempting to live up to your examples.

I have to thank my wonderful wife, Jennifer, for the countless hours you spent watching the kids so I could write and follow my dreams, including during the many, many hours of training, traveling, speaking, and racing that took me away from you all. We have an amazing family, and I wouldn't be who I am without you.

I have had many coaches and teachers over the years, and I could write a whole book on you alone. Thank you for all the time and energy you spent in helping me achieve greatness. Specifically, thank you, Coach Olliff, for teaching me the meaning of grit, and Kevin Hansen, for always believing in me and who once said you knew I could win if all I had was a shoebox on Rollerblade wheels.

I also want to thank Joe De Sena for your amazing introduction to this book and for creating a race that pushes me to rise up every day. I can't wait to see if you can break me.

I am grateful to Sarah Morrison and Rebecca Thomas for helping me develop this book and not making fun of me for my horrible writing.

I would also like to thank all of my fellow Spartans. I have found a family I didn't know I needed.

Lastly, I have to thank you. If you are reading this book, you have helped me become who I am. I have received many messages containing your stories on how my life has helped you overcome your challenges.

# ABOUT THE AUTHOR

KACEY MCCALLISTER IS A MOTIVATIONAL speaker, teacher, and coach. He has been a foster parent and is an adoptive parent to a wonderful special-needs boy.

Kacey has earned many awards and honors, including being inducted into the Oregon Wrestling Hall of Fame and being the first double amputee to complete his Spartan Trifecta unsupported. Kacey's Spartan Race videos have been viewed more than a hundred million times, inspiring people all over the world to rise above their own obstacles in life. Kacey is living proof that the word *impossible* only exists in our minds.

He currently lives in Oregon with his wife, five kids, three dogs, three alpacas, a cat, and some fish.